GULFS OF BLUE AIR

Other titles by Jim Crumley

GULFS *of* BLUE AIR

A Highland Journey

JIM CRUMLEY

MAINSTREAM
PUBLISHING

EDINBURGH AND LONDON

Copyright © Jim Crumley, 1997

First published in Great Britain in 1997 by
MAINSTREAM PUBLISHING COMPANY (EDINBURGH) LTD
7 Albany Street
Edinburgh EH1 3UG

ISBN 1 85158 889 2

A catalogue record of this book is available from the British Library

Typeset in Berkeley
Printed and bound in Great Britain by Butler & Tanner Ltd, Frome

Remember Well

Norman MacCaig
George Mackay Brown
W.H. Murray
Sorley MacLean

Contents

Acknowledgements

The author would like to thank the following for assisting the cause of this book: Marion Campbell, for her kindness, her understanding, her hospitality and her vision. Anne Murray for her permission to quote from the work of her late husband, W.H. Murray. Random House, UK Limited for permission to quote from Norman MacCaig's poem, *High Up On Suilven*.

Prologue – Tracks in the Snow

Gulfs of blue air, two lochs like spectacles,
A frog (this height) and Harris in the sky –
There are more reasons for hills
Than being steep and reaching only high.

Norman MacCaig
High Up On Suilven

The Highlands of Scotland have been on my skyline all my life, beckoning. I grew tall craning from the highest of the low-lying ground towards the north and the north-west where hills steepened and reached high. Through childhood, youth and adulthood I grew increasingly accustomed to crossing that frontier of landscapes. Now I do it almost daily in pursuit of my nature-writer's life.

Out of all that Highland wandering and watching (the one thing I do more joyfully in the Highlands than walking is sitting still), there has emerged the notion of a long journey for the sake of the journey. It is hardly an original idea. The Highland Journey is a writer's subject with a centuries-old pedigree, but then there are no new themes for a writer, only new ways of setting down old themes, new eyes to wander among old rocks. So I was looking for a new way through the Highlands.

I had got as far as the ruminative stage, and I had a picture of Suilven in my head for no other reason than that I often do. Norman MacCaig's *Collected Poems* was open on my desk (same reason). It is the most thumbed of all my poetry books, the thumbprints all mine. It was open at *High Up On Suilven*. There was a title, a destination and a philosophy in the first verse. So I blame Norman MacCaig. I blame him for crystallising in those four lines what I have tried to say in a dozen different books. There was a title, a destination and a philosophy in the first verse. So I blame him for being lucid in my preferred landscapes. It is a quite unwarranted show of lucidity.

But then, even as the book's contract was being finalised, Norman MacCaig died – on 24 January 1996 – uncharitably compelling hundreds of Burns Supper bores to write him hastily into their Immortal Memories. I was on Mull (I will go a long way to avoid a Burns Supper). I heard news of his death on the car radio driving back to Kilninian after a long day tramping alone across the island's empty north-west. Radio reception on Mull's west coast is like listening to the sea rattling pebbles, thanks to the befuddlement of island hills and mainland mountains. Typical, I thought, that even news of his death should reach me couched in the difficult speech of Highland landscapes. It was that speech he rendered lucid.

Inevitably, his own words make his best epitaph, although they were written to mark a different death, that of his great friend Angus MacLeod who lived in the landscapes of Suilven:

> *He is gone: but you can see*
> *his tracks still, in the snow of the world.*

And the purpose of my journey? It is threefold: I will explore the reasons for hills, I will bridge the gulfs of blue air, I will look for tracks in the snow of the world.

1

The View from the Edge

'Let me have a companion of my way,' says Sterne, 'were it but to remark how the shadows lengthen as the sun goes down.' It is beautifully said, but in my opinion this continual comparing of notes interferes with the involuntary impression of things upon the mind and hurts the sentiment.

William Hazlitt
On Going A Journey

Sheriffmuir, the lengthening shadows of a late spring sun going down. The only discernible movement on the face of the land was the steady furrowing of a short-eared owl turning over pale fields of air. I shivered. I had been watching her for an hour, off and on. I would lose her occasionally when she dipped into a gully or rounded a hill shoulder. She flew so close to the ground, hunting between ten and zero feet that it did not take much to lose her. The moor's rippling contours could snatch her from sight without warning. But always she hove to again, adrift on her airy shallows, pale as the summer-bleached grasses, high-winged, head-down huntress. When she lifted her head she would see the mountains.

Many mountains. A frontier landscape like no other, a barrier taut and ragged and ancient, the Highland Edge. The traveller going north from Sheriffmuir as I proposed to do, and whether owl-watcher or owl, must contend with that barrier and the psychologies of threading a path through the mountain realm which lies beyond it. Sheriffmuir is a wide and wide-horizoned shelf on the north slopes of the Ochil Hills. It is a doubly-blessed landscape, for it is the best place I know to look at the Highlands from beyond, and it has a good inn in one corner. For the last

25 years, which is half my life, I have been accustomed to climbing up from Stirling a couple of miles to the south to look at the Highlands, to watch for the owl, and to push open the inn door. Keeping that company – moor, mountain profile and owl – I have slaked all kinds of thirsts.

At the heart of that northern skyline are the Siamese twin mountains of Ben Vorlich and Stuc a' Chroin, joined at the hip by the Bealach an Dubh Chorein, and almost as often as I have tramped the moor, I have trekked up to that great landscape hinge of the bealach *en route* to the mountain summits or some exploration of their corries and wildlife. It is a fragment of the southern Highlands I hold in particular reverence. In an earlier book, *Among Mountains*, I assessed it thus:

> The Bealach an Dubh Chorein is much more than a mountain crossroads. It is also a bridge through half a lifetime, solidly founded on mountain truths, and in that high pass, that watershed, that launchpad for adventure and philosophy and eagles, is an idea called home.

So, like the moor-quartering owl, each time I raise my head to my own workaday skyline (assuming the whole mountain mass is not cordoned off by mists and storms: it vanishes periodically for a week at a time) it is that pair of mountains which meets my eyes. But I write this at a time when my own horizons are changing, or at least undergoing the most thorough re-examination, and I am having second thoughts about which of all my life's landscapes is the most potent 'idea called home'. The one which challenges the Bealach an Dubh Chorein is the first of all my landscapes, Dundee on its seagoing firth and its Angus hinterland. Here is one more assessment from *Among Mountains* on the subject of my earliest mountain explorations in Glen Clova, an acknowledgement which, now that I think about it, did as much as anything to set my life's journey on the climb towards the watershed where it now stands:

> Roots go deep in one so thirled to the land. I found my 'idea called home' far from here on the Bealach an Dubh Chorein, and pressed to cough up a top ten of favourite mountains or mountain landscapes (not at all the same thing), I'm not sure that the gathering around Milton of Clova would have crept into the list. And yet, whenever I haunt my oldest mountain footsteps and stir my earliest mountain memories, I have to acknowledge that between Clova and Glen Doll and that great fork of peaks from the Dreish to Broad Cairn and Craig Mellon . . . I encounter unfailingly a set of circumstances

which push me deeper into myself than elsewhere. I am more tellingly aware here, too, of the debt my life owes to the mountain landscape than elsewhere . . . Because the Clova hills (these days at least) bring out the contemplative in me (and because that fact in turns stems from the fact that Clova is where my mountainness comes from, its native heath), I have come to think of them as a set-aside place. For that matter it is a place where I set myself aside, and therefore, not a place I seek out lightly, not any more . . . In the too recent past I lost my mother and in the too distant past my father, and because Clova is where that part of me that matters most comes from, it is perhaps here that I remember them best, or here that I like to remember them best . . . I come back to Clova to restore in my own mind who I am and what I stand for.

Writing down that acknowledgement was the beginning of the reappraisal, the first of my second thoughts. The idea so grew, so compelled my thoughts back to where I come from that the writer in me grabbed the seed and made of it a book called *The Road and the Miles*. It was a homage to Dundee, a thing of the streets and the folk rather than the mountains and solitude, but it was fashioned out of the same thought process. Most crucially, it made me scrutinise my own place, made me uncover the depth and tenacity of my own roots. As I write, the prevailing frame of mind is that I should step down from the moor with its view of the Highland Edge and head for home, for good.

The owl came close, making little or nothing out of my hunched and seated stillness in the lee of a monolithic rock. She flew 20 feet away at eye level, the downstroke of her wings all but brushing the heather. She could do that. When she was higher off the ground, the wings would climb to almost a five-to-one position, the downstroke almost as low as 25-to-five, and in that way bounce gently across the moor's level airspace, keeping pace with her huge shadow. But when she came close to the surface of the land she reined in her downstroke so that it cut no lower than 20-to-four, quarter to three if she was too close for vole comfort.

She turned and flew tail-to-the-sunset so that her face was a shroud and her shadow began to forge ahead of her with the obvious advantage of a ten-feet wingspan to her four feet. The sun ran along her spine turning it gold, but the wing she raised towards me was that troubling blend of shadowed depths and whiteness which is the shade of ghosts. Her further wing was unfathomable darkness except for its trailing edge and its upraised tip and these were the same sunset-gold as her spine. As the wings fell with that long slow cleaving rhythm which is hers alone among all owls, the near wing closed off its whiteness, caught a touch of the gold as it brushed down, then darkened to the blackness of silhouettes just as the far wing's white underside was hit by the sun and dazzled with all the fervour of snowfields. The upstroke began and the sequence played itself backwards again while the shadow mimicked massively in monochrome. The bird passed beyond the limit of my craning vision. I sat on, secure in my stillness, the patience of hours rewarded with the spectacle of seconds. The bird would be back.

It occurred to me to try and photograph the bird as it flew past. I am a reluctant nature photographer. I don't believe in setting things up so that a wild creature performs on cue, and I loathe passing off tame birds and beasts for what they are not. What I have is a clutch of pictures caught on the wing, as it were, and these please me. I thought I might catch the owl on the wing, freeze a moment of wild theatre wondrously lit. I leaned into the shadow of the rock, produced camera and film box and started to load a new film. I put the empty box down carelessly and it fell against my knee, hit my boot and bounced just out of reach in the sunlight. Leave it. It will not rot soon enough. No. It still contains the return envelope. Besides, its red and yellow livery snags in the corner of an eye. If it snags in my eye it will certainly snag in the owl's. Pick it up. Irritation suddenly settled, deadly as midges. I don't like litter in wild places, especially my own. But I was trying to be a rock. Rocks, if they move at all, don't roll over a yard and reach out a limb then withdraw it and roll back. And this rock I was leaning against was probably the stillest thing on the whole moor. It is called the Wallace Stone because of its associations with William of that Ilk, so it's been still for 700 years at least, and probably something nearer 7,000 at a reasonable guess. I was unlikely to fool the owl, wherever it now was, given that such owls have the kind of eyesight which detects vole blinks at 50 feet in a whiteout. She was probably suspicious already. Such rocks don't drop red and yellow film boxes.

Suddenly she was a quarter of a mile away, hunting in deep shadow. She wouldn't see from there. My irritation at the dropped box won. I rolled over, reached out an arm, grasped the box, rolled back thrusting the box into my pocket as I rolled. Neat. The rolling back was not so well judged. My shoulder hit the rock and made the movement untidy. I checked the owl. Still hunting in deep shadow, quarter of a mile away.

Shit. Wrong owl.

A missile was pointed at my face, 50 yards and closing. I remember the white saltire on her face, the diagonals meeting between her eyes. A splash of blue either side would have made the perfect Braveheart face, the ghost of Wallace haunting his old war theatres, hung, drawn and quartering the moor. The missile banked. In the banking, one pale wing pointed far up the sky and a mountain appeared beneath it with its slope perfectly parallel to the wing; the other stretched to the eastern horizon. Where the wings joined, slung under the heart of their span like a lit cockpit, was the molten-gold epicentre of the creature, the staring fire-eyes of the short-eared owl.

She passed in utter silence. Then her shadow crossed, a vast chill, a House of Hammer shape. God knows what it does to crouching voles. She banked again to stare, glided a dozen yards with her wings held stiffly just above the horizontal, dipped a wing (a manoeuvre which drenched her entire canted wingspan in the sunset gold) and dived away down the moor chased by her shadow to where – presumably – her mate was hunting a quarter of a mile off.

Breathe out, unstiffen and stand. She's not coming back. A light at the inn window. Stow the camera, cross the moor to the road, drink in the mountains beyond Strathallan, their hardening blue-grey shapes as the sun dived below them. Next time, load the camera before you leave the car.

I ordered a drink, a whisky the colour of the owl's eyes, the fire in it wondrously smoothed by the maltman's art, a taste which put islands in my mind. The inn was empty, the barman idle, pleased to have company. I told him this:

'Short-eared owl is a name chosen by a dolt.'

He frowned. He'd expected something about the weather.

'What?'

'Here is a bird of limitless charisma, of unique characteristics and some natural beauty.'

He shifted on his feet and concentrated on the glass he was polishing. It was clear it did not need to be polished. His every gesture said 'Nutter'.

'Its ears do not rate an entry among any lists of its many attributes. Worse! They're not ears at all! They are rarely seen tufts – feathers, not ears! – which the bird raises to alert others of its tribe to a perceived threat.'

He put the glass down, rested his hands on the bar and looked at me feigning interest. The gesture said:

'Let's get it over with.'

'Here is the only ground-nesting owl. Here is an owl which flies by day. An owl with brilliant low-level aerobatic skills. It claps its wings and booms its territorial proclamation. You must have heard it in the spring!'

'Nope. Usually got Kenny Rogers on, or some compilation of '90s hits.'

It was my turn to frown, then shrug.

'Do you know it's enslaved to a remarkably specialised and sophisticated relationship with its prey – voles – and it can abandon territory and become a nomad when food grows short? Thought not. You should know these things. They've been on this moor longer than the inn.'

'Don't know about that,' he said, 'only got here in April.'

'It ranges from the Highland Edge to the ocean edge. It discriminates among islands – Orkney, not Shetland, for example; Skye, not Lewis . . . and it has the most alarming and alluring eyes in the wilds, eyes to out-stare eagles.

'Faced with all these possibilities, the dolt came up with the one thing the owl hasn't got – short ears. I've never forgiven him.'

'Who was he?'

'No idea.'

The phone rang. He answered it a mite too quickly, I thought. I took my drink to the fire. Then I sat alone and told myself:

'Ah, but Linnaeus knew better! He it was who first gave birds their Latin scientific names. For a scientist, he had a hint of the poet about him, or the painter. He considered the short-eared owl and came up with *Asio Flammeus*. Flaming Eyes! If only I'd known about this at Harris Academy, Dundee, when at the age of 12 I side-stepped the prospect of Latin with alacrity and took German instead.'

Outside again, the mountains were darkening, the moor paling. I saw no owls. I looked out from the moor across the misting-over gulf where the A9 never quite grew silent even at this almost-midnight to the inky shapes of Ben Vorlich and Stuc a' Chroin. The bealach was a slung hammock between them, or the clasp which bound them in their eternity. I felt love. Love for their very familiarity. It could be the worst day of my life down in the town, but I could always raise my eyes and see just this, this distant pair of mountains waiting. I resumed the soliloquist mood I had carried to the inn fire:

'If you went back east you would miss this. But you've always been that way, haven't you? Always missing somewhere else wherever you are . . . shores when you're land-locked, mountain plateaux when you're island-locked. Anyway, the idea of going back is different from this, it's been smouldering for so long now, hasn't it? Besides, there are other mountain familiarities where you come from. Other mountains to love. It's not like loving a woman. It's okay to love more than one mountain at once.'

And I remembered the love poem I once wrote to mountains and the woman who told me it should have been written to a woman:

18

LOVE OF MOUNTAINS

If love is
a perfect exchange of souls
my love is a mountain.

If love is
the embrace of unfailing arms
my love is the corrie of the mountain.

If love is
a song under the stars
my love is the mountain of the night.

If love is
tranquil in turmoil
silent in trust
rock in shifting sand
my love is the unfailing mountain.

If love is
eagle-loyal
lichen-tenacious
berry-bright
my love is the living mountain.

If love is
true
if love is
forever
if love is

my love is the eternal mountain.

I walked back up to the car. I had left it at the top of the road which squirms across the moor, knowing I would relish this last-of-the-light quarter-of-a-mile. There is no more familiar feeling than this, this end of the day solitary stroll back to the car, the tent, or whatever kind of base I have fashioned for myself in a thousand different Scottish scenes. So much of my mountain travelling has been solitary that now and again I wonder about myself, for it can be as miserable a condition as it can be uplifting. The writer certainly thrives on the solitude: to hark back to that quotation from William Hazlitt with which I began this chapter, the writer I have become thrives on – of all things – 'the involuntary impression of things upon the mind'. But my preference for the companionship of solitude in wild places goes much farther back than the last decade, which is all the time that has lapsed since I abandoned the newspaper office to write my books. And yet, how often I reach back in the writing to rifle through memory's store and find conclusions and perspectives hardly changed. Hazlitt offers a case in point.

I encountered him at school, aged about 15, the Dundee connections again. Our class was trudging wearily through the essayists – Lamb, Bacon, Addison and the rest – wondering what it all had to do with us. I was as weary a trudger as any, little suspecting that the next flicked page would alight on William Hazlitt's *On Going A Journey*. I read its first sentence:

> *One of the pleasantest things in the world is going a journey; but I like to go by myself.*

I was hooked. I read on:

> *I can enjoy society in a room; but out of doors, nature is company enough for me. I am then never less alone than when alone. I cannot see the wit of walking and talking at the same time.*

There was much more in that vein. The man spoke my language, he had pilfered my instincts and articulated them for me. Then I discovered that he lived from 1778 to 1830. How could he know these things? I carried snatches of Hazlitt in my head for years, but school things dulled into a kind of brown fog which I rarely stirred. Then, about five years ago, with a book or two of my own to my name, I stumbled on a paperback of William Hazlitt's *Selected Writings*. I stood in the shop and flicked through the pages to find *On Going A Journey* and found all my teenage instincts intact. The piece was a miracle of enlightenment. It took me where I stood (Princes Street, Edinburgh) round a whistlestop of all my favourite landscapes, journeys made alone when the alone-ness of the journey was its principal celebration. As I read, I was thinking, 'Where is the bit about the wild rose?' for it had a sentiment attached to it which had struck me as supremely valid at the age of 15, though I had long since forgotten the form of words. Then I found it:

Is not this wild rose sweet without a comment? Does not this daisy leap to my heart, set in its coat of emerald? Yet if I were to explain to you the circumstance that has so endeared it to me, you would only smile. Had I better then keep it to myself, and let it serve me to brood over, from here to yonder craggy point, and from thence onward to the far-distant horizon? I should be but bad company all that way, and therefore prefer being alone.

So, I would journey alone, acknowledging the sweetness of my wild roses, my daisies, my birches, otters and eagles without a word.

Mine is that undisturbed silence of the heart which alone is perfect eloquence.

The old Fiat was packed, primed for the journeying. This would be a flexible expedition: one set of four wheels, and in the back one set of two wheels and fourfold choice of footwear, a borrowed tent with a small hole in the floor, a 20-year-old sleeping-bag. One concession to luxury – a new single burner stove, the smallest on the market. If I left now on this midnight and drove flat out through the night I could be 'High Up On Suilven' for breakfast. But I wouldn't have much of a book.

2

The Mountain Thunder

It was still and hot and the only view was down. Late morning belied early morning's promise of a classic mountain day and drew immense curtains round the mountain. These hung lank and still. The sun glared down at them and they glared back. If you looked in any direction but down, your eyes winced before the blazing mass of air. Ben Vorlich was not a comfortable mountain-top.

The start had been full of early-June birdsong. Glen Ample was cool, but warming up fast. The climbing had quickly outstripped the climber to the waist. The plan had been to follow the Allt a' Choire Fhuadaraich from the glen to the corrie, storm the corrie headwall (a canny storming, it is no fortress) onto the Bealach an Dubh Chorein, then skip up the long curve of Ben Vorlich's skyline to its narrow double summit. Every step of the way would be as familiar to me as any mountain anywhere, but the plan was fankled by the deer. Because I was going quietly and alone (a state of affairs which permits a more noticing frame of mind than climbing in company: Hazlitt had nothing about how solitude sharpens the senses) I had noticed a cluster of stags on the lower rim of the corrie, so I cut away from the burn on a steep detour which would take me and my scent away on the tiny breeze. A good rock, an old haunt much perched upon by a young golden eagle for a single season 20 years before, would let me watch the deer from above.

As well to climb alone, I reassured myself. I know few enough folk who would thole this heathery purgatory of a detour to avoid disturbing a few deer . . . 'I am never less alone than when alone . . .'

The rock was awkward from the back, but smooth and warm on top with a fat golden eagle pellet among its tufts of moss and lichens. That cluster of stags now proved to be the fringe of a great herd. The corrie floor wore a tawny carpet, glossy with sweat and the heat of the day, upwards of 400 red deer, almost all of them lying down. If I had blundered on up the burn I would have set the mountain moving, and almost certainly I would have seen nothing of that spectacular disturbance, although I might have heard the stampede and felt the mountain tremble.

I lay on my rock and watched them steam. The burns rattled among their stones. Cuckoos havered. Pipits fizzed and swifts fizzed higher. A kestrel dawdled up among the fat folds of the heat haze constantly testing out its own fulcrum. A wren stuttered salvos of ire somewhere between my left ear and the burn. But not a sound rose from the herd. Not a grunt. Not a syllable of that quiet conversation which so often moves among hinds. Not a footfall. It was 11 a.m. and hot. It was as if they had sensed early the greater heat that was to come and folded themselves away in the coolest part of the mountain, the peaty ooze of the floor of the corrie that faces north-west, the floor still moist from weeks of rain, the floor which lies in shadow for more of the day than any other part of the mountain, the last part of the mountain to heat up on such a day. But now it steamed.

Only the stags stood. There were ten on the corrie rim where I had first seen them from below. But they stood the way cattle stand in a river. There was nothing to do but lie down or stand. So they stood. Perhaps on the rim there was a waft of cooler air. They neither grazed nor skirmished nor kept watch. They merely stood while every other deer lay down. All that moved among the herd were ears, hundreds of flicked ears swatting away hundreds of thousands of flies. The sun cruised up into its noon and turned their cool sanctuary into an oven, but the torpor which enfolded the herd was a collective burden to be borne by them all. Individualist action was out of the question. So they lay or stood still and tholed that rarest of Highland oppressions.

But it was too much for me. The rock became too hot for my comfort. The heat made me restless. I considered going down. A dip in the river would be good, but retracing my steps would be insufferable. The summit might be cooler, but what would I see? Perhaps if I contoured round to the north-facing slopes I might stumble on nesting ptarmigan in that bouldery realm. I reversed back down the rock's tilted crown and slithered to the ground keeping the bulk of the rock between me and the deer. By the time I had to show myself on the open ground I would be too far off and too high to trouble the herd, if they saw me at all, for I was sure now that their watchfulness was dulled by the nature of the hour.

The mountain did not grow cooler higher up. No wind stirred the haze. The hung folds seemed to advance and close in on me. If there were ptarmigan on the boulderfields they were sitting still, which is something ptarmigan do uncommonly well, their three-moults-a-year uncannily timed to match the changing shades of bareness of their high homelands. Only in snowless midwinter does it let them down. Three times I sat down where I know the birds like to linger, and though I scoured the rocks painstakingly with the glasses, I found nothing and felt outwitted. I found their droppings several times. These look unconvincingly like little cheese straws which a certain kind of cocktail party dishes up. I always avoid cheese straws, but then I always avoid cocktail parties too. I imagined a sitting hen, boulder-tinted and panting and watching my advance round the mountain. I could feel her crouch closer to the bedrock in response to nature's command while my boots thumped closer and receded. And still she sat and one of those other nearby rocks was not a rock at all but her watching mate. The heat would make them stiller than ever, which is a mighty stillness.

I trudged to the summit and sat and lunched, and because of the glare from the haze I looked down, down into the corrie, down onto the bealach, down into the Dubh Chorein which lie the far side of the bealach from the deer corrie (for the bealach teeters like a rope bridge slung between two great geological yawns). I sat, and in the solitude and the heat and the ptarmigan stillness, the boulder stillness, the couched-deer stillness, I felt suddenly shackled by the power of the mountain.

I could sense, in a way I had never done before and have not since, the spreading mass of the mountain beneath me. I sensed the great weight, the immeasurable weight (thousands of millions of tons shaped and reordered by thousands of millions of years) of its rock torso pushing down into the core of the earth, spreading as it deepened, colliding and battling in its depths with the bases of other mountains, other mountain systems. I sat atop all that, flimsy as eggshells, a transient thing of no more account in the mountain's scheme of things than a hailstone if one should fall now into this heatwave.

I sat. And without the distance which mountain-tops usually allow, without the blatter of summit weather to concentrate the mind, without a single distinguishing aspect to that most distinguished of realms, I felt quite defeated by the mountain.

Here is the lie to that hollowest of human boasts – the word is used as often as it is thoughtless – that to climb the mountain is to *conquer* it. Here was a mountain climbed, and its climber conquered, and conquered not by cold or storm or avalanche or disaster but by the adversary of the mountain's own massive aura. It is a crushing thing to feel if, like me, you crave a welcoming place in the mountain's scheme of things. For I have climbed, not to pronounce a thing conquered but to keep its company, not to tick off its name on a careless list but to enfold its namelessness into my own treasury of hours spent with wildest nature. Mountains to me *are* nature. They are where I shed something of my formal humanness, the outermost layer of the mind's skin, to be something else, something more of nature, something harking back to earlier eras when my own species was more integral to nature, to the mountain world, than it has since become. Nan Shepherd's *The Living Mountain* is a hymn to all that. She wrote:

> *Yet often the mountain gives itself most completely when I have no destination, when I reach nowhere in particular, but have gone out merely to be with the mountain as one visits a friend with no intention but to be with him.*

Now there is a sentiment to which I nod companionably. So much of my own mountain journeying has that 'visiting a friend' philosophy at its core, which is why I find myself again and again in the same places, and why, come to think of it, I find the Munro-bagger's pursuit of nothing but a listful of summits a frothy game. But now look what you've done, I rebuked myself on the summit of Ben Vorlich: you've yoked yourself to this destination-driven Journey, and the thing has stalled at its first stumbling block. I remembered Hazlitt, and the determination to travel alone, the better to acknowledge 'the involuntary impression of things upon the mind'. What a two-edged sword it is! Where was the hill-heady spring in the step of the early morning now? Where the optimism of the first footsteps on the Journey?

The Journey! Something nudged me in the ribs and pronounced a warning, some agent of St Christopher or whatever deity of travellers was looking down. Between here and journey's end, the warning counselled, there would be many mountains, and some of them would strew the journey's path with adversities. I had better find a sounder way of encountering them than this.

So I sat on the mountain's summit and thought about that and the heat beat down on me, and the mountain massed conspiratorially beneath me. And because there was no view at all in any direction other than down, down to the bealach and the corries on either side of it, I stared down. And then the mountain thundered.

Somewhere far down the burn where my own climbing had begun, two figures in white tee-shirts were on the hillside. Because they were in white, and because they were two rather than one (so as absorbed in each other's company as they were in their surroundings) they had not detoured away from the deer, perhaps not even seen the deer. The deer had seen them, however, and that alien white-shirted presence on their hill dissolved their torpor. In an instant, the floor of Choire Fhuadaraich changed colour and texture as 400 couched beasts stood. Four hundred heads craned north-west and downhill. Then the same heads faced south-east and uphill. Then they ran. And when they ran, the mountain thundered.

It began as a far-off rumble, the way thunder does – low, throaty and soft – before it begins to swell and grow ominous. It began to swell and grow ominous as the unanimity of panic gathered pace and purpose and chose its direction. The herd had been scattered loosely all across the corrie floor, a quarter of a mile wide. But as the instinct to flee gathered coherence and wedded it to the herd's intimate knowledge of the ground, the looseness tightened, the mass of beasts narrowed and funnelled upwards. In the disciplined ranks of orchestrated nature, they charged the bealach. As they charged and climbed I looked down on them. I was 1,000 feet above the bealach but I saw, heard, felt them rise like a lump in the mountain's throat. As they rose, the thunder grew.

As they rose, too, they reordered themselves. The bealach has only one crossing, perhaps four red deer wide. As the first of the deer reached the crest, they were already four abreast, and the funnel behind them was forming a short four-abreast column even as it climbed and charged. Then the herd as it crossed the bealach was hooves on hard ground and the thunder troubled the heart of the mountain. The sun seared at the sweating flanks of the runners and struck lightning there. The leaders plunged over and the river of animals at their backs became its own waterfall. Forelegs reached down, hind legs anglepoised acutely under themselves and the herd took the steepest of routes down into the Dubh Chorein. Now the descending column grew longer than the ascending one. The tight mass of the deer still in the first corrie had shrunk to half the herd. The rest were on the way up to the bealach, on the bealach, or coursing down the far side. The moving herd looked like something being poured, a glittering-and-dull whisky tipped from a decanter with a neck the width of four-abreast deer on the charge.

But the profoundest aspect of the spectacle was the sound, the ground bass, the thunder, rising on eagle-scoured thermals to my perch on the summit, rising higher to dissipate and fragment in the white-hot haze beyond the scope of all listening ears. I had heard the birth of the sound, heard its first ragged percussive overture, heard it coalesce and grow articulate. Now as the herd cataracted into the Dubh Chorein, it began to loosen stones and their clatter struck thin cymbal notes into that welter of drumming. On that river of deer flowed and on, up and up and over and over and down and down, until the shape of the funnel in Choire Fhuadaraich had gone and its mirror image had welled down into the Dubh Chorein. The last of the deer crossed the bealach, their flight and their thundering no less headlong and percussive than the first of them. Far down in the Dubh Chorein, the deer had fanned out and slowed up. A few stopped and looked back. Stones still clattered on the headwall. The last few deer skittered down with the same headlong confidence as the first. Finally the whole herd was still. Finally the thunder was spent. In the glasses I could see flanks heave, sweat glisten, backs steam. In the very hottest hour of what would prove to be the year's hottest day, 400 red deer had been stung into the most frantic exertion out of a state of the most profound langour by the distant appearance of two white tee-shirts. My preference for mountain clothes the colour of rocks or peat bogs or hill grasses, and for going alone were vindicated then, to me at least. And if you could have cross-examined the herd, they would have agreed, breathlessly.

I put down the glasses, and for the first time in what seemed like hours I looked in directions other than down. But still the haze blazed, and still the heavy curtains hung, and still the weight of high summer bore down. But I was smiling to myself now. Nature had given me back the companionship of mountains. This paradox was not lost on me: if the white tee-shirts had not barged in on the day, if the deer had not been stung into the splendour of their flight over the bealach, if I had not been on the one rock in all that mountain mass which was the perfect viewing stance for what happened . . . what might I have taken away from the first of the journey's mountain days beyond a defeated frame of mind?

I moved slowly back from the edge of the summit ridge, rose only when the deer were out of sight, began the long curving descent towards Loch Earn. I was low on the mountain by the time I found shade and water and a pool deep enough to immerse in.

I think I had never been so hot on a mountain before. The heat had only intensified on the descent, heat like a burden, heat like an extra rucksack on my back. I think, too, I never stripped off with such alacrity (well, not to swim at least), nor greeted the cooling benison of water with such gratitude. As I dawdled in the dark pool and flirted with the summer-tamed force of its waterfall, and daydreamed through the day's events, a queer feeling seeped into me. It was a quiet force which was at work, and it had the effect of stilling me, body and mind, so that I felt, briefly, a creature more primitive than myself. I had become a listening creature, rather than a seeing one; I heard the speech of the water, marked the layers of its sound, sensed the coherence of its orchestration as though a Sibelius had spelled it out for me. A dipper came to a rock below the pool and perched there, six feet away. Only my head was above the water and the bird perceived nothing untoward in that sunburned rock shape. I held my stillness while the dipper fidgeted. I looked into its eye across the level surface of the pool, a bird's-eye view of a bird's eye. That eye was a dark pool of its own. I saw the eyelid fall and rise and I swear I heard it. Absurd swearing, that, for blinking is silent, but in that moment of heightened perceptions, there seemed no sensitivity of which I was incapable. The bird bounced off into the fast shallows beyond its rock and left me to my daydream.

I think I must have spent an hour in that pool, although it could just as easily have been ten minutes. Time stalled. The burn was a wholly benevolent force, nature's counterbalance of the oppressive hours on the heights. The relief of that great cooling was such that it seemed almost the experience of nature itself, or of a creature wilder than I. Like the deer couched in the corrie, I had sought out (eventually, being a slower and less articulate mountain thinker than the deer) nature's response to the heat, to be still and cool. Where were the deer now? Had they trekked round the east side of the mountain, or were they compacted under the bealach, still in the Dubh Chorein, knowing that the first shadows would fall there when the sun eventually began to lower itself down the western sky? It was weeks later, and in a room far from Ben Vorlich with the scent and sound of the Atlantic at its open window, that I fingered through my Gaelic-English dictionary and stumbled across a familiar word. *Fuarachadh* it said. It was familiar and yet unfamiliar, or at least not as familiar as I thought it should be. Then I remembered Choire Fhuadaraich where the deer sought out that great relief of cooling. *Fuadaraich* did not appear in the book, but there was *fuarachadh* and there was *fuaraich*. For fuarachadh it said 'relief; cooling', and for *fuaraich* 'cool, become cool'. So my eyes were not the first to linger on that corrie while a herd of red deer tholed a mountain heatwave and sought cooling there.

3

Landseerscapes

No sooner had the Journey begun than it started to resist its self-imposed strictures. Good, I told myself, the nature of this particular journeying beast was coming to the fore, and in good heart. I was suddenly demanding freedom for myself to linger, freedom from the notional schedule of the proposed route march to sit still and think. In particular, I wanted to think back to earlier seasons in whichever landscape I happened to choose to sit still and think. If you can compare, say, an old winter ordeal with this spring-into-summer tranquillity on the same mountainside, you learn more about the mountainside, more about how you cross it or climb it.

This is my fiftieth year, and only among the dimmest horizons of memory is there a time when I was not accustomed to travelling among Highland landscapes. So there are more than 40 years of memories, a personal archive to plunder and bring to bear on the Journey. The deer, for example, had dragged me back to an old autumn, a hillside to the west, above Loch Lubnaig, facing Ben Ledi. Suddenly I wanted to stand there again and smell the place, and suddenly I was irritated with myself for setting out on such a Journey without visiting that hillside as a kind of Rubicon. In the last 20 years I have come closest to the landscapes that hillside contemplates, and in the last ten those landscapes have been a crucial hub around which much of my nature writing has revolved. So I plodded late in the day not to ease and respite by Loch Earn, but up the darkening slopes of Glen Ample. I crossed a watershed, found the larch-shaded end of a benevolently overgrown forest track, and let its slow, green curve ferry me round the hill shoulder to a scramble among boulders and a ledge high above the bend in the loch, that ledge where, autumns ago, I crept through mist towards the sound of a rutting red deer stag . . . Late October, late afternoon, belly-flat in the flaming mountain grasses. How does grass of all mundane and dull-green things ever achieve this colour, this reverberating orange, this cold fire? I walk October mountainsides just to watch its thin flames creep uphill, just to hear it crackle frostily under my own boots. Now I was wading through it with my face towards a rock, that rock which would conceal me from the Landseerscape of rutting stag and auburn mountain and falling, shifting, billowing mist. Always, whenever I try and stalk deer like this, crawling on elbows and belly, eyes only for a bit of cover, senses straining only for some betrayal in the wind, a vision steals over me. It is that 50 yards behind me, there is another stag, crawling along on its belly, mimicking the stalker, and laughing its coarse stag-laugh.

I reached the rock. There was no pursuing stag. There never is. My throat was tight, my breathing too heavy. Relax. Look around.

Autumn. Autumn on a Highland hillside. I think there is no other state in which I would rather find myself, just above the treeline, looking down on birches, larches, ashes, and the dark greeny-black swathe of the spruces which look well enough in the company of these goldening, bronzing, coppering flame-fanners. The grasses and dead brackens drag that fiery theme up to the high, bare places. And there, as if all this show wasn't splendour enough, as if nature hadn't already overreached itself in daring, there was a high trimming of new snow. The sky was fraying above Ben Ledi, baring its whitened shoulders, setting a skull-cap the shape of a small secondary mountain on its summit.

The dullest days make the most of the show. The land glows and the snow shines. Blue skies and sunlight dampen the fires and vie for attention. But low grey skies seal the colours in and let them blaze away until nature tires of its own bravura and summons the shades of winter down.

I rolled over onto my front, the reverie snapped shut by the grunt of a stag too near for any more daydreaming among the seasons and their scene-shifters. I put my eyes to the top of the rock and found the deer had drifted to within 100 yards. I could see only hinds, but the unseen stag suddenly unleashed a foghorn bellow. It was as if the mountain had roared. The sound rose and gathered itself and swelled into such a fat and raucous crescendo that I fancied I could see it as a shape, an unfurling breaker which overwhelmed the hinds' knoll, then exploded into a series of short grunts, a ragged diminuendo, the breaker burst apart by its rock shore.

The mist closed in again. I rested the glasses comfortably on the rock, settled a hip bone more tolerably on a stone beneath me and watched.

The tips of the stag's antlers showed first as he contoured below the knoll. They lashed about like the tips of birch twigs in a gale. Then they stopped. Then they rushed uphill at speed and the whole beast suddenly emerged in a dark brown blur. He was fast and lean and blackened by peat wallowing. He drove two hinds before him, old done creatures. He was driving them out. He turned again, downhill, towards his harem, still running. He was full of running. He wore the hallmark of a new master stag, imposing himself by formidable example, shaking up the old order. So somewhere across the mountain was a greying, hoary, thick-necked veteran licking his wounds and nursing the tatters of his pride. There is no sentiment for old age in wildest nature, no place for the deposed stag, no place for the chivvied old hinds. The winter ahead would probably account for them all.

The young stag trotted round the loose knot of his 16 hinds. He looked more than capable of serving them all and defending them against all-comers. He worked at speed, like a collie among so many truculent ewes. Then he stopped. He stopped on the very edge of the hill, silhouetted against the greying sky. His head faced uphill, his back raked steeply away from his neck at an angle which matched perfectly the hill skyline. His weight sat back on his haunches and they looked lean and hard and braced against the mountainside. His cloven feet dug into the fiery grasses so that they leapt like flames up his legs. His head carried eight points, nothing to carry home as a trophy, not yet, but there was a wide spread to his antlers, and if nature, poachers, and the perverse philosophy of the 'sporting estate' spared him, he would grow into a wondrous specimen.

The old hinds edged closer again, trying to integrate quietly back into the society of hinds. But the stag galvanised at their approach and chased them 50 yards straight uphill until they put a small gully between themselves and his pursuit and he stopped. By then, his harem below had begun to wander, so he turned and ran, stiff-legged, high-headed, back to his duties. The burden of a master stag in the rut is a relentless one.

His sprint brought him to within 50 yards of my rock. I put the glasses on him. He steamed. He turned his head so that it faced along his spine, and he roared again, huge lungfuls of granite-edged sound, the same towering climax and grunting anti-climax, voice as war-drum. From far round the mountain, and from the slopes across the loch, unseen answers and echoes poured. Another from nearer by, above and behind me, the deer coming down as the dusk encroached, the sound of them growing vaguely risky in my mind as the light faded.

31

I love red deer, hate what we have done to them in Highland Scotland. The economics of sporting estates are an affront, to the animal and to the land. Sustaining huge herds of deer so that they can be shot at great expense by people with no feeling for where they are and no responsibility for the wellbeing of land and landscape, nature and deer and Highlander . . . it does not amount to a very satisfactory definition of land use. All across the Highlands, landowners from every corner of the planet turn up for a few weeks' shooting, then leave again, turning their backs on 'their' estate, locking it up and running it down, pleased with their diversion, uncaring of the loss they inflict upon the land, the people, the nation. Why on earth do we let it happen?

LANDSEERSCAPE

Smouldery October catches
in the mountain's thrapple,
corries belch a song of stags
— lusty cadenzas in the hags

where black broths of peat
embalm the wallowing flanks
of rancid rogues, royals, and all
the rut's also-rans. Wall-to-wall

rock-to-rock echoes
of stag-to-stag challenge
rebound, rebound among
the coy curved heads of hinds. Flung

winds stir the cauldron's brew
to steamy fermentations
of Landseerscapes, but brushed with fire
— autumn's flamed attire's

a garb Victoriana
dared not wear, too gay,
un-grey, undismally intruding on
propriety's palette. Now sun

ignites a hill of pungent autumn dreams.
It is not all it seems.

Other peat-black ruts
imprint their lusts
upon the hill (they also roar)
— the scarry spoor of 4x4

sheik-encrusted convoys
climb with quadraphonic
air-conditioned ease to play
hedonic games, to slay

this stag or that
without so much as breaking sweat
or chilling to the bone.
And how could they have known

that fourteen generations of Mackays
(the ghillie's tribe!) were swept
from here to Canada for sheep
then deer, then accents rooted deep

in Sussex or Saudi? And how
were they to know the ghillie's gaze
blackly bore them courteous hate
for blood that flowed in spate

a human Gulf Stream rampant in reverse?
They jargonised his birthright
in The Scotsman *and* The Field
— 'sporting estate' — a bargain sealed

in whispered millions over lunch
his week's wage couldn't buy,
and played with their life-size Landseer
three weeks a year.

The June evening of the Journey was soft and warm. I pulled the bivvy bag from my pack, sipped malt whisky and nibbled biscuits, pillowed my head on a sweater and dozed until dawn. I dreamed of an old, grey stag which walked slowly away from his native mountainside, downhill to the lochside. There he waded out until he swam, then he swam until he drowned.

33

4

Beyond the Edge

If you have grown accustomed to the faces of Ben Vorlich and Stuc a' Chroin from Sheriffmuir and Stirling, you might pause halfway up Glen Ogle and look back and find that the mountains are suddenly the other way round. You have stepped beyond the Highland Edge, irrevocable crossing that it is. Moor-cruising shadows up here are more likely to be eagle than owl.

This glen which begins a bend or two above Lochearnhead wears the scars of many travellers. A wheen of history-makers have paused at Lochearnhead's T-junction, swithering, for the wide trough of Strathearn begins here too, just as irrevocably aimed at the Lowland east and the sea. Highland or Lowland? Advance or retreat? Whether to go with the ebb or the flow of the affairs of man? The curiously introverting landscape of Glen Ogle, narrowing as it climbs, has exercised them all – clansmen, soldiers, drovers, fleers from and pursuers of justice, military road builders, railway builders, new road builders, pylon-inflicters – with the extremes of optimism and despair and a climate that is as unmistakably Highland as the craggy walled labyrinth the landscape suddenly becomes.

And now tourism has oozed into the glen. The Glen Ogle Trail picks a path through low fields before stitching a section of the military road onto a section of the railway to create a six-mile walking route which begins and ends in the same place. I don't much like waymarked anythings, and walking the dead-straight, tree-shrouded, stone-and-gravel bed of a derelict railway is hardly characteristic of walking Highland glens, nor is it the most charismatic introduction for strangers. The obligatory information board turns the real natural virtues of the glen into a dirge of bureaucratspeak, concluding with the breathtaking information that the route can be walked in either a clockwise or an anti-clockwise direction. Look! Freedom of Choice!

I realise that waymarked trails are not going to go away just because I think they are crass, meddlesome, insidious, tasteless, wasteful of conservation's limited resources and an insult to the landscapes on which they are inflicted. But is it asking too much to have enlightened information boards? They should be written, not by bureaucrats and rangers and PR people but by poets. Stirling Council (for this is *their* contribution to the art of the waymarked trail), for example, could commission the Bard of Glen Ogle (which is one of my many self-anointed titles) at great expense to write a poem board for the beginning and end of the Glen Ogle Trail. Such a board might read:

GLEN OGLE TRAIL
INFORMATION

Nae gratuitous trash fae me
aboo' what wey tae walk,
yer chyse o shoon or what tae feel an' see:
yer in the Highlands – feel free!

Brook an' futtret maybe lie in wait (maybe no'!)
an furtive trooties in ablo a rock
whar otters ooze in drought an' spate:
be like the burn – gang yer ain gate!

Owerheid the ravens craik an' caa
an' lairds an' ither nobs are ta'en wi the stalk.
The laird o a' steps oot fae a mountain waa;
be like the eagle – soar wharawa!

All this unfolded as I trudged unenthused through head-high bracken and sheep-levelled fields which is what the trail inflicts on the summer walker at the low end of the glen. It is necessary to remind yourself when waymarkers lead you by the nose that if you don't like where you're being led, you don't *have* to follow. A great deal of wholly futile hot air has been expended in recent years about access to Scottish hills, as though there was a problem. There is no problem. You choose your route and you just go, and if you want to vary your chosen route on the spur of the moment, you just go where your spurred moment inclines you. Access problems exist in the minds of committee members and a handful of bullying landowners. We permit the bullies to rule 'their' land at our peril. Freedom to roam is the birthright of the Scot on his native heath, and it is a right he extends to visitors in his country. The day we ever settle for anything less – and 'access' legislation in any shape or form is infinitely less – is the day we impoverish ourselves forever. Do not be dissuaded, not by the bureaucratspeakers or the bullies or the access-obsessed, from gangin yer ain gate. So speaks the Bard of Glen Ogle.

Perhaps the enlightenment which will flourish after the creation of an independent Scotland will insist on a presumption against so-called sporting estates (and if you detect a hint of contempt in that 'so-called', you detect correctly), and pursue a more thoughtful way of working the land – more people in the glens working a small-scale partnership between subsidised conservation and a much expanded crofting regime. Perhaps too the crucial transport links to sustain such a regime will be re-invented and the bureaucrats and politicians who pronounced the extinction of railways like the one up there on the high western flank of Glen Ogle when a landslide offered the excuse they were looking for, will be shown up for the shortsighted oafs they were.

You see what happens when bureaucracy leaves its fingerprints on a Highland hillside and its waymarkers lead you by the nose? It is easy enough to close your eyes to the thumbprints of the waymarkers and the information boards and to the dereliction which is setting in on all the artefacts of the 'trail' (bridges, styles, posts) in the absence of a maintenance budget. But only if you are as soulless as the thumbprint makers. If you walk thoughtfully and softly with the consequences of their work, you will recognise that it has nothing to do with where you stand, a false thing pinned down onto the landscape and just as easily blown away as a leaf in a gale. The motivating force behind such things is often tourism, and tourism is the last thing which should shape our thinking about handling Highland landscapes. Rather than shaping the landscape to what we think tourism might like to spend its money on, we should give nature its head wherever we can, and encourage our tourists to admire and marvel at the naturalness of our landscape, and leave it as they find it. That way we will be spared the absurdity of, for example, the Forestry Commission plastering temporary notices on the permanent notices at the beginning of waymarked trails warning that the path is closed because of snow and ice. Someone might slip, you see, and sue them . . .

Glen Ogle grows natural by its river. The waymarked route is elsewhere, but the straggling thicket of alders where the water becalms is a precious, ungrazed place. A lightweight canopy switches the sun on and off and dapples the dark waters. Through the gaps there are crags, high up. The ingredients of the real world are still in place. I sat in the small shade of the alders, grateful for the coolness. I drank from the burn and thanked it, a mildly self-conscious habit. The habit says that when nature, in whatever guise, assists the state of wellbeing, nature should be acknowledged. So I say thank you. The burn is neutral in all this, of course, but that is not the point. The point is to keep the relationship with nature to the forefront of my mind. Every small gesture (and I can only make small ones in the face of nature's planet-sized ones) helps to reinforce the landscape bond, the intimacy of my association with the landscape I traverse. So I say thank you to a burn which slakes my thirst.

Beyond the trees I waded through a knee-high patch of bog myrtle. It would have been easier to walk round it. But not to walk through bog myrtle, rubbing hands and fingers there, brushing against it, picking a small sprig . . . anything to release its scent . . . not to do that is to decline enchantment.

> *Bog myrtle smells*
> *like curlews sound,*
> *curved pibroch of scent*
> *low on the moor, clinging*
>
> *to legs and trailed fingers,*
> *tangible as summer rain*
> *but sweeter, sharper, wilder,*
> *headier a brew,*
>
> *fit-sipping*
> *for Argus wings drinking*
> *in only the sunlight,*
> *thirsting in scented shadow.*
>
> *Brushing by*
> *we also drink in*
> *– scent, sound, sunflier -*
> *bending low, curved*
>
> *as a curlew.*

Beyond the trees, beyond the bog myrtle, the rough floor of the glen is suddenly level and smooth, such a marvellous discovery that you find yourself looking down as you walk, down to where you place your feet, and this with mountain walls all round. You have found the military road. Oh, but the military road boys knew a thing about road building! No Romans these, no railway line makers either. No straight lines. Instead there is a gentle uncoiling, as if a long green rope had been carefully laid on the landscape, easy gradients athwart natural contours, the laws of civil engineering deferentially yoked to the laws of nature in a mountain landscape. No one has built with the same reverence in Glen Ogle since. That road is organic, green and growing, not imposed like the railway, the modern road and the pylon line. Nothing jars. Walk it, and sense the builders' gratitude – you have honoured his purpose. I have found that kind of response rise in me unbidden wherever old hand-made ways lead through the land, where the skills of the builders rise above the mundane purpose of their labours . . . a rock-cut staircase at Croig on the north shore of Mull, a stone-flagged path which crosses a watershed to the sea near Glen Uig . . .

A higher order of builders – stonemasons, not engineers – laboured on the military road of Glen Ogle, feeling their way up the glen to the watershed. They were also coy about their greatest achievement – their bridges. You can cross them without knowing you have crossed. There are no parapets, no rise in the ground, nothing which proclaims the crossing of troublesome waters. But you *must* dismount from the track each time you cross a burn to marvel and pay homage.

A single simple arch, 30 slim stones set on end, each clamped to its neighbours by the weight of all the others . . . that is what you see when you dismount. The thing is such a marvel of pretty simplicity, a fractured, dun-coloured rainbow springing from bank to bank, that you are inclined to forget at first that the bridge has depth, that the 30 arcing stones are just the edge.

Lunch in the cool shade of the bridge's underside is like a sacrament in a moist chapel. Only fish and dippers, burns and heatwave lunchers understand bridges like these. You should go under them, not over. Underneath, they inhabit a different planet, a cross-section of shadows cut through the sunlit day. The sunlight stands at its open ends but makes no impression inside the bridge. Instead, the water takes the sunlight, bends its rays and plays them across the stone curve of the roof, a mesmeric dance. Its movement is musical silence, stone deafness. Perhaps Beethoven, in his stone deafness, composed under bridges.

Every sense heightens in that elemental shadow, where all is rock and water and rebuffed light. Sounds are the water, your own breathing, flutey robin-song from a small willow by the edge of the bridge. Nothing else. The sound of water breaks down as you listen, the splatter of a six-inch fall just before it enters the shadow, the soft companionable mutter as it idles deeply through the bridge, the thinner chatter where it grows sunny again and slithers over gravel. I took out a penny whistle in that wondrous chamber and made it sound like the Hallé Orchestra. Beethoven, where were you?

There is a conundrum on the watershed, a small dark loch, dark because although it lies out on the broad neck of the pass, it has been planted close with the worst kind of forestry, a dark green monotoned shroud. The Ordnance Survey map calls it Loch Lairig Cheile, which means nothing at all. Lairig is 'pass', and ceile (the 'h' is a confusion of grammar only) means 'fellow' or 'spouse'. But that is not the conundrum. There are plenty of instances all across the country of Gaelic place names which are seemingly meaningless. But there are just as many where the place names are singularly appropriate.

Two winters ago, crossing the pass in the snow, I saw two whooper swans on the loch. I know the habits of the swan population in this part of the world well: I have studied them for 25 years, and never once had I seen swans on Loch Lairig Cheile. I was intrigued enough to pull out a map and trace possible flightlines between whooper swan haunts I knew. But the map I pulled out was not the modern sheet, but an old inch-to-the-mile one from the early 1970s. On that map the name is not Loch Lairig Cheile but Loch Lairig *Eala* . . . the Loch of the Pass of the Swan!

I was intrigued enough to write to the Ordnance Survey in Southampton. The reply was disappointing:

> *I have checked the current names book and there is no reference to a name change. On the contrary, it would seem that the name Loch Lairig Cheile has always been used. Therefore, I can only conclude that the use of Loch Lairig Eala was an aberration peculiar to the 1" to the mile, seventh series. Certainly the very first 1:50,000 bore the former, as did the previous 1" edition.*

Now when the OS says it would seem a particular name 'has always been used' it is natural enough to believe. It is after all our National Mapping Agency. Then I found an old small-scale (non-OS) map hanging on the wall of a Callander coffee shop, and there was Loch Lairig Eala. So I asked John Fallon who lives in the glen and runs the wee snack bar in the car park on the watershed, and he said it was called Cheile, but the locals called it the Dying Swan Loch. Then I found an OS Tourist Map of Loch Lomond and the Trossachs: Loch Lairig Eala. Curiouser and curiouser.

What I think is that my Ordnance Survey correspondent is the aberration. Before the tree plantations crowded in on the loch, it would have been much more to the liking of swans and much more conspicuous to flying swans. The two names are not too different in pronunciation. Someone has taken down the wrong word and implanted it on the map, but Eala is the true name. That's what I think. That's why I'm looking for older maps. The swans have used it three winters in a row now . . .

The mountains have begun. West lies their first maze. Climb the steeps above the loch to the locked horns of Creag MacRanaich's tortured corrie walls and stand on the summit. For the first time, every sightline is Highland. There are no obvious exits, no escape routes to softer realms. A key of nature has turned. I'm locked in. This unsung summit stands in the midst of a mountain land, a landscape which will dictate every subsequent step of the Journey. It is also an outpost of a massif much riven by north-south passes, lesser troughs than Glen Ogle but troughs enough to make a quite pointless ordeal if I were to traverse them all in succession. I did not climb Creag MacRanaich for that reason.

Greater east-west troughs bound the massif to the north (Glen Dochart) and south (Balquhidder) and Glen Falloch (which opens southward to accommodate the super-trough where Loch Lomond swills) lies to the west. But cross any of these four great defiles and there are only more mountains beyond, more troughs, more airy townships of grey rock populated by streetwise ravens and smash-and-grab peregrine falcons, overlorded by eagles. If you would make a long Highland Journey, it is as well to pause here and take a long, lingering look around. If you do not take instinctively to the mountain realm and all its slung barriers, if you feel reluctant in its midst, wary of its mute testimony, this is as far as you should go. But if you can take this *ad infinitum* and occasionally *ad nauseam* (say if you catch the wrong end of equinoctial unrest steaming in from the Atlantic on a high flank of Beinn Sgritheall), if you crave it, you are equipped inside your head for the journey. Inside your heart . . . there lies what you make of the Journey.

In me, it is a different heart which is brought to bear on all my mountain journeys once I am locked into the mountain maze, once there is a slung barrier behind as well as before me. This second heart beats with an unsettling pulse, leaps at the landscape with a hopeless and almost lustful infatuation. It is as different from the heart which propels me cool and relaxed and trusting among my familiar Highland Edge mountains as a mistress from a marriage. All sensation is heightened, nerves are tauter, every savour is more ardently relished, just as ardently mistrusted. So I pursue those Highland-locked mountain innards with unequal, unbalancing surges of unease and arousal, comprehensively seduced by landscapes. It is yet one more of those distinctions which arise out of that solitary nature of the Journey, another 'involuntary impression of things upon the mind'.

So on Creag MacRanaich's summit, I have felt the mountains close in and steepen, and I have heard a great geological bolt rattle home behind me. The tempo of things is at once more erratic. My pursuit of the eternally unattainable has resumed.

I think I first felt the sensation on Jock's Road, going north, as a slim and uncertain 20-year-old. I had made the traditional progress which my home town of Dundee demanded – apprenticeship in the Sidlaw Hills to the north of the town, besotted by the mountains of Glen Clova to the north of the Sidlaws, enslaved to the addiction of the Cairngorms to the north of Clova. The Sidlaws were where you learned to stand up, fall down, get lost and find your way home and ponder the distant mysteries of mountains. Clova was where you tasted the forbidden fruit and found it palatable, grappled with a different scale of climbing enterprise, nudged clouds, wondered at the distant mysteries of that northmost skyline of midsummer snows.

For long enough, the wrap of Clova was mountain enough, and it never crossed your mind that it might also be a thoroughfare to the Promised Land. There was no barrier at your back when you wandered into Glen Clova from the south, only lowly Sidlaws and the road home. But the day would dawn when you walked through Clova, through Glen Doll beyond, and thought the unthinkable – go straight up that mountain wall which had until now formed the natural limit of the hills of home, and having reached the watershed, hitch your star to the uncanny highway of Jock's Road and keep going, your eye irrevocably thirled to the rising, widening, whitening skyline of the Cairngorms. As you dropped towards Braemar, you heard the geological bolt rattle home for the first time, and you were alarmed for the first time by the nature of the enterprise to which you were committed – to march along the ultimate skyline, to push open skylights in the false ceilings of your mountaineering ambition and step out onto the very roof of the land.

The bolt which rattles at your back on Creag MacRanaich is the one which compels you to contemplate not the north but the west, not the roof of the land but its bared soul.

5

Eagles of the Mountain Maze

I have a favourite way through the mountain maze. It leans into the contours, slips unobtrusively over watersheds, necklaces hill lochans. It takes the mountains in their stride, the way a fox or a deer or a wildcat would. It mostly avoids summits unless they are useful to the journey. Avoiding summits is the privilege of one unobsessed by the perversity of peak-bagging. I am such a one.

But one summit, lowly and unvisited by the standards of that cabal of giants glowering above the western end of the maze . . . one summit was about to prove useful to me. Useful because it overlooks a certain crag well known to me over the last two late winters, springs and summers, but known to me only from the floor and slopes of its own glen. From the unsung summit, I could pinpoint its place in the maze, and get an idea of how it looks to its inhabitants. So the summit was a diversion with a purpose, the more so when I discovered (the result of a casual browse among skylines and airspaces with binoculars) that one of the inhabitants was perched on the summit, fortune favouring the speculative. The glasses glided gently past her, hesitated, swung back and stopped. She stood erect and utterly still like a stunted totem pole and she stared west to where the mountain gods crowded round Ben More.

I lay full length in the fragrant hill grass. The sun hovered endearingly above my back and struck gold in the nape of the totem. It was the first time I had watched a crag-born golden eagle and been completely comfortable and warm.

But which eagle? It is the happiest consequence of regular and repeated study of a single piece of mountain terrain, a single crag-sided glen, a single nest site through its long nursery season, that you learn not just to recognise the ways of the species, but also to differentiate among individuals. There are those – and they are the majority – who travel, even live, in the Highlands and who never see a golden eagle. I have seen them on a hundred mountainsides from Ben Vorlich to Suilven, from Angus to Ardnamurchan, and in such outposts of their territory as the Lake District and St Kilda (the latter an eagle on an away day from Harris, 40 miles to the east). That makes me lucky as well as watchful, but here in the mountain maze I had watched often enough, been lucky often enough in the past two years, to consider the totem on the small summit and ask myself 'which eagle?'

The story of these eagles is remarkable. It is this:

Ten years ago, and for every one of the following eight years, the eyrie was robbed of its eggs. Not one eaglet flew from the crag's dark shadow, not one, for all the eagles' persistence. A small nucleus of conservationists decided to try and reverse that most depressing of trends by recruiting volunteers to keep watch in seven-hour shifts through the crucial weeks of nesting and early fledgling. Eagles are among the earliest of nesters. March and April in such a glen as this are months which belong incontrovertibly to winter. Two days spring to mind. The first from two seasons ago, the calendar professing April, the weight of snow on the mountain such that the nest was hidden by a white wall which had consolidated on the nest ledge, the eagles negotiating what must have been an awkwardly narrow gap between snow wall and rock face as they flew in and out. The second, from last year, a sequence of snow, thaw and big freeze, the glen's every rock face (including the eyrie ledge) columned with icicles the size of trees, then the day of sudden sun which was punctuated for two hours either side of noon by the explosive snap of hundreds of icicles grown too heavy for their own survival, the crash of each icicle onto rocks below. At every snap, the sitting eagle's head would jerk round testily, an untranquil day for eagle and eagle watcher.

By the end of the first summer, more than 100 volunteers had stood guard, many of them local people, some of them watching eagles for the first time, a few having their lives changed forever by the raw forces of nature which coloured the hours of their vigils. If you would put the soundest principles of conservation into practice, there is no more telling way to do it than by introducing local people to whatever it is you want to conserve, and having nature speak for itself. The excitement was crackling like lightning between two walkie-talkies when one pronounced the first sighting of one tiny white floundering chick, then after a few minutes' pause (minutes of eye glued to telescope and hardly daring to breathe for some uncertain reason) pronounced again, memorably ungrammatical:

'There's two!'

So the robbers had been thwarted. All the eaglets had to do now was survive. Two eaglets is comparatively rare. That it should happen here, before so many wondering eyes, and with an adult pair which had known no breeding success in almost ten years . . . we were all holding our breath now. We had telescope close-ups of the stronger of the two eaglets repeatedly beating up the weaker, the harsh realities of golden eagle life articulated in the nursery. The adults never intervened. Why should they? Tactics for survival were being learned, rehearsed and effected. In the world of the golden eagle it is never too early to learn these.

At the end of it all, both survived to fly free in midsummer, to fly above and through the mountain maze, wearing the white wing patches and tail feathers of their youth. Among the watchers there was much celebrating. National newspaper headlines proclaimed the occasion. The celebrations proved to be premature.

Before the end of the winter, a shepherd reported finding a dead eagle high above Glen Ogle. But he didn't bring it down, nor did he remove the ring from its leg. The irresistible conclusion was made: it was 'one of ours'. Then, at the end of the winter, the second bird was found dead in a crow trap. It had probably taken a week to die in a trap which should have been checked – by law – every 24 hours.

Despondency was countered by a redoubled determination to do better the second year. But then, as the second winter relented and something like spring set in, a mystery turned up. There was the male bird doing his short spell on the eyrie between the longer vigils of the female. There was the female, newly liberated after four hours on her eggs, but instead of flying off to feed she suddenly soared 1,000 feet (my roughest of instant estimates) then fell to meet the climbing advance of a third bird. Here was news! For several of the most unforgettable moments of my life, these two birds fell and rose and jetted and jousted through a range of high-up, high-speed aerobatics which challenged the evidence of my own eyes, all this at speeds from a flying standstill to a blur, and rarely more than a few yards apart, often within talon-touching distance.

I watched for a while through the glasses, then lowered them so that I could look just with my eyes. I have good nature-watching eyes. Now I put them to work to gauge the true scope of the eagles' flight, liberating it from the enclosing rim of the lenses, setting it tinily in the vastness of an eagle's portion of the Highland sky. Those of us who study such things tend to mark out our idea of a golden eagle territory in terms of square miles – bounded by a certain watershed, this lochside, that mountain skyline. We discount the vertical territory at the bird's disposal. I have stood, for example, on the summit of Meall a' Choire Leith, a single contour line above 3,000 feet, and watched two golden eagles rise together into a clear sky. They rose until they were simply too small to see and my eyes began to hurt with the strain of trying to keep even the idea of them secure in the sky. How much higher had they climbed before I lost them? Three thousand feet? Four thousand? Five? How high did they climb before they tired of their game, that game which reduces Glen Lyon to the size of a birch twig? Ten thousand feet?

On such a day of encouraging thermals, a golden eagle territory might be limited only by its own inclination.

I remembered that old summer now, as I watched the female and the interloper, watched them wizen and dwindle to the size of thrushes. Had I not seen herself leave the eyrie ledge and climb as only an eagle can, following her every wingbeat of the way, would my casual glance across and above the glen have made anything at all of these high eagle scratches on the surface of the sky?

Finally, one of the birds broke free, a long, shallow, gliding dive which brought it low along the skyline at my back. I had it close enough in the glasses for long enough to see the white wing patches and tail feathers.

Volunteer watchers saw the bird frequently after that, a state of affairs which suggested that the adult birds were relaxed enough about its presence not to drive it out of their territory, another rarity in the life cycles of eagles. It all made us wonder, and the wondering began with the same question . . . what if . . . ?

It was the end of the summer before RSPB and Forest Enterprise staff went looking for the dead 'eagle' which the shepherd had found in Glen Ogle. They found the carcass, what was left of it, and were able to confirm from a ring on its leg that it was a hen harrier. There was little doubt now that the young eagle which so intrigued the volunteer watchers was one of the previous year's eaglets. What a boost for eagle-watching morale! It was followed by one more eaglet flying from the same eyrie the second summer.

Another fragment of news percolated back to the eagle watch. Police investigating the theft of eggs from another eyrie found the nest-robber's diary. It confirmed that he and an accomplice had been through the eagle glen, but they had noted the conspicuous presence of the watch, and simply wandered on. It works, it works!

So all that explains how it was that my journeying self, tackling the mountain maze and easing towards a certain unsung summit, could spy a perching golden eagle there and wonder 'which eagle?' The bird – of course – would have been aware of me long before I was aware of the bird, and now that my casual movement had ceased abruptly, it converted wariness to flight, and in the spreading of stiff wings and its banking turn out into the glen's airspace, I saw the white patches and tail of last year's youngster. The eagle glided past me in a wide arc at about 50 yards, and perhaps 50 feet lower, studying me as it flew, head cocked and curious rather than fearful, and the sun glared down on the eagle and lit up that thick mane of neck feathers and there was no doubting in that moment what it was which persuaded men to name this bird 'golden'.

What had lured me up here was the opportunity to peer over the rim of the glen and study the territory of these birds I had begun to assess as individuals, and to fit the eyrie crag into that territory, not as the dark and skyline-bulging mass known to the watchers on the floor of the glen, but as a fragment of the mountain maze. Perhaps I could briefly assume the position of a perched eagle to see if their preferred choice of eyrie site made sense. So I sat where the eagle had been perching and looked down, down to where the countless crags of the eyrie glen adhered to their mountainside and I could not begin to separate the eyrie ledge from the mass. The nature of the light was not helping, but neither was the fact that although I had borrowed the eagle's perch, I was not scanning the glen with the eagle's eyes. But the next time I sit by the watcher's rock low in the glen and the male eagle free-falls from 1,000 feet up to 50 feet below the nest ledge, brings his wings to bear on the thunderous air, curves and climbs to alight by his mate as gently as a discarded feather, to deliver a bloodied leg of deer carrion, I will have in my mind's eye the image of that airspace which spilled him earthwards, and the tilt of the mountain maze as he folded his wings and fell. I will have half an idea too (or maybe less than half, maybe a tenth of an idea, maybe a fiftieth!) of how a tiny sloping nick in the black and annihilated rock mass of the glen's shadowiest mountainside grows and grows and hurtles up to rest at last under the reassuring grasp of your one taloned foot (the one which is not clutching the deer leg); and of how it feels to perform such miracles of landscape transformation as a humdrum ritual of the workaday golden eagle world.

Spending a night out alone on the hill changes everything. The kind of night you might spend begins to insinuate itself into the mid-afternoon. The car, the tent, the road home, the hotel room . . . whatever sanctuary you might fall back on at the end of your mountain day . . . all these are elsewhere. Tonight it will be the hill wind, the voices of hill winds in all their moods, blowing you snatches of curlew conversation through the night, perhaps the yap of a fox; the ground where you lie will be a thing of scratching feet you cannot identify, of rustling grass shifted not by winds but by . . . by *what* for God's sake? What *is* that noise? Is that a rock beyond the burn, or did it just move? How long till dawn removes the uncertainty from the mind? Why did you think this was a good idea? Hang on, it's only four in the afternoon.

You take more trouble over the weather, scan every sky shadow for hints of impending storm, no matter that the weather has been set fair in its earliest June rut of sublime benevolence for over a week and this morning's radio has promised only more of the same. 'The involuntary impression of things upon the mind . . .'

I wandered away from the eagle perch, and the idea which impressed itself on my mind as soon as the eagles had vacated it was that I wasn't going down tonight. I was staying high. I was going to walk the high shoulders and ridges through the late afternoon into the evening, then find a high burn with a heathery couch. There I would eat and drink, stroll around my encampment with hands-in-pooches contentment, and bed down in a sleeping-bag (with a bivvy to ward off the arctic chill which occasionally graces midsummer 3 a.m.s . . . I've been here before!) and watch the stars until I was too tired to watch. I began to scan the map, plotting a path through the mountain maze which would keep me high, and bring me and my journey to a suitable watershed in, say, a couple of hours of none-too-energetic wandering. I picked a spot, checked a compass bearing and wandered on. And because the mind's purpose as I wandered was to make an account of the wandering, it found something else to linger on. I had the sun in my face, a gentle wind in my hair, I felt fit and exhilarated, and I moved to the rhythm of my own boots on the mountain earth. No matter that I would dine on tinned potatoes and mince tonight, I felt like hunter-gatherer man moving through the landscape by its highest highways, profoundly content with the simplicity of the expedition and its motives. As always in such circumstances, I found myself craving a closer alliance with the land. I wished I was more articulate in its ways, I wished I shared more of its languages, I wished I knew what the forebears of my tribe knew, the mountain travellers who mountain-travelled because that was their way of life . . . it was where they lived, and how they lived, they were mountaineers because life required them to be mountaineers. They knew nothing of crampons, lightweight artefacts, fleece jackets, Goretex, all the accoutrements which safety bores insist we must carry before we set foot on a hillside. Yet they travelled in greater safety, greater certainty, because their relationship with the mountain was one of greater intimacy.

The best of all our climber-writers, W.H. Murray, caught the sense of them in his matchless biography of Rob Roy:

> *Many days and nights together had to be spent on the hills, hunting and tracking, which meant careful, close observation of all wildlife, weather, landforms, sun and stars, the conscious, constant use of eyes, ears, nose, and the sense of touch in response to wind shifts, until the four senses remained alert all day long without conscious effort: recording, warning, informing, guiding, in ways now lost to man in the Highlands where by comparison he is now only half alive. No compasses were used for navigation in mist nor watches for time. In traversing the hills and moors in mist, direction was held by the wind, and even the lightest air sufficed when men were sensitive to its touch on skin, and from the sun by gradations of light in the cloud, by which lowlanders were blind. The flight of birds could bring news. The slow, heavy flight of a heron, reluctantly moving from one bay to another on Loch Katrine, differed subtly from its more purposeful search for a fishing ground, and gave early warning of man's hidden approach. High on the hills, the scuttle of ptarmigans, the quick twist of a hind's head, the line taken by a darting hare or suddenly moving goats or ponies were seen at long distance by the sharp eyes of Rob and his clansmen; they knew in every detail the lie of the land and could judge the source of disturbance. Their sight had a keenness rarely matched now by men who read much. Their powers of observation by the four senses were trained by the necessities of a life lived at one with nature, free of the artificial aids that blunt them.*
>
> *Every scene, therefore, was much more meaningful to Rob and his compatriots than to men of later times, or townsmen of their own day, and much richer, both in its seen context and by their ability to interpret. This fact of their life rewarded them with a deeper love of their Highland ground than Lowlanders could appreciate or be expected to understand. They did not understand, for example, that to deprive such men of land was to uproot them as a tree is uprooted. They might exist, but no longer feel alive.*

It is a preposterous notion that a night out on a mountainside in June, even a night without a tent, could restore that kind of awareness, or even a thousandth of it. By the time Rob Roy Macgregor was born in 1671, hundreds of generations had contributed to the kind of awareness his generation could bring to bear on their landscape. The awareness would be both inherited and taught. The value of such continuity is immeasurable. In the thoughtful analogy of Bill Murray's uprooted tree, it is the process by which a single Scots pine might reach back through 30 generations of its own direct descendants to the Ice Age, each descendant passing on the skills of survival, the scent and the sense of the brush of a wolf or a boar, a beaver or a bear.

The sun stayed late on the face of the hill. I found a level terrace above a burn, established a niche for the night there, unpacked my tinned meal and stove (Rob might have skinned a hare earlier in the day, or plucked a brace of pigeons, or settled for a bag of oatmeal to make into porridge, and he certainly wouldn't be cooking it on a gas stove), let it warm slowly on a low heat, uncorked the hip-flask and let a mouthful or two of mountain burnwater spill into the single malt whisky, the better to unleash its bouquet, its fragrance, and to liberate all its incarcerated mischiefs. I tried to guess the time from the position of the sun. I was 45 minutes out, and I had last consulted my watch only two hours previously. I shrugged and raised the flask to the land, an all-embracing toast to landscape, nature, and those elements of my own tribe which had once felt at home here.

The air was clear after the heat of the day, and long sightlines were opening into the north-west, Beinn Dorain at Bridge of Orchy, Glencoe beyond, Ben Nevis inevitably. A distant mountain shape in the north caught a fluke of sunlight. I guessed at the aloof mass of Ben Alder. East, the wondrous rumples of the Tarmachan ridge, the all-but-4,000-feet heapings of Ben Lawers and its acolytes. Nearby in the west, the brutish bulk of Ben More, a far glint through a gap in the south-west, unmistakably Jura . . . the riches which unfurl from any scrap of high ground in the middle of Scotland. Yet what I craved at that moment, alone on that sun-graced yellowing June evening a notch below 3,000 feet as the distances grew like an opening flower, were sightlines into the past. Not the straw-clutching deliberation over a knee-high wall of broken stones or winter sun-and-snow delineating the gone-to-seed fertility or old lazybeds, but the real thing . . . the way the landscape actually was, the way the lost wildlife tribes went about their lives, the way Rob and his lost generations of predecessors went about theirs. It is a preoccupation which grows the more intense in me the older I get, and because it only ever resolves itself into frustrations or the best guesses and half-truths of poets and novelists, the intensity only deepens and every new plumbed depth cloaks in ever darker frustration. From time to time

I revert to a couple of cornerstones among my bookshelves. Marion Campbell's *Argyll* layers her archaeologist's expertise in sublime shades of poetry, and her novel *The Dark Twin* reinvents a Highland Bronze Age world with astounding clarity. The latter book was the consequence of a series of waking dreams, so perhaps it is as close as any of us can reach now, now that the Highland Clearances and the emergence of the Victorian sporting estate – a devastating concurrence – have made deserts of glens and despatched their people to Glasgow and Cape Breton, their wildlife tribes to oblivion. William Golding delved further back, dared a remarkably plausible fantasy in *The Inheritors*, inventing the time of the Neanderthals:

> At last Mal finished his cough. He began to straighten himself by bearing down on the thorn bush and by making his hands walk over each other up the stick. He looked at the river then at each of the people in turn, and they waited.
>
> 'I have a picture.'
>
> He freed a hand and put it flat on his head as if confining the images that flickered there.
>
> 'Mal is not old but clinging to his mother's back. There is more water not only here but along the trail where we came. A man is wise. He makes men take a tree that has fallen and –'
>
> His eyes deep in their hollows turned to the people imploring them to share a picture with him. He coughed again softly. The old woman carefully lifted her burden.
>
> At last Ha spoke.
>
> 'I do not see this picture.'
>
> The old man sighed and took his hand away from his head.
>
> 'Find a tree that has fallen.'

All this intrigues me, and for an hour, with these ideas at work in my head, I scrutinised the mountain air high above Glen Dochart for truths, hints, scraps of lost realities. They rose like bubbles through deep and dark water, their truths sealed in, until they surfaced, glittered for a tantalising second so that the watching mind gasped, then they burst and the wind had the seed of them to itself, took them and scattered them God knows where. In any case, I wanted to see the hand that carved the tall stones, the brow that furrowed as the caves were painted, the eye that narrowed as the stone axe was well fashioned. I didn't want bubbles.

A snipe drummed high overhead. The best that I could hope for is that the cave painter, the bear hunter, the Macgregor doing his chieftain's bidding, would have raised the same involuntary glance as I did to pinpoint the sky-diving, bleating bird, and marvel at its voice and its dance. And at what point in all that bird-scrutiny did it dawn on the watcher that the voice is not the voice at all but a peculiar adaptation of tail feather reverberating in the wind forces set up by a fast dive? The Gaelic for snipe is *meann-athair*, the roe deer kid of the air, for want of a more concise translation. But such a specific designation suggests a comparison of voices, the young roe's thin piping cry to its mother, and the rhythmic vibrato of snipe-flight.

The snipe was high, a bird from a bubble. There is the only continuity – the natives of nature. These and the rocks. Nothing else. Munro-baggers and tourists are not much of a substitute, and neither for that matter am I, for my presence may be more frequent hereabouts than theirs but it is no less fleeting. A forkful of mince, a swig at the flask, the soothing elixir of the snipe, the mountains locked into the maze at every compass point . . . these were my mighty consolations.

There is also this. Simply by being here, simply by climbing alone and forsaking an occasional night of comfort for a roof of stars and the companionship of mountain birds, I had laid myself open to as many of the forces of landscape as it is still possible to acknowledge, kept in touch with the idea at least of what I look for every time I step out into the company of nature. And who knows what nature's undiminished capacity to surprise will confront you with simply because you have laid yourself open to the possibility. Not to go, not to taste the pure single malt of the landscape, not to embrace the primitive whenever the opportunity arises . . . that is the unforgivable sin of omission.

Away in the west, in Marion Campbell's portion of Argyll, there is a fragment of the landscape where all these things – the sense of place, the sense of the people's past, the sense of nature through all its ages – coincide on a single small and sacred hilltop. The Journey would weave Dunadd's thread into its tapestry in due course, but sitting on my unnamed hillside above Glen Dochart, I thought about Dunadd, thought about how it was illuminated by its earliest civilisations when such a place as this was still darkness, nature's place, impassably forested. Folk moved round the island by its seas, settled if they settled at all where they could see their drawn-up boats. The singer Dougie MacLean has a song about the island of Lewis which stems from a remark made to him by an old islander; 'This is such a thin place,' he said. What he meant by that, he said, was that the island past was so near the surface of things. The past informs the present more than in most places. I envy the old Lewis man that inner awareness, for it is a sense of history and a sense of place immune to outsiders and tourism. It is untouchable, a thing of personal ownership, sacred almost. It is perhaps as close as any of us will ever get to knowing the hands which carved the tall stones and painted the caves.

So I sat on my Glen Dochart hillside writing these things down more or less as they occurred to me, and why I was contemplating Lewis from as land-locked a Highland landscape as Glen Dochart I cannot say. The train of thought which casts off on a mountainside where you know you will spend the night is a free-running conveyance, freighted with the involuntary impression of things upon the mind. I value it as I value the Lewis man's assessment of his own place.

Midnight. The sky finally dark, except in the north where there is royal blue, turquoise, yellow, in short vertical bands, and a patch more colourless than rain. I stared at it for unbroken minutes trying to put the name of a colour to it, but none would do. I settled my sleeping-bag inside the bivvy bag, leaned over a yard to the left, lit my tiny stove and brewed fresh coffee, made with mountain water. I leaned back and stared at the stars. I was pleased to see the Plough was in its 'pan' formation. There are times when it stands on end and looks like a question mark. I don't like question marks that size in my sky. It is as if some Omnipotence or other has chosen to interrogate me silently, so that I have to invent the questions as well as the answers. The sky is always a more tranquil place when the Plough is a pan, catching shooting stars.

The coffee muttered. The smell of it in the open almost ranks with bog myrtle. I poured, cupped my hands around the furnace of the cup, and as the giant shapes of the mountains gathered blackly round I drank, and in the moon-shadow of Ben More was Elysium.

The cold woke me at two o'clock. I sat up, pulled on a second jacket, looked round, recognised nothing. A thick darkness was on the mountain, not troublesome to me but an alien kind of darkness. I tried to think why it felt alien, but sleep had clouded my head, and all it wanted was more sleep. I pulled the sleeping-bag back up over the second jacket, and that was anaesthetic enough. I slept in half-hour fits and starts until five, and by then a snipe was drumming in my sky, there was pink and grey in the north-east. I lit the stove from inside the sleeping-bag, and heated what was left of midnight's coffee. It had lost its charm in the cool hours, and I threw it out after the first mouthful. Action. The day was galvanised.

6

Rob Roy Was Here

The Allt Coire Chaorach claws at the very highest flanks of Ben More and Meall na Dige for its sustenance, and having swallowed a clutch of tiny tributaries, it slaloms down through its own corrie, darkens under a conifer forest, emerges unscathed into a shallower stretch among glacial moraines before diving down under two bridges (one decrepit carrying a stretch of mossy track of unguessable vintage, the other all too modern, carrying the main road west) to an uneventful tryst with the River Dochart. It was as good a way down the mountain as any, and as I had washed and breakfasted among its highest tendrils, and as the Journey's landmark stood within earshot of its lowest turbulence where it negotiates the bridges, I decided we should lose 2,500 feet in each other's company. There is a sense of lifeblood about such a burn, emanating from the hidden mountain heart with arterial zeal. It has an unstoppable pulse, an unshakable conviction in its own destiny. It will hit the wide floor of the glen beyond the bridges, slither into its own niche in the dark deceptions of the Dochart, rattle over the falls at Killin, delve into the 500 feet depths of Loch Tay, comingle with the waters of Glen Lyon, storm through Aberfeldy, Dunkeld and Perth, season its mountain sweetness with salt, gather in the Earn (where it might encounter its mountainous kin, the Allt Coire Buidhe born high on Ben Vorlich), and growing mightier by the mile, unravel through the Carse of Gowrie as the Firth of Tay, the first of all my life's waters. The view from the end of the garden path of the first house I ever lived in – in Dundee – was of sunsets over the Tay.

It is a simple thing, the logic which binds a life and a landscape together, when you can reduce it to the most basic, elemental components, when you can let a thread of mountain water bind you to your city and the inevitability of the sea beyond. Scotland is, after all, a small country, and even such a land-locked heartland mountain as Ben More is but a day's determined travelling from either of my two favourite lighthouses – the Bell Rock off the Tay estuary and the Rubha nan Gall, the Headland of the Stranger, on Mull. Primary school geography taught us about Scotland's watersheds, the long slow rivers which travelled east, the short fast ones west. Here is the lesson in the flesh and bone. You have to go 20 miles further west to where Ben Lui stands with one foot in Argyll before you reach the first west-flowing waters. And even Ben Lui harbours headwaters of the Tay, the highest and westmost reaches of the drouthiest catchment area in the land, the furthest source from the sea, a tiny lochan under summit crags. If you were to stand there, by that primitive source, you would be not 25 miles from the sea at Oban, not 50 to the Headland of the Stranger, but over 80 miles to the Bell Rock. You see with the evidence of your own eyes, the canted-over spine of Scotland, the lie of the land both literally and metaphorically. When you stare into the Highland heart from such as Ben Lui or Ben More, you see only the press of mountains. There is no sense, none at all, of the hundreds of thousands of restless waterways, the millions of watery miles they travel before they are buffeted and seasoned by the seas, no hint of their sound beyond the single syllable of that lochan's first slippage across its own lip. Stand in such places and marvel, and revere, for they are sacred places, where mountains gods would do well to dwell.

But the Journey has slipped ahead of itself. I have held as close to the Allt Coire Chaorach as the fankling forestry plantation permitted, and eased beyond that dark stiflement with some relief, out onto a wide and level terrace that stands 50 feet above the main road. A gable end stands there, you see it from the road as you blur past, and I have known it from childhood (holidays at Benderloch passed this way and my mother was a generous distributor of roadside bric-à-brac, every detail from banks of primroses to waterfalls to craggy gables – she and Hazlitt would not have lasted a minute in each other's company!) as 'the house where Rob Roy lived'.

I learned as I grew and read about the Highlands for myself, then began to explore them for myself, to discard all such claims until proven otherwise, the Bruce's Caves, the Bonnie Prince Charlie's Caves, the inn windows where Robert Burns scratched love poems or tirades against the Hanoverian succession . . . and I carelessly lobbed the Glen Dochart gable end into the same rag-bag labelled 'rubbish until proven innocent', except that I was to discover in time that it was more or less true. 'More or less' because Rob Roy did live on that moraine-sculpted shelf called Auchinchisallen, but not in any four walls which included the half-surviving gable. Its walls are too thin and the points of its corners too sharp to have been built in the 17th century (walls twice that girth and corners rounded to deflect the wind – and the sound of the wind – were the order of the day in Highland Scotland). There lies the outline of Rob's house, knee high and smothered in moss and turf, and it could be that its stones were reordered into a later house and you see some of them in that free-standing ruin.

Rob Roy came to Auchinchisallen in 1713, bankrupt and outlawed, his family brutally evicted in his absence from their home at Inversnaid on Loch Lomond by the Duke of Montrose's men, Montrose being one of his creditors. The astounding life and times, as well as the landscape at the untranquil hour in Highland history, laid bare with vivid eloquence by the late W.H. Murray in his *Rob Roy MacGregor*, an unsurpassed model of what a historical biography should be. A helpful savour for the Journey through Glen Dochart and concerning Rob's acquisition of Auchinchisallen from the Earl of Breadalbane:

> It suited Breadalbane well to have on his land a man of Rob Roy's resource, the more so when outrage had maddened him against that obnoxious Whig Montrose. Like most other great men of the Highlands, Breadalbane had use for a body of men living in contempt of the law, provided they were sufficiently resolute to savage the lands of his enemies, and disciplined enough to give him no trouble at home. James Graham was a man to be brought down if that could be done, and Iain Glas relished the idea of providing a base of operations for Rob Roy. If Montrose were ineffective in defending his own land, who would trust him with the nation's? Government of course would know that Breadalbane could halt his raids if he chose, and that would enhance his negotiating position in certain affairs.
>
> Rob Roy was pleased with this new refuge . . . The house overlooked the flat grasslands of the River Dochart about a hundred feet below. Along its banks went the drove road used by the Skye and Lochaber herds, with a night-stance at Luib one mile east. The house was well sited for gathering news . . .
>
> By the early summer of 1713, Rob and his family were established in Auchinchisallen, and Rob had reorganised his life. He did so most efficiently, for he grasped the simple principle on which he had to work, and applied it methodically. For him, the king's law no longer

ran. Its rejection had to be mutual. He would substitute for it his own conception of natural justice as he had been led to see it (amending it over the coming years in light of experience).

Lowland society had outlawed him; therefore, since he had no means of living or supporting dependents other than by the life of an outlaw, that should be his profession, and his prey those who had unjustly imposed the outlawry. The lands of Montrose were the prime target . . .

How tellingly he conducted his redefined lifestyle can be gauged by the fact that within two years he had a charge of treason against him, and having withdrawn into his Trossachs heartlands, a troop of mercenaries under General William Cadogan burned Auchinchisallen to the ground, believing that it would ingratiate the general with the upwardly mobile Montrose.

Murray tells how Rob had laid an ambush for the troopers, but the party was too strong, so he lay in hiding and fury watching until he could take no more and ordered his men to open fire. There were casualties on both sides, but the Macgregors stole away into Glen Chaorach, and crossed into Balquhidder, climbing the very burn where I had just descended. It is not hard to see why Rob Roy would appeal to Murray as a subject. Murray was the writer-mountaineer incarnate, a fearless climber with the soul of a poet, who produced two of the most extraordinary books any man will ever write about the mountains of Scotland. He also espoused the very highest standards of ethics and fairness in his dealings with his fellow man, and he would find in Rob Roy a kindred spirit, a man who was a mountaineer for a living because an intimacy with mountains was fundamental to his wellbeing, and a man whose fairness, and his compassion even in the harshest of adversity, are fundamental to the wellbeing of his reputation which still endures more than 250 years after his death. Murray gave him this memorable tribute:

While Rob was waiting through December [1734] for his God to call him away, perhaps he thought less of his deep despairs, or the long-drawn hardship that shortened his life, and his memory brought him images of the land he loved so well that the power of the great men around had not sufficed to break his will to live on it, or his grasp on happiness. No man could have maintained his ground as he did for 20 years, however disciplined his body and quick his mind in the skills of living off the land like a wild animal, unless the energy fountained from deep wells of love. His land and people were a well from which his generosity of mind drew life.

So it is an unsatisfactory relic which stands above the road to Crianlarich. The gable end, which was not Rob's in any case, is dwarfed by the late 20th-century's gesture towards history and the landscape of Glen Dochart, an electricity pylon. The chimney does not reach one-third of the way up the pylon, and that gaunt presence does not invite a lingering appraisal of the site or Rob's memory. The slumberous ruin of Rob's house is unmarked, which is fair enough, and it was always an outpost of that heartland between Balquhidder and Loch Lomondside which shaped him, and sustained him. But I have lingered long and often in Glen Dochart, mostly it should be said for reasons which cling to a winter watersheet a mile upstream from here, but also because in my countless lesser journeys across the Highland Edge, it is when you swerve out of Glen Ogle into Glen Dochart and catch your first alpine glance of Ben More, that you have the new status of the landscape confirmed. It may be above the watershed of Glen Ogle that the bolt draws closed behind you, but it is the first sight of Ben More above Glen Dochart that speaks to you of a mountain realm with an unambiguous Highland voice. When Rob Roy lived, that was as true of the Trossachs, but times change and it is no longer true. So the significance of what is left of Auchinchisallen is that it is history which is still true to a sense of place. Or perhaps it should be the other way round. Glen Dochart's sense of place is still true to its history. The pylon does not assist its cause, but nor does it obliterate it. And if you happen to come on the ruin from above, as Rob Roy did with his ambush party, and after a night out on the hill at that, you drain every dreg you can from that greened-over outline of stones in the ground; your mind is full of your own idea of that house which stood in the summer of 1713 and the man who moved in here, and the frame of mind he brought to bear on it. And perhaps, if you revered the life and work of Bill Murray, you might catch yourself standing a little way off, looking out as Murray must have done, as Rob Roy must have done before Murray, raising your eyes to where Sgiath Chuil and Meall Glas lounge across the northern horizon, and loving the land where you stand because of the way it looks, because of the way it can make pulp of your emotions for no reason whatsoever other than the fact that you were born to it, that your foot is on your native heath. You might glance back at the shrouded stones and wish you could interrogate them. What was it like then? What was he like? Oh, for the sweet mute speech of stones.

What service we might tender
– one to the other –
if we could teach to stones
the speech of tongues and bones
or – better! – learn
the sweet mute speech of stones.

How might stones render
the ping-pong zest of avalanche
the vice of ice, the smoothing
gusto of spates, how re-define
the arts of standing and silence?

We could tell them
– if we dare – how jauntily
they wear the haute couture
of lichens, and in time, in time,
teach them how to rhyme.
And in return request

shed light on the runes of mystery
or the spilled beans of history.

There are oak trees in the small grove which the Allt Coire Chaorach cuts down through the moraines. Strangers hereabouts, oak trees. Not that they should be, but it's noticeable that wherever you find them now, they cling to the steep flanks of small gorges where the grazing sheep and deer has been less pervasive, less devastating than on the open ground. An oak wood should be such a fundamental part of the Highland landscape, as appropriate and elemental as mountain burns, but where they have flourished they have mostly been felled, and where they have clung on the sheep and the deer have nipped natural regeneration in the bud. I scanned the tiny gorge by Rob's old home for young trees. There was not one. This relic of a wood which, as recently as Rob's day, would have lightly cloaked the mountain for another thousand feet, will be extinct in another hundred years; our own time will mark the extinction of trees which have flourished here since before men came, which paused in their flourishing only to accommodate ice ages, then rushed back into leafage as soon as the ice relented.

An oak is an uncanny creature. It may live for 200 to 300 years. In that time, it is likely to be a hospitable host for anything up to 200 different organisms from weevils, fungi and gall wasps to tawny owls, woodpeckers and root-dwelling foxes and badgers. Its canopy is a benevolent shelter for countless wildflowers, and for landscape dawdlers like me, and in the wild bare places, mosses and lichens and ferns cling to it as affectionately as bairns to a mother's skirts. It has given us many gifts – building timbers, mansion house panelling, hulls for sea-going tribes from Viking longboats to east coast trawlers, cartwheels, church pews, fence posts, and oak casks beloved of brewers, vintners and distillers. But it is a slow-growing tree, and our own era has run out of patience for slow-growing things, as we will run out of oak trees, unless . . . As I write this, the Woodland Trust has just announced its acquisition of Glen Finglas south of Balquhidder (and another haunt of Rob Roy MacGregor), 10,000 acres of all-too-typically atrophied landscape, browsed to the bone from lochside to mountain-top over the last 200 years. Encouraged by the scattered survival of smatterings of native trees, the Trust plans to plant 1,000,000 new trees, including many oaks, and by removing sheep and culling deer, let trees thrive again. It is absolutely the only way to begin to redress a hideous imbalance. Set parcels of land aside – and 10,000 acres should be considered a small parcel, a minimum (the desolation of Highland treelessness is millions of acres wide) – with only one purpose, the re-establishment of nature's diversity. For with the trees will come all the eager tree-thirled tribes, spores on the winds of all nature, avid for return, thirsting to reclaim the birthright they have been denied for so long. Thereafter, nature conservation's possibilities will be limited only by the scope of our own imagination. Beaver is already on the way back, a commitment made at Government level (for what that's worth). Wild boar is a possibility. And when we have restored habitat enough, so is the wolf. The Journey will revisit the theme of wolves, for there is a place in the north where my mind's eye places them, but already you see the scope of what unfurls from beneath the June canopy of a cluster of oak trees. It is a mighty tree, and a mighty symbol of past and future, the Highland oakwood. Only its present is derelict. Only today's living generations can pronounce its fate. Only *this* moment, of all the moments of the Highland oakwoods' evolution, must be seized so that oak trees like the one at my back clamber up out of the furtive gullies and swarm across the land again, until they are as thick on the ground as sheep.

A roar at my back, an intrusive belch, a bridge-shuddering oak-trembling bellow, a convoy four-strong of articulated forestry trucks heading east, groaning under the piled-high burden of spruce trees . . . no roof timbers or trawler hulls there, but paper mill pulp, chipboard, forestry's answer to junk food. The work of clear-felling harvests of timber from mountainsides all across the land goes on and on. Public opinion wrinkles its nose in profound distaste. As a land use, as a landscape abuse, we think it stinks. Here is the oak tree's real dilemma: the same generations – those living now – who are responsible for turning the work of the Forestry Commission from a landscape-conscious publicly-owned source of rural employment teaching the skills of silviculture into privatised and shallow-minded cash crop mercenaries accountable to no one . . . those same generations of people are the last hope of future generations of oak trees. The portents are poor, but there are scraps of hope, straws in the wind, a fistful of acorns from which to clothe lightly the mountain flanks of the Allt Coire Chaorach again, oak trees in the Corrie of the Rowan Berries. And a better remembrance than pylons for the life of Robert C. Campbell, also known as Rob Roy MacGregor, sometime of this parish.

7

The Soul of Wildness

Broken bits of the old railway line, placid stretches of riverbank pock-marked with otter spraints (the river deep and dark and slowly going the other way), a necklace of small lochs, and Ben More massive over your left shoulder so that you keep turning round, looking, vast unchancy mountain that it is; then a wide wetland mile where the river is hesitant and sluggish and given to flooding at the least encouragement as though it is no longer satisfied with the channel it has cut for itself through the peaty ooze of mud and reeds and tall grass . . . such is the landscape mix between Auchinchisallen and Crianlarich. It's a desultory landscape, an unsatisfying conclusion to the broad power of Glen Dochart. I've always thought Glen Dochart should emerge bursting into sunlight from a great watershed like the Pass of Glencoe, maybe, or Brander. Instead, it emerges from a bog on the edge of Crianlarich.

But the bog has its focal point, its one undeniable beauty, though its June greeneries are not how I remember it, not the shades I associate it with; when I think of Loch Dochart, I think of it in the fire shades of autumn, the greys and whites and hard metallic blues of winter, the daffodil yellow of winter-into-spring. June makes it look as if it has borrowed someone else's frock, and it doesn't quite fit. The shape is too rounded, the textures too soft, the shores too fertile, the trees too leafy. I'm too warm, too comfortable, too suspicious that nature is playing games with me. Where's the catch? The ruined castle on its mid-loch island is pretty, not gaunt. The island itself is so thickly wooded that you might think an otter would have trouble squirming between the tree trunks, buffeting through the density of the understorey. One does, though, and quite possibly several do, to the concerted mistrust and disapproval of the wildfowl hordes which thicken the darkest parts of the loch, under the crags on the north shore. Ducks like these – teal, wigeon, tufted, mallard by the hundred, goosanders, mergansers, and kindred spirits like grebes, moorhens, coots – reproduce on the safety-in-numbers principle, and by June a water like this is chaotic with infancy. To the otter, and for that matter the pike and the peregrine, all that reverberating, rippling life is just so many sitting ducks. A brood of ten which takes to the water for the first time on Monday can be quite extinct by Friday, the bewildered mother duck the last to go. So ducks play the percentage game. Survival is for the lucky ones, and long life is not a prospect worth contemplating. The survival of the species is all.

So I stood warm and as unruffled as the oaks on the north shore (another sparse oaken survival, how wondrous with oaks the glen must have been, once; wondrous too with human living and the passage of drover herds looking over their shoulders askance and in admiration at the howl of wolves). I stood, masked by the benevolence of alder and birch which hide the summer loch from the road, and the June evening sun was yellowing the west. The loch glowed with the light and its own abundance and all it felt was strange, strange that there were no knives in the wind, no great shadows under the north cliffs, no deer on the low ground mooching down to get below the snow line, no unrolling carpet of ice on the water. Strangest of all – no whooper swans. The whoopers, Icelandic itinerants, turn up here in October, and stay in fluctuating numbers (anything between one and 80 in my experience) until April, and in my book they are the very soul of wildness.

The very soul of wildness . . . I look at the phrase on the page and I think 'what the hell does it mean?' So I thought about it and it means this. Among my preferred landscapes between the Highland Edge and Shetland, and between the Angus coast and the west coast of the Western Isles, there are dear places, landscapes within landscapes; places I visit again and again for no reason other than that each place affords me peace of mind. To keep the company of the landscape because it is all the company I crave, to occupy the best seat in the house in theatres of nature, to be moved beyond joy or tears by performances of nature, starring rock and bog, water and light, landform and creatures, and to know that each new venture into any one of these landscapes will provide reliably what I seek, always constant, never the same . . . these are the motives for my journeys. Then, slowly, over many years, and quite possibly subconsciously at first, I would discover that every one of these dear places was a whooper swan haunt. For no reason which is obvious to me yet (although it is not for the want of trying to unearth it) I adopted the whooper swan as a kind of talisman. I fancied it (the idea stands up to no biological scrutiny whatsoever) as something almost beyond nature, something which inhabits nature's world but is of a different plane, another dimension, a thing not of the flesh and blood and feathers but of the soul, the soul of wildness. And I have found it here on Loch Dochart.

But not in that summer season in which I now stood, watching fleets and squadrons of wildfowl trundle across the yellowing evening, or zapping across it, or flying or flirting or dizzying or diving or (in the lugubrious case of the heron) plying a stiff and solitary dignity across it, a cortege for one. It was still early enough in June, but the hot spell made it feel as if summer was further advanced than it really was, and then and there, a seed of doubt rooted and began to niggle. Did I really want a Journey through summer, when mostly I made a point of staying away from wild places in summer – too many people on the move, too many midges, clegs, ticks, too much bracken, trees too heavy, mountains too green. The seed would grow fast. I saw suddenly an otter slide down from the island into the water, dive and disappear, saw the ultimate amphibian move seamlessly between his two elements – a coalescence of quite magical fluency. His underwatering added bubbles to the surface wakes of birds and panic to the demeanour of a family of mallard. Mallard are not wise birds, and a family of new-born ducklings sometimes looks as if it has been put on the water by nature to entertain and die young. At two or three days old they are preposterously pretty. They spend much of the day cavorting over the surface snapping up at that layer of insects which drones and hovers six inches above the water. Parental control is almost completely absent. They resemble nothing so much as a toymaker's workshop gone berserk. But while they are berserk they are completely unprotected. A pike, for example, is spoiled for choice. Or the young birds cram together in their mother's wake as she leads them (for reasons best known to herself) across the middle of the loch away from the safety of shallows and reedbeds, and an underwatering otter can't miss, or at least it shouldn't.

I saw the bubbles. I saw the duck at the head of her brood drift suddenly sideways, the tight yellow-brown phalanx behind her follow suit, then she was thrashing the water and squawking and that square yard of loch at her back was a killing field as the otter moved in. The duck lifted off the water, flew round in a tight circle and crashed down again. The otter surfaced and she was off again, but this time she was not three feet in the air before she seemed to burst apart. Feathers fell where the otter's head had been moments before; there was a thick splash as the

duck hit the water out of control and probably already dead. None of us
– otter, mallard, ducklings or me – had seen the peregrine, but it had
homed in unerringly on the commotion.

Not quite unerringly. The duck had fallen onto water. The falcon turned
(an object lesson to mallards in the art of the tight circle), the slate blue
of its back gleaming dully in the yellow light, hurtled low over the
floating bird, turned again and saw the bird begin to move, slowly, on its
side towards the island, propelled there by the jaws of an otter. There was
not a duckling to be seen.

Some you win . . .

Otter slunk ashore. Falcon disappeared behind the island, probably
perched to wait and watch and try again. The air was full of wildfowl
panicked by the drama of the moment. On the topmost stone of the castle
ruin a cormorant stood. It had been there for as long as I had, and
remained just as still, wings akimbo. It looked like a gendarme on points
duty, controlling the traffic movements of some avian Paris with nods of
its head. Only one crash in the evening rush hour. Not bad, not bad. You
can never legislate for nutters with turbochargers and pointy wings.

Now that I began to think about it, now that there was time to think in
a lull between dramas (the sense of wild theatre again), I was
remembering an old September, a late September, a pause on a journey
to Skye, an 'oh-you-never-know' kind of pause, a different otter
encounter with a different outcome. I had crossed the river to sit among
the rocks and oaks of the north shore, saw the otter head rounding the
end of the island, trailing a wake which rippled oddly across the surface
between island and shore. I had been watching handfuls of gulls drifting
through the glen because there was not much else to watch. They passed
me more or less at eye level, and their reflections moved through the dark
depths of the loch below me. The otter turned my head, and its rippling
wake began to break up the reflections of the flying gulls, abstracting the
bird shapes, elongating and splintering them into more and more
horizontals, like pieces of white slate. I was briefly captivated, nature as
cartoonist. When one more white reflection crossed the rippling water
and transformed more weirdly than all the others, I was enthralled. The
rippling was at its widest, the reflection scattered into a hundred bits, but
then as I watched, it began to reform, compacting itself into a more and
more credible bird shape; it climbed sharply up through the water
towards the surface until it splashed and glittered and there was a
whooper swan sitting on it.

It had been a half-hearted stop in the first place, too early autumn for
realistic expectations of seeing whoopers. It became an object lesson, as

Milestone on the road to the
Mull of Kintyre

'Heir lies the corpss . . .' burial
ground, Kilnaish, Argyll

Paps of Jura centre stage for a spectacular Kintyre sunset

Leaning, standing stone, Gigha

Sea pinks and daisies thicken a roadside on Gigha

*The view from the tent, Kintyre
coast*

Stone figure, Kintyre

The Mist Rolling in from the sea . . . Kintyre at sunrise

Ardnamurch lighthouse, an exhilarating place in a hurricane

Stating the obvious at Ardnamurchan Point

Eerie sunlight illuminates the summit of Beinn Sgritheall

Ladhar-Bheinn and Loch Hourn, dawn

The vexing Skye Bridge, subject of many controversies

Gavin Maxwell's last home, the lighthouse cottages of Eilean Bhan

Travel weary. The old Fiat estate survives the double crossing of the Bealach na Ba

Cul Mor from the Inverkirkaig track

Stac Pollaidh breathing fire from the north

Journey's end – Suilven with its head high in the gulfs of blue air

persuasive an argument as I know for the case for taking the trouble to stop. Having stopped, I took the trouble to cross to the quiet side of the loch, away from the road so I saw the otter, the ripples, the reflections. I would almost certainly have seen the swan fly in even if I had not crossed, but I would not have seen it alight on its own reflection. I might have picked up the otter's circumnavigation of the island, but I would not have been in the right place at the right time to see it meet the swan head-on. I wrote the moment down, not long after it happened, in an earlier book, *Waters of the Wild Swan*:

> The whooper, having landed on itself and sat on itself, promptly stood on itself in that heraldically supreme gesture of high and wide wings which so often follows almost any aspect of sudden swan activity. The otter, having rounded the further end of the island, was lured back by the sound of the swan just as it reared. I have often wondered since then how that must have looked from ten yards away through eyes at water level – just possibly too impressive for comfort, I should think. The otter's response was remarkably cool, considering it was the first swan he would have seen since April; he sank. The swan swung leisurely round to follow the bubbling underwatering, like a small boat on a bow rope. Then the otter resurfaced and stopped, facing the swan which had now turned through 180 degrees. For five minutes, the two creatures circled each other, sizing each other up, the otter making a slit on the water, the swan a swirling wake as she swung through tighter circles than the otter. As I watched I was aware that my heart was thumping, my throat dry and tight, and I realised then that I was in there with them. There were not two creatures on the water with me as passive observer, but three creatures, two on the water and one on the crag, all sizing each other up.
>
> The otter was certainly on to me, turning away from the swan for a few moments to work the wind with his nose, to dive and swim for a few yards towards me and resurface and stare, then turn back to the swan. The swan caught the otter's inquiry, muttered a monosyllable, looked at me, then swung through a new arc to face the otter's new direction. To be a part of such a trinity of awareness was to be elevated briefly beyond anything I have ever known watching wildlife, and I sensed that for as long as the episode lasted, I had shed something of my formal humanness, and become something more elementally appropriate, some old throwback, something nearer the animal state. I felt lighter, looser, freer than I

could ever remember, so charged with purposeful energy that I might race up the crag at my back without a thought, or dive into the loch from my 20-feet-high ledge and swim to the island underwater, perhaps coming up between swan and otter and throwing them a confusing wake of my own. The otter was porpoising now, a playful gesture which seemed almost calculated to persuade the swan to participate, but the bird simply sat pretty and swung through lazy arcs on its unseen rope, and watched. I felt so strongly this wild fellow-feeling that the urge grew in me to participate, but it was then that the door which some god-of-the-wilds had opened for me slammed shut, and I realised that what they – otter and swan – were prepared to accept was my stillness. I was, after all, human, predator, threat, alien, and as welcome in their midst as an oil slick. But a remnant of that older throwback instinct demanded an audience, and I stood and moved stealthily down the crag's easy ledges to a woody shelf just above the water and stepped darkly among its small shadowy trees. Otter and swan watched intently. Then the otter swam to within 20 feet, snorted, dived and was gone. He resurfaced out by the island and stared back, but the whole thing was done, the spell in shreds, the swan perturbed and swimming strongly away as I trudged round the shore and across the river to the car in a black depression. I was angered by my own arrogance. To think that a swan and an otter might somehow see me as different, acceptable; that my frustrations could demand not just stillness and quiet observation but participation – what stupid, futile and unworthy creatures we humans have become, I thought. It will take hundreds of years of reverse evolution to win back a semblance of the animal state we once inhabited. My five elevated minutes were nothing more than a freakish privilege accorded by nature and my own willingness to be still in wild places. If I had not suddenly become unwilling, who knows what I might have seen, what deeper insights I might have won, but I disobeyed those instincts which have always served me best in the wilds to try and be something which I was not.

Hours later, in a calmer frame of mind, I could cherish the richness of the encounter, and although there was much truth in the train of thought which followed it, I had watched a small episode of nature which had a quite magical aura about it, and in my own subsequent behaviour I had learned something new. All that nature can ask of us is that we respect its wishes. We are what we have become, and if there is a way to a closer human co-existence with *nature, it is a long road and those of us who would tread it must do so a step at a time, seeking to accomplish only that which is humanly possible. The miracles take a little longer.*

The Journey that paused on an early June evening, eight years after the event, remembered vividly, recognised with some satisfaction that in the intervening years the lesson had been taken to heart. I pulled back from the trees, and neither bird nor beast saw me go. I stepped into the yellow light filtering down along the old railway line. Next stop Crianlarich.

8

Runny-egg Yellow

Crianlarich is the most signposted nowhere on the planet. From Oban, Fort William, Glasgow, Stirling and Perth to name but a few which spring to mind without copious research, more roads lead to Crianlarich than can possibly be good for it. What you find when you get there (and how it must tantalise then confound tourists and other strangers) is a T-junction in a raincloud, an over-large hotel which seems mostly closed, and a hideous double bend under a railway bridge where you invariably meet articulated trucks from Belgium as big as the hotel in the middle of the road. To be fair, there is a road sign which warns you about traffic in the middle of the road. What it does not do is offer solutions about what to do when you meet it head-on. Reversing round one half of a blind double bend on an EC-designated trunk road is not recommended by the police drivers' manual, *Roadcraft*, nor by the Highway Code. And it is an undeniable truth that if you are driving through Crianlarich (which is what most people do with it) you will miss out on its solitary cultural experience, the station tearoom. Yes, Crianlarich has a station. And unlike most Highland villages which have stations, Station Hotels, Station Roads, and Station Tearooms, Crianlarich Station has railway lines and trains stop there. One can only imagine that when Dr Beeching was wielding his mad axemanship about the Highlands in the 1960s he had his concentration broken in Crianlarich by something large and Belgian oncoming in the middle of the road.

It is an endearing station too, storm-lashed by winds from every compass point, but endearing, and it has a tearoom. Crianlarich Station Tearoom is a legend. People have missed trains just to while away an extra hour in its ambience. If your idea of railway cuisine is the stuff they cellophane-wrap on the Waverley Station concourse, here is an instant culture shock stained runny-egg yellow. It was here, one sodden February afternoon, that I fell into conversation with a shepherd and his two collies, two back-packing mountaineers who were also Austrian power station technicians, and a doctor from Bristol. We all sat down, more or less independently, at the one table which had any seats left (it is a very small tearoom), and all suffered the same spontaneous combustion of laughter as one by one we put our food order on the table, a cup of tea and a runny-egg roll. Five mouths grinned and giggled and chattered idly as they yellowed. Crianlarich tearoom will be forever runny-egg yellow in my mind and a blessed haven of catering pared to the bone.

There are three ways to leave Crianlarich going north. If you drive you must negotiate the middle-of-the-road, double-blind-bend-under-the-railway-bridge, articulated Belgian oncomers. If you walk, you must shackle and hamstring yourself to that travesty (dictionary definition 2, 'a ridiculous misrepresentation') of the Highland Journey, the West Highland Way. Travesty because it breeds a mentality at odds with the landscape and the landscape tradition. It swallows whole the Sassenach preoccupation with rights of way, but if you believe in freedom to roam, which is the Highland tradition, then feel free and *roam* and sod the guidebook, and sod the clamourers after rights of access. We *have* a right of access implicit in the fact of being a Scot on his or her native heath, and being a hospitable tribe (to all but landowners who argue otherwise) we extend the hospitality of our landscape to allcomers, allcomers, that is, who treat it with respect and leave it as they find it.

Or you can leave by train, snooze to Bridge of Orchy (you won't miss much, just Tyndrum), then prepare for the train ride of your life, short, sweet and sensational. I looked at the train timetable. Two hours. Two hours in Crianlarich is a long time. I could subject myself to purgatory, five miles on the West Highland Way, those five which deposit the unwary at Tyndrum. I am wary. I've been to Tyndrum, got the dish towel. But I've been enjoying this Journey too much. A little masochism seemed called for. It's only five miles. I could enlist in the monstrous regiment.

A waymarker. Aargh.

The morning was hot, the path was hot, hot and crowded, by which I mean I could see ten people ahead of me in scattered groups. I am unaccustomed to paths of ten. Perhaps I could spurt into clear air. I had hauled in five or six of the ten and began to relish the game when I realised that instead of four ahead of me there were 20, and as the track opened onto a straight 50 . . . more. I thought miserably of a Lake District expedition a few years ago which began at 8.30 a.m. on The Band, a

69

turgid bit of Bowfell, and there were 50 purple rucksacks on the first slope ahead of me. The West Highland Way is like The Band without the contours.

I met a couple with the map out, looking forlornly over their shoulders, pointing back the way they had come towards the shrugging mass of Beinn Dubhcraig. Problem?

'We cannot climb? Shame. Not to climb?'

'You want to climb it?'

'Yes. Want.'

'So why don't you climb it?'

They frowned in unison as though I had pronounced heresy.

'Fence. Guidebook. B and B man . . .'

They grinned at each other. 'B and B man' was a private joke. I said:

'Can I give you some advice?'

'Advice. Okay.'

'Climb the fence. Throw away the guidebook. Shoot B and B man. Then go and climb the mountain.'

'Climb is okay?'

I made a widespread gesture of my arms towards every mountain I could see.

'Climb is okay. Climb them all if you want to. In Scotland, to climb is okay.'

They grinned again. He said to her:

'Shoot B and B man. Yes!' They laughed and I laughed with them.

'*Buenos Dias!*'

'*Hasta la vista.*'

I don't know if they climbed. I plodded for a while, saddened that there were those in my own country who perpetrated such negative propaganda in the name of tourism. A party of four stomped past me, one of the groups I had overhauled earlier. A passing Yorkshire voice counselled me thus:

'Slow and steady, mate. Take it slow and steady. That's the way to take stuff like this.'

'Thanks.'

I stopped in my tracks. What was I doing? What was I doing here? I was trying to chart a Journey of my own choosing across landscapes of my own choosing. What the hell did the West Highland Way have to do with it? What did it have to do with me? I turned on my heel.

I pushed open the door. Forty-five minutes to go. I said:

'Cup of tea and an egg roll, please.'

70

Tyndrum Upper. I was awake. The train window faced down towards the village, and through it I recognised all the hallmarks of an embryonic Aviemore. There are more neon signs than residents. A huge new hotel, bus parties a speciality, a new street full of new houses (quite nice houses actually, cottagey, Scottish, a pleasant surprise when you see what else has been built here), enough food and drink places to feed and water a small town, or 20 coach parties should they all choose to stop at once (they do, they do), shops that sell whisky and fudge and smell violently of pot pourri. I can never work that one out: why pot pourri? What's Highland about pot pourri? I just know that down in the foyer of the Clifton the video screen will be playing an overweight man in a kilt singing *The Dark Island* to the accompaniment of an electric organ and a drum machine. All this, and they've just reopened the gold mines of Cononish up the Ben Lui track. I fear for Ben Lui and that small still opalescent lochan under its summit when gold fever strikes. They say opals are unlucky. All that's missing here now is skiing, but if you have gold mines, who needs it?

The train shuddered, groaned, and crept off. As far as I could see, I had the train to myself, a two-car Sprinter, which had declined to sprint thus far, and in this heat, who could blame it? I felt like a hi-jacker. Take this train to Rannoch. It is a curious feeling, being alone in an empty train. The guard came through calling for Tyndrum tickets, saw that the complement of passengers was unaltered from Crianlarich, caught my eye and said:

'What! You again!'

I shrugged, returned his cheerful grin.

'I'll change seats if you like.'

'No. You'll just get them dirty. Where you headed?'

'The Moor.'

'Rannoch?'

'The same.'

'What the hell for?'

'Why the hell not?'

'Too wild.'

'That's what the hell for. Exactly that.'

'Suit yourself. Thought maybe you'd given up on the West Highland Way and decided to skip the hard bit. Look at 'em . . .'

He gestured through the window to where the footpath trudged along just below the railway line, and we sprinted past one technicolour group of walkers after another.

'That's why the train's empty. They're all *walking* to Fort William. It's not healthy. It's daft, too. Mind you, Rannoch's dafter.'

'If I was to tell you that I'm spending the night out on the Moor to get the feel of the place as a future sanctuary for wolves . . .?'

'Wolves.' He said it deadpan, matter-of-fact, cool. I nodded.

'My brother-in-law could help you,' he said, in the same measured tones.

'Is your brother-in-law a wolf expert?'

He shook his head, heavily, exaggerating the shaking.

'Psychiatrist.'

'I'll let you know,' I said. He went off, muttering 'Wolves!' with theatrical incredulity. 'Thought I'd heard 'em all. But . . . wolves . . .'

We trundled round the long loop which hugs the hills huddled into Auch Gleann. The road is far across the river at this point so that if you are driving, you drive looking sideways at the mountains. The Way is down by the river so that if you are walking you walk looking sideways and upwards, so you probably stumble a lot. But the train digs into the flank of Beinn Odhar, lets the curve of the hill horseshoe it east, at which point one of the best hill shapes in all the Highlands materialises perfectly formed in the window. Beinn Dorain is suddenly there, a pyramidal prow, perfect almost, except that I prefer it with snow on the pow of the prow. Beinn Dorain is a centrepiece, the hooked beak of an eagle shape made from high contours, the mountains fan out and back north-east and south-east, great wings to hold the eagle head steady, coldly eyeing the West.

The train kinks north, and a handsome viaduct pulls you away from the mountainside and puts space about you, although there is little enough of the sense of a viaduct when you're on it. I thought: 'Glen Ogle was like this. Glen Ogle should still be like this. It must have been some train journey – Stirling, Callander, the sudden transition from Lowland to Highland at the Pass of Leny, under Ben Ledi, a collision of landscapes so sudden you could almost mark the spot with a cairn, north up the dark side of Loch Lubnaig to Strathyre, a longing glance into Balquhidder Glen with sawn-off Stobinian head-butting the snow clouds, down to Lochearnhead, then the long grind up Glen Ogle, the Highlands instantly more convincing, more grandiose, more intimate, more intimidating if that is the way you see dark precipices, then the teetering descent and the long curve west and the sudden exhilaration of the breadth of Glen Dochart, the muscular torso of Ben More, Crianlarich Station Tearoom, runny-egg rolls, then on to this, clattering a hundred feet above the waters of the Allt Chonoghail that breenge through Auch Gleann. Would any engine driver worth the rank ever tire of all that?

You would think the tourism potential was limitless. Countries like

Switzerland which value their rail network would find this situation incomprehensible. There are the jostling coach parties and get-rich-quick architecture of Tyndrum, there is the caravan cortege crawling up the A82 towards Glencoe and jousting with Eurotrucks, and here is an empty train rubbing the flank of Beinn Dorain. I changed seats to watch Auch Gleann advance and recede, and caught a glimpse, far up the glen, of an old adversary – Beinn Mhanach.

I was younger and less discriminating then, and although I was mercifully unsmitten by the disease myself, I even consorted with Munro-baggers. Weekends were for mountains, almost all weekends, especially winter ones, although even then I had a profound distaste for high summer. Expeditions almost thrived on adversity. I can no longer remember whose idea Beinn Mhanach was, nor whose was the prevailing voice which urged the expedition on when wiser counsel would have ushered us towards a long, lazy lunch in the Bridge of Orchy Hotel. The conditions were not exceptional, just run-of-the-mill midwinter atrocious. You could drive the Auch Gleann track then. There were no forbidding 'Private' signs at the road end, but 25 years ago, the Munro disease was not the epidemic it has become these last few silly years. Today's track could not stand the traffic which would want to use it.

I remember it was my car, I remember that the track tossed it about like a Pittenweem trawler in a North Sea gale. I remember that getting out of the car felt like standing on the deck of a Pittenweem trawler in a North Sea gale, only wetter and not salty. I remember only this of the rest of the day, that we came off the mountain in the dark. Of the mountain itself there is nothing. Not a scrap. I don't know what it looks like, what it feels like, what wildlife might have watched us go, how it stands in its landscape. It was an utterly pointless exercise. No. It was a mostly pointless exercise. It was part of the learning process. It helped to teach me to rely more on my own judgement than the judgement of others. It helped to persuade me that mountains are richer experiences when you go there on your own. It convinced me at a stroke that Munro-bagging (where that is the only reason for climbing) is as big an insult to the Highland landscape as sheep. If all you do is climb the mountain to pronounce it climbed, to tick it off on a list so that once they're all ticked off, you can have your name added to another list, which is the list of Munroists . . . if that's the height of your ambition, then I wish you every one a Beinn Mhanach.

Bridge of Orchy. The train stopped expectantly, though it seemed to have little enough reason to expect.

Another layer of Highlands begins here, something more indefinably of

the West, a sharper distillation of the landscape essence. The roads grow
lonelier, and the stranger going north begins to be impressed – or
appalled – by the emptiness of places. Mountains begin to make greater
demands, trekking country away to the north-west, and Glencoe just
over the next horizon where the mountains go beyond landscape and
become – briefly – all the world there is. And it is about Bridge of Orchy
on countless journeys to Skye and other north-west places that I begin to
count buzzards on telegraph poles. If you are travelling south, it is at
Bridge of Orchy that you feel the Highlands begin to relent.

The train panted. If I got off now and headed up that burn, straight up
all the way, I would hit the watershed between Beinn Dorain and its
soulmate Beinn an Dothaidh. I know that burn. On a day like this it
would be like climbing a ladder of stained-glass slabs. Pools and falls
glitter and glow, square edged and flat backed, the right-angle as art form,
nature proving its own rules with its own exception. I looked up and saw
it flash yellow in the sun, thought of it cool in the heat, the jade clarity of
its pools closing over my head, looking back up from deep in a pool (I
know the one, its rock bottom bears my footprint) to rocks and jellying
clouds, bursting up into sunlight. The urge stole over me to gather my
pack and boots and step from the train right then, at which point a door
opened, six passengers clattered aboard, each carrying packs the size of
waterfalls. The door slammed, the train groaned and eased forward, all
patience rewarded. Besides, the Journey wanted its flirtation with the
Moor and its wolves.

The train stitches together the hems of Dorain and Dothaidh, Beinn
Achaladair of the long ridges and the unsung Beinn a' Chreachain (but
it's a Munro too, for its sorrows, so it isn't *that* unsung). Chreachain was
another Mhanach, but many years later I went back (I could never think
of a good enough reason to go back to Mhanach) because I remembered
the wretchedness of trying to navigate the twists of its high ridge in a
sealed and steaming envelope of cloud, and because near what proved
to be the summit (I bumped into a cairn with one hand holding the
compass and the other trying to keep it free enough of wetness to be
legible) there was a shaft of non-cloud with a lochan in it and I like high
mountain lochans. The second time I zigged the zags without cloud or
compass, the loch was a sheet of tinfoil, and a second tiny lochan hard
under the summit was the bluest thing I ever saw. That second lochan
alarmed me, for it had not registered at all in my recollections of the
first climb, in which case I was probably in mortal danger of stepping
off its small crag and falling more feet than would be good for me onto
its snowed-over ice. There but for the grace . . . but it was a good

discovery the second time. And because it was May and the day as blithe as it was long and the start had been early enough, I took the ridge to Achaladair, and a canny contour above Coire a' Ghabhalach from which I stepped onto the bealach between Dorain and Dothaidh. It was on the way down from that cherished watershed that I lingered in a certain pool on the glass staircase and my feet touched bottom and the clouds above jellied.

An hour later, I sat with my skin sun-stiffened and my throat sun-dried before a pint of the black-and-white stuff in the Bridge of Orchy Hotel, and I raised the glass to the ridge-maker and the lochan-painter and the staircase glass-stainer. And when the second glass was to hand, I pulled a notebook from my pocket and scribbled down the title of a something that had been rummaging around in my head for half the day. What trickled down, in Norman MacCaig's phrase, from beneath the title was this:

MOUNTAINEER, MOUNTAIN AIR

He gulps it. The overhanging
cornice compounding the gully,
last straw, camel-back-snapping.
He gulps it, and drugged on it,
finds the strength he knew
– moments ago – was beyond him.

He pants it. Won through,
won over, one up, the ridge
is his to cramp on,
pant-and-axe, pant-and-axe,
that deep grey ritual bit every winter
mountain extracts, extracts, extracts.

He swills it. High on summitry,
distilled in crystal chambers
the single malt of almost-madness
avalanche of relish, good vintage,
good mountain, fusion of savours,
mountaineer, mountain air.

Under Beinn a' Chreachain the train slips between a tiny fort called Dun Laoghan and the bothy at Gorton, then steps away from the hills, to cling

75

to the very shore of that moor-sea called Rannoch. Neil Munro called it thus:

> . . . *the moor stretched flat and naked as a Sound . . . all untracked and desert-melancholy . . . God-forgotten, man-forsworn, wild Rannoch, with the birds above it screaming, was the oddest thing, the eeriest in nature he had ever seen. It charmed and repelled him . . . Half a dozen times before the noon that day he walked up the brae from which the moor was widest seen, and looked across it with uneasy breast, and drank, as one might say, the spirit of the wilderness, so strange and so forlorn . . .*

Even the mountains seemed to share that view, for suddenly they no longer hurtled down to the carriage window. They frowned down to where the tiny train set its course on a huge curve round the eastern fringe of the moor, a foolhardy crawler; they shook hoary heads in disapproving incomprehension and withdrew so that suddenly the train's only possible destination was distance. To the north, the sense of space grew and grew, undeniable even through the liberally grimed windows, and the 'spirit of the wilderness, so strange and so forlorn', was a canopy stretched taut across miles of loch and lochan, rock and bog, heather and peat-hag and not a single bird was above it, screaming or otherwise.

The train shouldered its way through all this, quietly rumbling neutral, as unconcerned as the tawny flanks of red deer herds which it began to brush past. No deer started away. The train was a moving fragment of their landscape, regular passage and harmless. It trembled their portion of bog as it approached. They recognised that trembling and knew it for what it was. It rumbled past and shook the ground under their feet. Then it trembled into its distance attending to its own mysterious purpose while the deer attended to theirs, scenting their disapproval of its dieselly odour before the moor's constant and many winds broke and banished it.

A long dull conifer plantation blurred past. Rannoch Station stood at its further end, a *cul de sac* of that civilisation which lives elsewhere and travels by road. Rannoch Station is where the road ends and where the moor washes up against the world of the road dwellers. It is possible I could have missed something, but as far as I could see and hear, nothing at all moved at Rannoch Station. No one and nothing met the train. No one boarded it and no one left it. It stopped, went quiet, paused in its quietude which the world beyond the moor felt quite unmoved to disturb, grunted, burped twice to itself and heaved gently out into the moor again, but it left me behind.

I had almost missed the stop. In my mind was an old journey on this train to the next stop up the line. I remembered more wide and wider miles, more deer as unconcerned as all the others, more rocky, peaty, heathery bog, more and more treelessness. I remembered too, that on that second leg of the railway's crossing of the moor, the train had begun to feel like something not so much in touch with the ground as low-flying. I eyeballed stags the way a hen harrier might. Or if a hen harrier were to cross the train's path, perhaps the train would slow and keep it company, the way those uncanny cameras do in TV documentaries of birds in flight.

Then the train stopped again. I got out and stood until it had gone, until even the sound of it had gone. They say the track floats on top of the moor, a technique invented by the Romans and only refined since then, not improved upon. Not that the Romans built railways or crossed Rannoch Moor, but the infusion of that ancient lineage is just one more charm that a train journey over Rannoch Moor delivers. It's just a pity that the train in question is as bland and smelly as the 10.28 from Stirling to Edinburgh Waverley.

Corrour. I had looked at it, looked at its nothing, and wondered how on earth its station and its trains' inclination to stop there still survived. I remembered a youth hostel, and a signal-box, especially the signal-box. It was, what . . . 20 years ago? There had been a long circuit round the hills above Loch Ossian, a long sodden circuit, and an hour to wait for the train back to Crianlarich at the end of the day. It might have been a miserable hour, but the stationmaster suggested using the signal-box to dry off and change – there was a good fire going there. It was a signal-box the way God made them, before the world was privatised and electrified. It was full of levers the size of men and brass things which shone in the firelight. Sometimes some of them rang . . . oh, I don't know. I know nothing about trains or signal boxes, but the Corrour signal-box was an oasis of warmth and sanity in all that sleety winter-dark madness which the outside world had suddenly become.

There was also the sense of an island about the place, conferred by the knowledge of the unseen night-black sea of Rannoch Moor that ebbed and flowed from here to the Glencoe road, and I wondered what manner of furies would while away the night out there while I brewed some more tea.

And now I stood in all that spring-into-summer light and another train had vanished into the maw of the moor. I took my shining-brass-and-firelight memories, stored them away in their stoorie corner marked 'dinosaur', and turned my back on the station, my face to the moor, God-forgotten, man-forsworn, wild Rannoch.

9

A Landscape Fit for Wolves

I walked for two hours then stopped. It was well into the afternoon and it was not the Rannoch Moor I had anticipated at all. The ground was firm and dry, the peat cracked and crumbling. The lochs and lochans lay blue. Some sparkled. No black depths. No crust of ice. No treacheries. And no birds screamed. Some drooled – curlews. Larks roped up and abseiled down severe ascents of singing cliffs. Pipits free-fell to soft landings on knolls with their hands in their pockets. A greenshank sighed in a bog. A smattering of black grouse broke cover, eight birds in a tight flying wedge, glossy black that was sometimes blue and sometimes green, a red pencil stub behind each ear, shirt tails flapping whitely in the breeze behind them, showy Celtic birds cut down from some mediaeval saint's chapel window somewhere, Iona probably. Who designed a black grouse?

Afternoon-tea-cum-late-lunch was bread, cheese, apple, and a fistful of licorice allsorts from the morale-booster pocket (a good piece of advice that, passed on by an ancient gangrel who also mostly preferred his own company to other people's). I met him 'up the Clovy' as we would say where I come from, which is to say in Glen Clova, and years ago. He greeted me on a high shoulder of the Dreish:

'Eh aye like tae see a laddie oo' on 'es ain,' he said, establishing his Dundee pedigree with his first vowel. I nodded agreeably.

'Best wey, eh?'

'Best wey. D'ye ken aboo' the morale-booster pocket?'

I shook my head. He plunged a leathery hand into a buckled down pocket of his knapsack and produced a half-eaten packet of custard creams.

'Staves aff the pangs,' he said. 'No the hunger pangs, the fed-up pangs.

Be'er nur some ahld fart blahin awa in yer lug, eh?'

He gestured for me to try one.

'Too true.' My endorsement through flying crumbs. And since then I've cushioned my solo voyages with morale boosters – licorice allsorts, marshmallows, custard creams, that kind of thing.

'Does whisky count?' I asked him, uncorking my wee hip-flask and passing it over.

'Na.' He swigged lustily, nodded his appreciation. 'Whisky's food.'

He said his name was Alfie. Deid now fur ah Eh ken.

I rolled over and started to scribble notes, a discipline of the Journey. Get something down while you're out there. I wondered how long all this summery benevolence would last. So far, the Journey had not coughed up a single raindrop, or even a cool day. I wrote down:

> The Moor is camouflaging itself in a false summer. The real Moor is hidden underneath. One day soon it will writhe free of the skin like an adder, and be venomous to travellers. Not tonight please, not tonight.

A traverse of Rannoch Moor was one of the first ideas I had pencilled in when I chose a first rough route for the journey. (The one I now proposed to follow was my third.) I had crossed the Moor once before, at the end of an old March, when it was hard and still and steely and ice-grey and dark, dark brown. I have wandered out into it in every season from Kingshouse for a mile or two at a time just sensing its difference. I have stared out at it from Beinn Dorain, Schiehallion, and the Buachaille's near-neighbour Beinn a' Chrulaiste, the last an occasion when it connived its own sunrise weather, fashioned it into a thunderous storm and hurled that monster of its own making at mighty Clach Lethad of the Black Mount, resuming (as I saw it, high and dry on my off-to-one-side mountain) ancient glacial hostilities. If you ever fall to wondering about the ice-bound forces which made the shape of the Highlands as we know them, then scratch your head over this: here was one high white plateau, like the Icelandic ice-cap. When things began to move, and the dragging weight of the ice began to fashion mountains, Rannoch Moor fell through its own roof and lay there, a reservoir of ice, and the glaciers of the embryonic Black Mount fed it. I have stood at the base of an Icelandic glacier: it is no great claim to fame (any number of tourists have done it), and although any number of films and glossy books can prepare you for the spectacle of it (although not the scale!), nothing had prepared me for the fact that it spoke. It continually groaned and growled and muttered and spat out lumps of itself. It sounded like the indecipherable musings of a parliament of plotting architects: should we have another lake here, another mountain? Or a mountain range? If we lay our moraines through that valley, will trees follow? It was a one millionth part – a billionth for all I know – of an awareness of what went on here when Rannoch Moor invented itself and began to leak glaciers of its own – Glen Orchy, Glen Etive, Glencoe, east to Loch Rannoch, even northwards, where Loch Ericht lies. My mind is not up to the task of imagining what that invention of landscapes must have looked like, but I have heard a few syllables of the language of the architects.

More than any other fragment of my Journey, crossing Rannoch Moor was the one I approached with something like trepidation. I hold the moor in a particularly rarified species of esteem. It is an extreme of landscape, as unique in Highland Scotland as the Cairngorms plateau. Its raw scope, its primitiveness, and its potential for urging the traveller into unwariness and therefore mistakes (a foot wrong in bad weather and it could be a long time before anyone found your remains) . . . all that dogged me like a shadow. When you turn your back on that tiny gathering of civilisation's artefacts at Corrour and put the moor before you, the feeling is akin, I would imagine, to the first few pulls of an ocean-going oarsman. I had even thought twice about crossing alone, for it is an undertaking demanding no less respect than the most arduous mountain trek. The fact that it is flat, flat and naked as a sound, all untracked and desert-melancholy (perhaps not just as 'untracked' as when Munro contemplated it) should enhance, not diminish the respect. So much is hidden. And because that which is hidden lies within the very visible scope of its sprawling distance, there is always as much likelihood of being repelled as charmed.

But Hazlitt was one of the Journey's guiding lights, and the 'involuntary impression of things upon the mind' should be unfettered here of all places.

Besides, it is a place I have always felt close to, even drawn to. Almost all my previous encounters with it had been constrained by company. Now I had Rannoch Moor in my mind as a kind of watershed of the Journey, the philosophy of Hazlitt carried to an extreme which he probably never contemplated. I was prepared for adversity, for an encounter with the forces of nature on the grand scale. I was not prepared for a summer blessing, the seduction of warm winds and sunlight. I finished scribbling, sat up and looked around. Then I had an idea.

I took out an orange bivvy bag from my pack, then put the pack inside it, then put a small rock on it to keep it still. I was satisfied that I would have no trouble finding it again. Then I stood up, tied a sweater round my waist, and carrying nothing but stick and compass, I set out on a southward bearing for the heart of the moor. I walked for perhaps a mile, in as straight a line as I could, dodging lochans, testing boggy bits with the stick, liberated by the simplicity of movement, relishing every step of the walking, the moor as a passport to a higher plane. I stopped when, for no reason I could judge, it felt like the right moment to stop. I climbed to the top of a small rise, no more than 50 feet above the lie of the land, and there I sat. I measured my sitting self against a rock, judged us to be near enough the same size, and of as much account as each other on the face of the moor, then tried to inhabit the rock. Suppose that rock was I and I that rock, would I feel anything, anything at all, but small? Would I know anything of adjectives but small and cold and old? Yet, if the stone had my inquiring mind and capacity for memory which reached as far back into its own lifetime as I could remember in mine . . .

I said: 'What's your earliest memory?'

Stone said: 'Shivering.'

I said: 'What next?'

Stone said: 'I stopped shivering.'

I said: 'Can't you do better than that? I'm trying to write a deeply philosophical piece here.'

Stone said: 'I remember trying to get comfortable.'

I said: 'Comfortable?'

Stone said: 'Comfortable. It's a long haul between ice ages. When the glaciers had finished rearranging things, I had been squirted up onto this pile of rock and mud and junk. It was a precarious existence. There is, as you can see, not much shelter. So the first age I lived through was the bedding down era, all of us trying to find our niche, trying to get comfortable before the vegetation came in and consolidated things.'

I said: 'How long did that last?'

Stone said: 'I don't understand the question.'

I said: 'Don't you have any grasp of time?'

Stone said: 'Don't you? Time is as long as it takes.'

I said: 'Are you comfortable now?'

Stone said: 'Yes. Are you?'

I said: 'No, not particularly, but I didn't come here to feel comfortable.'

Stone said: 'Why did you come here?'

I said: 'To feel small. To sense the pulse of the moor. To try and make sense of the place.'

Stone said: 'Oh. You are an odd fish.'

I said: 'Help me. Can you remember trees coming?'

Stone said: 'Yes. They came so slowly at first, skinny things, dwarf trees at first, toeholds, nothing more, around the edges, along the moraines, like the scouts of a great army of your people.'

I said: 'You know about armies, battles?'

Stone said: 'Who doesn't who hangs around the Highlands for a few ages. What else have you done here but fight, fight each other and fight nature? You ask if I remember trees coming. Yes, but not as clearly as I remember them going. Snap your fingers.'

I said: 'What?'

Stone said: 'Go on, just snap your fingers.'

So I snapped them, once.

Stone said: 'That's how quickly the trees went. That's how quickly this place became what you call a moor. It was never a moor before. Look there. And there. And there. Look anywhere. What do you see? Trees. Or rather what's left of them. It is not a moor you have made here. It is a burial ground. Do I remember the trees coming? Yes. Let me tell you what I remember. The ice has gone, right? Then there is a lull, a lull in which nature reconsiders the possibilities of the place. This, you will understand, is not the first time the ice has been and gone, only the most recent. Then nature does that – snap your fingers again! – that, and says "forest", and the forest begins. It creeps in, from the edges, and as it creeps, and gets a toehold, it improves the land for the trees that come behind, the army, whose mission is pacific by the way, and healing, binding together the land which was wounded and loosened. Do I know about battles? Did you really ask me that? Have you ever seen a glacier fight a volcano? I sit here through my ages and sometimes wonder if there is not a better way of making the land comfortable, but who am I to question nature? Where was I?'

I said: 'The healing army, the trees.'

Stone said: 'So the willows paved the way for the birches, the birches for the pines, and when the pines got going, all things were possible, and soon – soon enough, before you ask – there was oak, aspen, hazel, alder, and this place could mark its seasons again. There are two things you have done which are unforgivable, crimes for which it is not possible to devise a severe enough sentence. The first is that you reduced this place to two seasons – the season of snow and the season without snow. Nothing else. You removed when you removed the trees – snap your fingers again! – like that, so fast, the green season of the new leaves, the dark green season of the fullness of the leaves, the yellow season of the resting of the leaves (their job is done), the gold season of the falling of the leaves which greets the season of snow. Four seasons, you took from this place, leaving only two.'

I said: 'We only count four seasons.'

Stone said: 'That does not surprise me. You're forever losing things.'

I said: 'What else? What is the other crime?'

Stone said: 'You silenced the wolves.'

I said: 'Not I. My predecessors. Wolves have friends again, among people.'

Stone said: 'Yes, you. You sought me out to represent all my own kind. I hold you similarly responsible. And where are the wolves you have befriended? There are no wolves for you to befriend. You silenced them all.'

I said: 'There are wolves in other lands. In some places things are changing for the better.'

Stone said: 'Do not let those in other lands absolve you. This place is what concerns me. You took the tree seasons away and you silenced the wolves. You are guilty of these things, are you not? You don't deny it?'

I said: 'Guilty. Yes.'

Stone said: 'You told me, traveller, that you came here to feel the pulse of the place, to try and make sense of it.'

I said: 'That was my intention. And to feel small in its midst.'

Stone said: 'Do you feel small now?'

I said: 'Small enough, now.'

Stone said: 'Right. As to the rest of it, you cannot feel the pulse, for this is a dead place. There is no pulse. And you cannot make sense of that which you have made dead.'

I said: 'No! Not dead. There is a big nature reserve over there, 3,000 acres secured by the Nature Conservancy Council, a huge blanket bog, a priceless thing, not dead, not . . .'

Stone said: 'Blanket bog! Blanket bog! Nature *reserve*! What's a blanket bog but a dead forest? What's a nature reserve but the acknowledgement of nature mutilated outside the reserve? What's a nature reserve compared to nature unreserved? What's a blanket bog compared to a wolf?'

I said: 'Why do you lament the silencing of the wolf so much?'

Stone said: 'The voice of the wolf in the night was the breath of this place when it lived. This place you call the moor that is a smothered forest, the mountains you see in every direction and for many mountains beyond these from the summit of all to the pyramid one . . .'

I said: 'The summit of all? The pyramid one?'

Stone said: 'The summit of all – the great flat-topped mountain in the north-west. The pyramid one – there, in the east.'

I said: 'Ben Nevis? Schiehallion?'

Stone said: 'All that land. West and south of west . . .'

I said: 'Black Mount? Glenorchy? Ardchattan? Etive?'

Stone said: 'And to the great loch in the north.'

I said: 'Ericht.'

Stone said: 'All that land is indebted to this place, all in thrall to this place, this was their womb, this the centre from which their lands were fashioned, from which all life flowed. It was a tumultuous place after the ice, when the trees came, the big trees, so many trees. Three thousand acres! Ha! Three hundred thousand maybe. Maybe more. It could have been chaos, but nature prefers balance to chaos, and so ushered in the wolf. The wolf was the keeper of the balance. The wolf was nature's disciple. Nature's bidding was achieved through the wolf in the forest, the eagle above the forest. Nature is strength. The wolf was the sinew which made the strength flexible. Nature is wisdom. The wolf was the brain which distributed the wisdom all across the land. You cannot say that since you took away the trees, since you silenced the wolf, the land has been ruled by wisdom, strength, balance. Under the wolf it thrived. Under what has replaced the wolf, it has died.'

Then Stone said: 'The wolf was my friend.'

I said: 'Some people want to bring the wolf back here.'

Stone said: 'You cannot reinvent what you have silenced.'

I said: 'Wolves from other lands.'

Stone said: 'It is not nature's way.'

I said: 'No. It is our way of owning up to our mistakes.'

Stone said: 'Three thousand acres won't do for wolves.'

I said: 'How much . . . of the old wolf lands?'

Stone said: 'All of it. But the wolf needs a homeland. By removing the tree seasons, you removed the homeland. First you must put back the homeland. You know how to put back trees?'

I said: 'Yes. In a few places it has been done, collecting seed from the few trees that survive, and planting, the right trees on the right kind of ground.'

Stone said: 'You say this will be done here. By you. Then the wolf.'

I said: 'It's possible. When there are more disciples for Nature. But people still fear the wolf . . .'

Stone said: 'Fear! People fear the wolf! Don't you think on the basis of historical evidence that the wolf has rather more to fear from the people than the people from the wolf? The wolf did not silence the people. The wolf did not destroy the homelands of the people. Are the ways of people so dismal? Is their land-greed so consuming? Are they so obsessed with self-interest that they cannot relinquish a little of what they took into their midst, one element in nature that is beyond their control? I pity you. Better I think to be a friendless stone in a treeless desert. Go, traveller. I have nothing more to say to you.'

My pack was where I had left it, wrapped in its orange bivvy bag. I sat down beside it, stared gloomily at the bared and bleached corpse of a tree, an ancient thing, or so it looked through the eyes of a species which thinks in terms of what might be achieved in three score years and ten. But in terms of the life of a stone on Rannoch Moor, it had died within the time it takes me to snap my fingers. We must learn to think beyond our own time, to consider before our own time, and to use our own time to link the two. Bringing back forests and wolves is not a task for our own time. It is a task for our own time to begin, knowing there will be others who come after whose time will advance the work. The task is to benefit not mankind but nature, to reintroduce the balance and the strength, which will mean advancing the cause of forests and wolves and withdrawing the cause of self. John Muir wrote that we abuse land because we think of it as a commodity which belongs to us. When we think of it as a community to which we belong, then we may learn to use it with love and respect. I reminded myself of that sentiment, as I stared at the tree, and in my ear was the voice of Stone. Stone said: 'And who do you think taught him that?'

Evening advanced. The moor grew quiet and cool. The sky behind the mountains of the Black Mount was a yellow band high up and a searing electric blue below. I looked at where the shapes of the mountains fitted round those wedges of vivid blue and saw how the oblique sunlight illuminated the depth of the mountains too. Gulfs of blue air.

I had written down the book's prologue before I had taken a step or turned a wheel of the Journey. I now reminded myself of its self-proclaimed purpose: I will bridge the gulfs of blue air. I will look for tracks in the snow of the world. Here's one bridge – a forest reaching from Ben Nevis to Schiehallion, Loch Etive to Loch Ericht, and wolf tracks in the snow of that resurrected world.

Of course it's possible. The only work anyone ever quotes on the history of the wolf in Scotland is J.E. Harting's *British Extinct Mammals*, published in 1880, a troublingly warped account with all the Victorians' hatred of all predators, whether hook-beaked, claw-footed, or well-toothed, and with a 19th-century English academic's misunderstanding and downright ignorance of the landscape of his own time or the wolves' time. I should have read this paragraph out to Stone. It is not untypical:

In the time of James V their numbers and ravages were formidable. At that period, great parts of Ross, Inverness, almost the whole of Cromarty, and large tracts of Perth and Argyleshire, were covered with forests of pine, birch and oak . . . and it is known from history and tradition that the braes of Moray, Nairn, and Glen Urcha [presumably Urquhart], the glens of Lochaber, and Loch Erroch [Ericht?], the moors of Rannach and the hills of Ardgour were covered in the same manner. [Fraser Darling, whose 20th-century scientific studies may be judged a safer bet thought that 'the Moor may have been extensively wooded as recently as Roman times'.] All these clouds of forests were more or less frequented by wolves. Bothius mentions their numbers and devastation in his time; and in various districts where they last remained, the traditions of their haunts are still familiarly remembered. Loch Sloigh and Strath Earn are still celebrated for their resort, and in 1848 there were living in Lochaber old people who related from their predecessors that, when all the country from the Lochie to Loch Erroch was covered by a continuous pine forest, the eastern tracts upon the Blackwater and the wild wilderness stretching towards Rannach were so dense and infested by the rabid droves, that they were almost impassable.

Modern studies have failed to unearth a single reliable piece of evidence which would support the idea that the presence of wolves would render a forest impassable. And by 1848, by which time wolves had been extinct for around 100 years, they had passed into the stuff of legend, and God knows what embellishments graced the word-of-mouth passage of wolf stories between generations.

The much quoted slaying of the 'last' wolf in 1743 on the Findhorn south-east of Inverness was not written down until 1829, yet the verbatim account of the wolf-slayer is faithfully reproduced as fact, despite the fact that it crumbles under close scrutiny based on what we now know of wolves.

I hear Stone say:

'What do you know of the last wolf? What you think you know is when the last wolf died which was killed by human hands. The last wolf of all died alone and lonely under a rock on Rannoch Moor, many years after you had pronounced his extinction.' I hope so. I do hope so.

Long before the true extinction, and particularly around the beginning of the 17th century, the work of removing the four tree seasons from the land and making a moor out of Rannoch was energetically begun. One historical record from 100 years later intoned:

'On the south side of Beann Nevis, a large pine forest, which extended from the western braes of Lochaber to the Black Water and the mosses of Rannach, was burned to expel the wolves.'

We stand alone among the creatures of the Highlands of Scotland in that we take beyond our needs. We kill not for what we might reasonably argue we need to sustain us, but also that which is inconvenient for us. That which is both inconvenient and a source of fear, we annihilate. At least that is the way it has been. But there are straws in the wind. They wear bureaucratic labels – conservation, environmentalism, green issues – and their best endeavours are often fankled by bureaucrats who value the report on the shelf more than the wolf on the ground. A beginning has been made. We may well have beavers back within two years. But the wolf, and the strides we will have to make in such as Rannoch Moor, to put back a landscape fit for wolves – that will always be the yardstick of the past which our future will have to live up to. The American naturalist Paul Errington wrote it as well as anyone in his 1967 book *Of Predation and Life*:

> *Of all the native biological constituents of a northern wilderness scene, I should say that wolves present the greatest test of human wisdom and good intentions.*

It won't be easy, putting the tree seasons and voice of the wolf back on Rannoch-that-was-once-a-Moor. But then neither was exterminating them. An equivalent zeal should get the job done – I snap my fingers – as quickly as that.

10

That Strange Too-fullness of the Heart

I felt small and not comfortable. The June evening felt as long as the moor and twice as wide. Mine seemed a dawdling, confused presence among so much that was certain of itself, rooted. Even the dead tree stumps. Dead certainties. I began to see them differently, almost to envy them for their place in the landscape, where they had lived and died. The confidence to set down roots here, committed to a century or three . . . here! . . . staunch as a lighthouse in a moor sea. But of course it was not a moor, not when the trees thrived. It was a plain of trees, a forested carpet which turned up at the edges to swarm up the lower mountain slopes until it ran out of sustenance and ran into that landscape zone where the forces of rock and wind mitigate against all tall, upstanding life. And of course the carpet would turn down at the edges too, thickening into the spoors of the old glaciers, more tracks in the snow of the world. Just as the moor was once its own reservoir of ice, so it became a reservoir of trees, as surely as it has since become a reservoir of treelessness. The traveller crossing the moor today, whether by road *en route* to Glencoe and looking east, or by train looking west, sees the archetypal bare Highland landscape, a shudder at 50 miles per hour, a roadside pause to photograph its barely credible harshness. But by walking across east-west, you brush up against its truth like a lost Lilliputian picking a path through a graveyard of Gullivers.

A thin high layer of cloud was growing in the west, advancing as I walked towards it, drawing a grey veil across the day, snuffing out sunlight and colour, calming and cooling, drawing light from the sky on the one night in the whole Journey when I desperately wanted there to be light. Let there be light, I had cajoled the Fates, and they sent me a clouded night. I found myself trying to prepare an instant philosophy, psychological weatherproofing against the forces of the moor. All you have to do, I told myself, is keep walking through the good light, or until you get too tired, then stop. Make a brew, eat, find a heathery couch, stretch out in sleeping-bag and bivvy bag, and keep the morale-boosting pocket handy. Then you scribble your notes for as long as you can see well enough to scribble, then you make yourself as comfortable as you can, and make what you can of the night. What are you worried about? Thieves? Wolves? You are where you are because you wanted to be here. You wanted to test the night embrace of Rannoch Moor, alone and without distractions, to record the 'involuntary impression of things upon the mind'. How can you come close to the landscape – that landscape bond you are always telling other people is at the core of your work! – when your head is trying to fend off the night, fend off the moor. Rannoch is still Rannoch at night, just less visible. The cloud moved in and covered the sky. The mountains dulled and blackened and edged closer. It felt suddenly as if the moor was shrinking itself to accommodate my frame of mind, and at once the landscape was a benevolent presence again, and the hour became a privileged one. How many people whose work was a commuter rush-hour grind of centrally heated, double-glazed noise would give much to feel the breath of Rannoch Moor on a June night and be able to call the sensation work? So I lay on my heather couch inside two layers of sleeping-bag with a pen in my hand and I wrote until 11 p.m. by which time what I was writing was making no sense at all, I was scoring out more than I was leaving unscored, and it was too dark to see what I was scoring out. I lay back and looked at the sky and listened to the night song of the moor – a breath of wind, the restlessness of curlews, the occasional passage of the grass-rustlers (mice, voles, shrews, who knows what else?) – and I wondered at the nature of the forces at work which had propelled me here, to this moment in this place. But my mind had drifted down that road more than once before and come up with nothing that was conclusive, only that the course life had taken was inevitable and that I was (mostly) profoundly grateful.

My mind drifted on, until it alighted on the wolves again. If one should howl now, how would I feel? But there was only the curlew's three-syllable jabber. I tried to imagine the moor as a forest, as a sunken ice-cap, as something else before the ice, but every thought I caught hold of turned to smoke. My mind would not give up the game of snatching at passing thoughts like a demented butterfly netter, nor would it hold on to a single butterfly for long enough to examine, admire . . . another passing thought, catch it, let it go, and another, and another. If only there were stars to stare at. But the sky was a blank page, an evenly spread darkness, and so was the moor, and in the midst of all its unfathomable square miles were its restless birds and foxes and grass-rustlers and mosses and flowers and tree graveyards and (as far as I knew) this single human being, this fish out of water, trying to come to terms with where it was and why it was there. I don't believe it ever quite did.

2 a.m. The sky blacker than any sky I have ever known. The moor quiet apart from the voice of the thinnest winds and the movement of a tiny burn; precious quiet.

3.15 a.m. Something four-footed and tiny sprinted into the middle of the bivvy bag's dewy, slippery contours, halted briefly in what must have been the most alien environment of its short life, sprinted on for the sanctuary of grasses.

4.30 a.m. A seepage of light. Low mist out among the lochans, scarves round the throats of the mountains.

7.00 a.m. I slept! Sunlight flooding out of the east, a reversing glacier of warmth. Every nagging, doubting thought banished, all the butterflies flown, and in their place the exhilaration of waking with the new day, the night outfaced, the day's business to attend to, the moor to cross, a new lap of the Journey.

The first thing to do was to remove the orange stain of the bivvy bag from the face of the moor before it offended eyes other than my own. Perhaps nature was watching. I washed where that skinniest of burns had muttered through the night, talking in its sleeplessness. The same burn sweetened fresh coffee and thickened into porridge. I count that solitary breakfast among the most untroubled and tranquil hours of my life. As the mist swithered off into its own oblivion and the mountains threw their grey scarves into the air, Rannoch Moor reasserted itself in its own landscape, restoration of the great primitive of the Central Highlands to all that its name and reputation commands. I watched it unwrap itself until every detail sharpened and glittered, and Rannoch Moor grew columns of lark song as profusely as it had once grown trees. The mountains had retreated again, the moor stretched to its furthest morning dimensions. I felt small again, small and profoundly comfortable. I remembered a line of Gavin Maxwell's from his first book, *Harpoon at a Venture*:

> *I had that strange too-fullness of the heart which the sensory sum of*
> *my surroundings would often bring.*

The solitude was part of it. Company would have chatted and laughed away the night, probably sung songs and swapped stories, coughed up a moothie and a penny whistle. I would have found it a convivial enough hour, but that morning was enriched far beyond the convivial by the nature of the night which had preceded it.

I wanted to thank something for the love that I felt for the situation and the moment, for the gift of sensibilities enough to relish them, but I didn't know who or what to thank. A God I could not define? The Great Spirit? The Stone? So I spoke the words 'thank you' and directed them out over the moor in the hope that the appropriate authority would heed my gratitude. Then I rinsed my cup (a last task for the burn with more thanks for services above and beyond the call of any burn's duty), shouldered my pack and walked west.

The day grew hot, almost too hot for comfortable walking, a rare enough experience in Highland Scotland and an unprecedented one for me on Rannoch Moor, but I walked anyway, reeling in the mountains of the Black Mount a yard at a time. I kept walking because now I wanted to put the crossing behind me. The moor had treated me with uncommon compassion, handled me with kid gloves, and I was concerned that I should not trespass unduly on its hospitality. You make these strange pacts with nature when you travel alone, supplications for a safe passage across the landscape. So I took the long miles (Rannoch Moor deals only in long miles) with steady strides until Kingshouse hove into sight, white and far off and faintly exotic in its shimmering distance.

Then I made out the vivid blue speck of the old Fiat. Logistical imagination had arranged for it to await my arrival there, but the sudden appearance of the safety net corrupted my demeanour. The crossing dwindled from the euphoric early morning to a tired and anti-climactic late-afternoon. That sweet sting of adrenalin which had been my shadow since I boarded the train at Crianlarich was suddenly absent because I was more or less in control of the situation again, the end in sight under clear skies.

I hit the bar running.

'Hot on the hill today, eh?'

'Hotter on the moor.'

'You come across the moor today?'

'Yup.'

'Sleep out last night?'

'Mmm. Not much sleep, but out, yes, no tent.'

'On your own?'

'Mmm.'

'Good for you, mate. Swallow that.'

91

Glen Orchy, the tent on a favourite spot by the river. I have pitched a tent more often here than anywhere else on the planet. Glen Orchy has helped me out of every shape and shade of my life's occasional crises. It's where I go to sort things or myself out, a quiet and unspectacular place. I wear it like a good glove. I remember the first time, a day trip during a family holiday near Oban, aged about 12, the river in spate. I think I had not seen a river in spate before. I was walking a bit of the bank when I was overtaken by a tree. It was in full leaf. For the previous 20 or 30 years it had stood on the river bank, shading anglers, rubbing up against passing otters, shading the singing perch of dippers, flinching in sleety winds, tholing spate and drought, and all the time the river was plotting its downfall.

I had seen rivers in mountainous places, of course. Glencoe, for example, where the mountains lean close and the river dives down into their deepest shadow and coils and cowers there. But Glen Orchy's mountains lean back, as though they were in thrall of the river, as though at any moment a heavy spate might send one of them spinning into Loch Awe the way it dealt with trees.

Then there was the way the river had of reinventing the waterfall. Not for the Orchy the rush towards the brim then the cataract's plunge. Rather it makes horizontal chaos of its waterfalls, trips them up and stretches them over rocks it has assembled and sculpted specially for the purpose. In the mind of my 12-year-old self, the Orchy was a highway through Wonderland. In the mind of my 50-year-old self it seems much the same.

Over the years, I have unearthed the glen's secret places, or at least some of them – the lost fragments of pine woods; the hidden corrie where raven and kestrel nest side by side; the high shielings; the wood which cloaks the ruin of a large house, a chapel and a tiny triangular chamber whose purpose escapes me utterly; the pools for summer swimming; the orchid fields; the nests of dipper and yellow wagtail. Over the years too, I have seen every one of Scotland's principal breeding birds of prey in the glen – eagle, buzzard, sparrowhawk, osprey, kestrel, merlin, hen harrier, peregrine falcon, and four different species of owl. Add kingfisher and cuckoo, whooper swans and ptarmigan, sandpiper and woodcock and more woodland and moorland birds and more wildfowl than I can remember, red squirrels, red foxes and red deer and (once!) a red-throated diver at 2,000 feet . . .

There are more trees and more bracken in the glen than there used to be, and the tree-planting has not been of the most enlightened variety, and there are many more summer (though not winter) visitors. But it has the capacity like no other place I know to wrap me round with the benevolence of hill shoulders. The song of its river has infiltrated my sleeping and waking dreams and its eagles' shadows have crossed my path more than once. To turn in at the road end in the old blue Fiat estate is to know that I am once again in the land of certainties, a reservoir of all or almost all the things I hold dearest in nature and in life.

A small fire of dead wood before the tent, tea made pungent and midges held at bay by its smoke, the art of the camper; a glass of island malt whisky the same shade as the summer-brown pool beyond the tent, the art of the distiller; the low throaty song of running water on stones and nudging curves out of boulders, the art of the river. The Journey was about to take an instinctive turn.

The plan had been a couple of days of rummaging among the glen's old haunts, catching up on tape-making and note-taking, then two long mountain days with a high camp on the ridges of the Mamores to Fort William. But Rannoch had been epic enough, mountain enough, for the moment, and the whole Journey thus far has been entirely land-locked. Instinct – nothing else – suggested a new direction, a change of pace, the cut a different landscape cloth, some Django Reinhardt after all those Ellington layers. I had crossed the very threshold of the Highlands in the south, cut a swathe through the heart of the Central Highlands. Why not take to the very edge of the land and travel north up its western edge? But where to start, where to break into that western edge so that it would be a fit beginning for the trek to Suilven?

Ash from the fire splashed onto a spread map on the grass. I brushed it away absentmindedly while I toyed with possibilities, old familiarities mostly, for I have known that coast for 40 years of sporadic reiving. Then, as idly as the ash alighted on the map, the thought lodged:

'But I've never been to the Mull of Kintyre.'

I rarely turn southwards instinctively. My preferred direction is north. Cairngorms, Skye, Sutherland, Orkney, Shetland, Iceland. But in the morning I drove down the glen, delved darkly into the shores of Loch Awe and headed for the Mull.

11

A Crown of Mysteries

So it should have begun again at the Mull of Kintyre. That was how I planned it as I drove. Whatever I might make of that first and last gesture of Argyll (I had imagined a high and classic lighthouse, a brazen jaw of land thrust out at Ireland and accustomed to taking the Atlantic and history's storms on the chin, the ocean full of sunset, the usual intoxications of Hebridean shapes), I was to mark its doorstep significance then turn pointedly on my heel and head for Suilven, a few hundred headlands to the north. But that was how it should have begun.

Such a beginning demanded a little discipline. Not much, and none of any significance for I was answerable to no one but myself. But I was to take no notes, no photographs, pay no heeds to the seductions of the landscape (what! not even that beckoning osprey hanging over a hidden watersheet near Loch Awe?) until I reached the Mull. It was necessary for the sudden contrast, necessary to mark the change of pace, necessary to note the new scent on the air, ocean after woodsmoke. But I broke all my rules for Dunadd.

Dunadd. The simplest of names, the Fort on the Add. The Add is the river which rises east of Loch Awe and uncoils a cartographer's nightmare as it trembles west to the sea at Crinan. Dunadd is mountain made miniature, heaped up from the flattened stuff of the low-lying flatlands at its feet, Am Moine Mhor, the Great Moss. Yet Dunadd seems to be more crouched down than heaped up, the way a hare crouches in a flat field. And it wears a crown of mysteries cut in stone, legacies of lost rituals. For here was a capital city, a place of kings, and a foundation stone. Scotland, the nation, glimpsed the first possibilities of its existence here.

But I knew all this, knew Dunadd of old, knew well the seductions of the place, so why not resist, pass by blind-eyed, head-down for the Mull of Kintyre as planned?

Well, my eyes failed to blind. I failed to be indifferent to the enchantment which radiates from that rock, tangible as lighthouse beams, but beams spun with the resilience of spiders' webs. My resolve succumbed to its provocative golden green evening dress. I saw its familiar profile against the shore of the Moss. I saw it beckon, just like the osprey. I stopped to watch. It was the last hour of sunlight, the light coming low from the unseen ocean. It lit Dunadd's north and west faces and shrouded the rest blacker than night. I looked straight at the dividing line, the sunlit and the shrouded, the golden green and the black. Every edge the sun touched was a gold rim, every leaf, tree, rock, fence post, fence wire, bird wing, bird bill . . . they all wore the same burnish. That gilding was my undoing, for I saw in my mind's eye that rock slab which lies just below the summit, that cold nest of ancient, enigmatic symbols, and I wanted to see them sculpted again by this hard-edging sun.

So I pointed the Fiat at the dustily rutted track once trodden by shoes fashioned by Dalriadan cobblers. I stood for a few minutes beyond the car, breathing in the changed air, listening to the fussy confusion of its bird sounds, trying to acclimatise. The dust of Rannoch was still on my boots. A cuckoo embellished its every other call with a triplet . . . 'ku-ku-ku, ku-ku, ku-ku-ku, ku-ku . . .'

I climbed the shroud. I have never yet climbed Dunadd alone without the sense of being one of a single file of climbers, sandalled and robed figures. It is the same every time – I suppose it's the same now because each time I expect it. They are perhaps 2,000 years removed, and I am in my own time. They treat me no differently from the way they treat each other. There are quiet words, some of them mine, none of them distinguishable. We curve, this file of unseen climbers and I, the way the Historic Scotland arrows direct you (yes, even here!); the procession is almost real when it reaches a rock gully which the path steepens through, the echo of the padding sandals almost audible in the gully's roofless chamber. It curves on, spirals left into the sunlight and onto a level shelf just below the summit. The sun and the wind and the airiness of the shelf disperse them all, and I am myself and alone. It is a pity. I want to ask them about the slab of rock on the ground, the cold nest of Dunadd's mysteries.

There is a basin cut deep and perfectly round into the rock. If you kneel to drink from it, there is a shallow curve for a knee to rest in. Who first knelt and drank? Was the knee-rest carved with the basin, or have kneelers worn it down? How many kneelers might it take?

There are two footprints. One is a bare foot, hardly visible. The other is a shod foot, a deep and vivid imprint. It is irresistible to try them on, like Cinderella's ugly sisters seeking an invitation to some stone age ball. Your feet are unlikely to fit them both, for one is probably prehistoric, the other a mere 1,500-or-so years old. But if it is the kind of day which permits such things, when you stand on the footprints you find yourself facing the far peaks of Beinn Cruachan, mountain masterpiece of all Argyll, and you find yourself thinking that that is more than coincidence. The sightline is north-east. Suppose (you find yourself thinking) the sun were to rise on Midsummer's Day between the peaks. That would be a moment to savour, and perhaps the savouring, if it was solitary and profound enough, might uncork . . . oh, I don't know, a genie, an undreamed of something or other. The idea lodged, anyway, a week before Midsummer's Day. It had been in my mind that the journey might like to see that sunrise from the summit of Ben Nevis, but so far, nothing much had gone according to plan, and suddenly I had a better idea. In any case, I prefer my journeys to have flexibility rather than schedules; the spur of the moment is all.

There is the outline carving of a wild boar, a symbol as ancient in Scotland as the presence of people.

There are two lines of script arranged along horizontal cracks in the rock, striving like a child's writing on a ruled page to be orderly. The script is Irish, it is called Ogam, it is very simple to read if you are an archaeologist (I am not – I stand and stare, I kneel and finger, I shake my head and marvel), but the Dunadd inscriptions have defied the minds of all archaeology's code-crackers.

'Once,' wrote Marion Campbell, 'as I watched one of the greatest living authorities kneeling beside it baffled, I heard the echo of a ghostly chuckle from the bare rock-boss behind me, a rock that forms no part of the defences but might have served other purposes – sacrifice perhaps, divination, or the composition of cryptic epigraphs.'

I would have thought that if it was the rock-chuckler's intention to reveal the inscription's meaning to today's inquiring minds, then the mind of one such as Marion Campbell might be where he would choose to plant the seed. She is both writer and archaeologist, and a more perceptive and attuned soul is not to be found in that woody hogsback of Argyll which lies between Loch Fyne and the Sound of Jura. Her rootedness in that landscape is an unbroken chain of 400 years. Her attachment to the place is at least partly responsible for an eerie series of troublesome waking dreams from which she constructed her astounding novel, *The Dark Twin*, and her *Argyll – The Enduring Heartland* reveals that the archaeologist and the historian in her are blessed with a poet's instinct for language. But she does not know the meaning of the Dunadd stone. And you sense that perhaps she cherishes the mystery more than she would cherish the knowledge. It is certainly a source of gratification to me that this Internet-surfing world can still be outwitted by a Pictish rock-chiseller, if the chiseller was a Pict.

But my journey has taken another liberty. Marion Campbell was to slip into the narrative – as was Dunadd – on the northward trek, when I had planned to loop west from Tarbert round the folded skirts of Knapdale to Kilberry, which is her specific place in the landscapes of Argyll. It is not time to meet her, not yet.

So I have climbed to the slab below the summit of Dunadd, egged on by that seductive sun which divided the hill into the golden green and the black. It has lingered long enough to illumine that cluster of rock-cut shapes so that I came on them in an unfamiliar light. The basin and the shod footprint benefited most. It was a frail and horizon-low sunlight which lipped them, but that rim of thinnest, palest gold inlay conferred on them an embellishment of veneration, and both are cut deep enough to throw their own internal shadows, so that the gold rim topped the darkest blackness of their shapes.

But all I can say for certain is that the gilding made their prosaic shapes briefly beautiful. It lit no insight, at least not for me. The sandal-wearers, the rock-chucklers, perhaps even the waking dreamers among the living . . . these might have seen things here which I did not. Yet I incline towards the idea of sacred landscapes much more so than sacred buildings, and here is a place which corresponds to my freewheeling definition of sanctity, and here is a light as benevolent as any church candle by which to bless the place and the journey.

The sun sank. Its small sorcery on the rock dimmed and guttered and died. But it still lay on the windings of the Add, that mysterious highway of the ancients, illuminating cornerstones of the river linked by spools of shadows. Dunadd is a plinth on a wide bog, only part of which has been reclaimed. In its civic heyday, between 400 and 800 AD when the sea rather than the land offered the way in, small ships from France are thought to have nosed into the Add from Crinan with cargoes of wine. What journeys! Did they set sail knowing their destination in advance, or were they travelling salesmen, claret reps, seeking clients as they voyaged? The notion of the *barques* dropping anchor here, French voices on the air, the bartering and the haggling over prices and payments lends ballast to a new voyage of thought. It is this:

Dunadd at that time was an oasis of culture and civilised living in a primitive landscape. You would look at it now and think of it as an oasis of the primitive in a civilised, even tamed landscape.

The Add has coiled through all its eras. It surges down out of the Forest of Kilmichael, out of Gleann Airidh, swithers out onto the low ground of the Great Moss and stalls. It is a journey not just through landscapes but through time, not just geological time but also among the scratches on the surface which mark the paltry few thousand years of human endeavour. The signposts of our own kind are surely more liberally scattered here than along any other Scottish river – standing stones in ones and twos and circles, carved stones, cairns, duns, forts (14 are visible from even today's Dunadd), cup and ring marks, carved crosses on hidden rocks, and sundry other old stone souvenirs punctuate the watercourse. Their perpetrators are gone, but you can see their tracks still, in the snow of their world.

The carved rock is not the summit of Dunadd but the centrepiece of a small shelf below the summit. The top is a wide grassy plateau. You see from here how the hills stand back, a respectful distance which confers stature on Dunadd. For a 54-metre-high rock, its command of its surroundings is total. Its sense of time comes at you in subterranean thrusts so that you catch yourself placing your feet carefully, softly, for fear of injuring . . . what? For fear perhaps of obliterating the footprints in the snow of the world.

You see, too, as you walk sunwise round the rim of the plateau, how the hill's natural contours have been enhanced to defend its old inhabitants, ramparts and ditches, a fragment of a wall, and all the while the gulls drift over, indifferent while you marvel, following the watercourse to roost on the safe shallows of Loch Crinan. Their voices mingle with the whine of a buzzard and the hiccups of a cuckoo and the booming of cattle. The wind dies and the midges rush out, the fly in Dunadd's soothing ointment. Down then, and damn them. There are southward miles to travel before I sleep.

12

The Road to Hell

The tent was on its shore. The tinned mince and new potatoes still in their jackets (the rotating menu was back on its preferred camping option) steamed softly on the stove. A spot of red wine ennobled the mince, made it miraculously palatable. The sea air put that edge on the appetite which makes a banquet out of dull fare. A glass of Islay malt raised towards the west – its foreground was Gigha, its background the hills where they make the stuff. If the tent had not been arranged so that one wing of the entrance cut off the wind from the stove, I would see Jura too. But I could always save Jura for afters. I drank to the islanders, to maltmen, all the distillers the world ever gave birth to so that the sum of all their art and evolving expertise might coalesce into the sorcery of the bottle by my side, the glass in my hand.

Here would be my new home for the next week. Apart from the fact that I have never yet devised a comfortable way of writing in a small tent – and I would have to do a lot of writing in this tent – I approved of the place immensely. While dinner cooked as slowly as a one-burner stove is capable of cooking anything, I walked the few yards from the tent to the edge of the sands, glass in hand, looking south. There was a swelling bruise of land thumped down into the Atlantic. Across a dozen miles of the ocean, a hazier island reared. A lighthouse blinked there where it had blinked all day. The bruise was where I had spent a long day, the Mull of Kintyre. The island was someone else's country. Ireland. And yet, and yet . . . 150 years ago, John Crumley, tinsmith, and Catherine Crumley, hawker, fled the desperate poverty of their homeland like so many of their kin. They washed up in Dundee, had five bairns. One of the five, Robert, married Jane Anderson from Forfar, had six bairns. One of the six, James Anderson Crumley, was my father.

Whatever the motives of the voyagers, from the nomads of prehistory to the Scotti who christened Argyll Dalriada after their Ulster homeland and set about subduing it, to Columba who came peddling his God, to the famine fleers who came just to keep living, to the Chinook helicopter which crashed on the Mull of Kintyre in 1994 killing 29 officers of the Royal Ulster Constabulary, the Army, the Royal Air Force and the Crown Service, it is a well-worn groove which flows and ebbs across the Atlantic between Ulster and Argyll. One far-flung ripple crossed the land and nudged up against the North Sea shore, and now it has rippled back and I am standing on the Kintyre shore where it reunites with its parent waters. It always seemed a good idea to let the Journey begin again at the Mull of Kintyre.

The lighthouse is famous enough to be signposted from nine miles away. I had in my mind a long and leisurely descent, through fields to a last dwindling ramp of rocks. Instead, there is the road to hell. The road to hell, I now know, is not paved with good intentions. It is paved with, well, practically nothing at all, other than potholes and broken edges, ruts and rain gullies. It writhes like the Add, but with hills, and what hills! All the way down the douce Kintyre peninsula I had nurtured doubts as the rich and low-lying fertility of the land slipped past. This isn't the Highlands! Campbeltown assists the illusion. It is a sturdy, rather than a pretty town, more like a Borders community than a West Highland one. Then the road divides among more fields and the signpost ushers you through still more fields towards the lighthouse. It is the lull, the first 'this isn't so bad' yards of the roller-coaster before your carriage starts flipping upside down and looping the loop. The road to the lighthouse doesn't exactly loop the loop, but it suddenly heaves you up into a landscape as Highland as Sutherland, and without so much as a Government health warning, it embarks on a demented relationship with the contours of the land and the miles grow longer and longer.

At one particularly perverse corner, a red and white sign proclaimed 'Road Ahead Closed'. How far ahead? How closed? Why closed? I drove on. I had the bike and the boots in the back, not that cycling this road was an enticing prospect. Two tortuous miles later I met the road closers. An amiable gaffer strolled over and explained:

'You'll get through in a few minutes. We're just replacing the culvert. We just put the sign up to let folk know they could be stopped for a while. The lads are just tidying up now. Mind you, we shouldn't have to be here at all. We did this yesterday. But it seems the culvert we put in was the wrong size . . . not too small, mind, too big. It was 500 [millimetres presumably], this one's a 480. They made us replace it. Well, I hope it floods. These are the jobs that cost money, you know? Where you off to – the lighthouse? Waste of time. There's nothing to see. But it's amazing the number of folk wants to see it.'

'I thought I'd take a chance on your sign,' I said. 'I've got the bike and the boots in the back, so I reckoned I could get there one way or the other – not that I fancy the cycling much on this.'

He smiled, a tolerant sort of smile. He was a good-natured soul glad of the excuse for a chat. His smile acknowledged cheerfully enough that there was a sub-species of humanity which somehow had contracted baffling disease of the brain, a disease manifested by a compulsion to trek to the extremities of the land. Obstacles like 'Road Closed' signs were not going to deter them. There was no accounting for them, the poor souls were beyond help, but they seemed harmless enough. The truck and the digger pulled off the road. Both drivers waved agreeably. They were altogether the most civil crew of road closers I had met. And doubtless they watched the Fiat's receding tailgate with shaking heads. Another nutter for the lighthouse.

So the nutter for the lighthouse paused at a small car park on a clifftop and let me out. It was the end of the public road, but not the end of the road. A heavy-handed rash of notices warned that unauthorised vehicles could go no further. It also warned authorised ones that This Hill Is Dangerous. Bureaucratic understatement. This Hill Is A Bloody Nightmare. It swooped to the lighthouse and the sea in a spectacular series of obscene gradients and hairy hairpins, each hairpin coaxed round its curves by red and white corrugated barriers, which seemed to rather labour the point.

The lighthouse squatted at the bottom of all that, low and fat and ugly like an angular toad. Clustered round it were white-painted, flat-roofed buildings, as alien to the landscape as minarets. They looked like the kind of buildings which used to illustrate children's editions of the Bible, and the story of the four friends who lowered the paralysed man through the hole in the roof so that Jesus could heal him in the crowded room. I think it was the same architect at work, although he understandably omitted the hole in the roof from the Kintyre buildings. It's not a hole in the roof kind of climate.

The day had gone grey and cool on me, the first sunless day of the Journey. The cliff turned out to be not so much a cliff as an all-but-vertical hillside with a small cliff at the foot. The Mull is a place of huge, blunt shapes, and the colour of elephants, which is appropriate enough for huge, blunt shapes. Somehow it did not look like itself, in the way that a mussel doesn't look like its shell. Its real self, the soft green fields with an Orcadian hankering for the sea, lay the other side of the Road to Hell. And the lighthouse was a sore disappointment. I had wanted a classical lighthouse monolith, tall and slender, pale and unflinching, not this cowering cube dug into the hillside. I declined the walk down the hairpins to see it at close quarters, and wandered off north high above the sea. I lunched on a ledge and scanned the world beyond Scotland for Viking invaders, Somerled's birlins, sea serpents, whatever.

Twelve miles away, the northmost headlands of Antrim loured hazily. In the field glasses their hillsides showed greener than this, and divided into small enclosures by miles and miles of climbing, contouring dykes. Not Scotland. Ulster. I remembered a scout camp, 1960, at Helen's Bay on Belfast Lough, swimming among seals, swapping jokes about accents with a uniformed guide at Stormont. I remembered then this morning's news bulletin on the car radio. At 12.30 p.m. the first plenary session of Irish peace talks was beginning, at Stormont. I glanced at my watch . . . 1.15. Right now, not 40 miles away as the gannet flies, that confused and confusing group of people, the politicians of Ulster, were at their seats. Sinn Fein were locked out in the absence of an IRA ceasefire, and the bomb which blew away the centre of Manchester was only a few days off. I was not sorry that John and Catherine Crumley crossed the Irish Sea 150 years before and made me a Scot.

So I sat on my Scottish hillside, 200 feet and a torture of hairpins above the lighthouse, and nearby my ledge another ripple of the Troubles had come ashore. A new path worn into the peaty hillside led to a new cairn which commemorates the 29 who died in the Chinook crash of 2 June 1994. Their names are on a plaque set into the cairn, a curious, mirror-like surface which somehow devalues the remembrance. Memorials used to be cut into stone, which made them endure. Nor is it a good cairn. It is almost as much concrete as stone and it has already acquired tawdry appendages. A bright blue cable has been tacked none too neatly round the base, presumably so that flowers can be held in place against the cairn in the face of the hillside's many winds. A sponge in a green plastic holder above the plaque is also designed to hold flowers. A plastic milk carton containing water (to keep the sponge moist?) 'hides' behind the cairn. A new spray of flowers in a plastic wrapper was withering in the salt wind. An old spray lay where it fell, only its plastic wrapper intact. Beneath the plaque there were two tiny wooden crosses, a single white ribbon. I caught sight of my own disapproving face in the mirroring surface of the plaque. It seemed to me that the one thing missing was dignity, for a memorial in such a place should serve two purposes: a fit remembrance for the dead, and a fit recognition of its landscape setting. It is a tricky assignment, a public remembrance, for it compels strangers to consider the grief of others and to scrutinise its public face. Perhaps the new cairn will settle into its landscape, but while it is still raw and the source of the grief almost daily fare for our world's headline writers, it sits uneasily on its hillside, scarring the land as it must also scar the minds of those who still mourn.

I forebore to join the ragged procession of hairpin-traipsing pedestrians between the car park and the lighthouse. Instead I worked a long diagonal down the hillside and away from the lighthouse fashioning hairpins of my own so that I shifted my weight from right boot to left. A buzzard, contemptuous of such crude ways of doing things (an executor of spirals rather than hairpins, a pedestrian of thermals rather than hillsides), angled past, whipped up and stopped on the air, and looked down with something like pity. There are circumstances in which even a six-foot, 14-stone human can feel vulnerable in the shadow of a buzzard. Here, looking up and off balance when I should have been looking down and achieving balance above all other considerations, I knew a brief fellow-feeling with the hillside rabbits. So I climbed desultorily down to the Atlantic, shorn of the descent's original purpose by my disappointment at the unprepossessing nature of the lighthouse. Perhaps the shore would cough up some other portentous beginning from which I could unfurl my Journey north.

It coughed up a bull Atlantic seal, which is a mighty cough, a brute mass of equipoise, 600lb of blubber wondrously slung beneath a head the size of Ailsa Craig, chins enough to call up the image of a ploughed field on a hillside. All this was held perfectly still without visible effort, as though it was a cork gripped by the meniscus of the ocean.

The beast stood in a vertical pose, his muzzle aimed roundly at the sky, his eyes shut, a pose which assisted the idea that here was a living definition of the word 'shapelessness'. At intervals, several minutes apart, the muzzle would lower heavily. It was as if the mechanism of an unseen crane was at work using a crawler gear. As the mottled grey mass lowered and the chins rippled to the realignment of their burden, the black pool of his shore-facing eye unveiled itself, a hypnotic moment. In the instant of awakening, the black orb was a rivet pinning me to my rock. I was a new shape in his perspective of the shore. I was to be scrutinised, assessed, disdained, discarded. Close the eye, up periscope, but slowly, mind, slowly. Each time the eye opened, the first task was to pin me down, as if I was an itch to be scratched. It was not difficult. Neither I, nor the eye's space in all that Atlantic greyness had moved since the previous unveiling. Occasionally the open-eyed phases would go into swivel mode, the seal head troubling Ireland with its gaze, or Gigha up the coast, or Islay loitering beyond Gigha like a buzzard over a rabbit. All quiet, up scope, slowly . . .

Mischief arrived in the shape of a gannet, which is a sublime guise for mischief. The bird muscled in on the seal's territory, all slim planes and points and hard edges, a hunter with attitude. There are times when you wonder about evolution and the creative process. How come, you wonder, that the single-cell origins of the stuff of life which emerged from the Green Slime should grow up so diversely that a fistful of aeons later they can be gannet and seal, wash up on the same fragment of all the world's oceans and compete for the same fish? Such a fish contrived to coincide with my arrival on this of all the Atlantic shores, a wrasse nudging in towards the seal's space and catching the gannet's eagle eye. My own eye simply watched the remarkable consequences of their three-way collision course. What happened was this:

The bull seal was in doze mode, so the gannet's arrival and the approach of the wrasse went unobserved. The gannet began quartering the inshore waters 200 yards out and 100 feet up, working a quarter of a mile up and down the shore, vivid in all that sky-wide greyness as quartz in a boulder-field. Its wings, long and slim and white and pointed as pencils, were quick and shallow. The flight was wide circles, looking down. The seal dozed on.

Then the gannet abruptly broke its circle and steamed ashore. It tilted on one black wing-point, drew its wings close and half-closed, and fell. It carved open a hole in the seal's portion of the ocean not five yards to the north, a towering splash. The seal galvanised, or at least that portion of the seal above its chins did – nothing else much seemed to move. That unseen crane working the rise and fall of the seal's head roared into overdrive and the head fell massively to the horizontal, wide-eyed. From there it whirled far round on its neck – no, on the cushion of its chins – to where the splash was already falling back on itself. What the . . . ? But by now the gannet was swerving down towards the bull seal's deeply submerged and unsuspecting tail, swimming hard downwards because the momentum of its crash dive was all but annulled by the great dull-grey body of the ocean. Its streamlined body was unbalanced by the 2lb wrasse now impaled on its lance. That fish dived in death as it has never dived in life, head and tail perfectly horizontal. It was killed not by the impalement which holed both its flanks but by the instant shock. As it was thrust beyond its comprehension down through the surface layers of the Atlantic, the last sight in its dying head was the blur of the seal's flanks sliding past like a grey wall.

At more or less the same instant, the seal registered the broken white shape of the diving bird beneath him. The seal's huge head was suddenly dipped downwards, chins compacting like closing accordion bellows, but the gannet was already rounding the Cape Horn of his tail and cleaving fish-first for the surface. A new commotion, not five yards to the south of the seal head, and again that blunt and bewildered mass spun round on its chins.

And there was the gannet, spread wide on the water, wings held out like a scarecrow's sleeves, white with black cuffs, a toff among scarecrows to be sure. The bird persuaded the limp fish off the point of its bill and down its gullet in a single slick manoeuvre.

Seal glared at bird. If it occurred to him at all that this was anything other than a particularly witless way to catch a fish, it did not show. He hauled his snout back to its sky-contemplation, and having briefly contemplated, he closed his eyes. The gannet heaved on its wings, lifted and flew and resumed its circling scrutiny of the ocean, looking down.

So I rose too, stiffly after that long stillness, and my movement brought one more head-lowering, eye-opening response from the bull. It seemed I was his last straw. He snorted massively and sank, doubtless in search of a less disturbed corner of the Atlantic, or perhaps to satisfy himself that fishing is nothing like as complicated and traumatising as a gannet tries to make out.

I took a long look south, south to the lighthouse, south to that downpour of contours with which the Mull of Kintyre greets its ocean, south-west to Ireland on a famous day which would prove one more false dawn in its search for a path to peace through its maze of bewildering conflicts. I feel for you, Ireland, but I don't understand you, any more than you appear to understand yourself. You see two Irelands. I see one from my Kintyre shore. The bull seal cruises between your place and mine and doesn't know the difference, far less the difference between your two Irelands. I wish you peace, I who think of myself as neither Catholic nor Protestant, and I ask you to celebrate the one thing which unites you all and gladdens my heart whenever I am in Irish company: your Irishness. Then I turned my back on it all, all that lay to the south, and I pointed myself up the Kintyre shore, and my Journey felt suddenly secure, now that it had reverted to its instinctive preferred direction. North, to where Suilven stands heroically patient, bulwark between two gulfs of blue air, staring out at Harris in the sky.

That first mile from the bull seal to Balmavicar, the land empty of everything but sheep and ruins, the companionable sea restless with birds, a spillage of yellow light among the islands seeping away the pervasive grey, a film-maker's trick, monochrome to colour, the sounds only of wind and my own footfall, a buzzard clamped on the air by its wingtips, the heather-dark steeps, crags ribbing the bare places, a far mountainous profile – Jura – to be reeled in and brought close as I walked up the slow miles of the land . . . these were the elemental fellow travellers, the footstep-haunters which had suddenly begun to gather, now that the Journey had harnessed itself to the West. They would become the ever-present themes varying only by degrees. Their familiarity from hundreds of lesser West Highland treks has always both troubled and comforted me. In their various ways they delineate the joys and the melancholy of the West.

They tell me too that I am a stranger in my own land. Do I not need a dictionary to unravel the names of the landscape? My coast, my native shore, is the east one, from which the mountains stand back. My mountain familiars are the land-locked ones . . . Angus and the Cairngorms, and all the Journey that lay behind me now from Sheriffmuir to Orchy. Yet there is a strain in me which clings to the West, to its mountains and its islands. I felt it first when childhood holidays turned a corner of the Dirie Mor and the window of my father's car showed me Torridon. It rose in me uninvited and unexplained, and while my mother commentated on the surroundings, finding them 'bleak', I hugged silently to myself the immensity of one of the most important discoveries of my life. That was the joy of it. And perhaps that strain in me was imported by John and Catherine Crumley 150 years ago, melancholy enough baggage, that.

Perhaps it goes back further. Crum, I was once told by no great authority on the subject, was a sept of the Macdonalds of Benderloch so perhaps the strain found the Irish Crumleys by way of the Lordship of the Isles. Crumerled. It has a certain ring to it.

In which case, though, why don't I feel more at ease here? Here on the Kintyre shore where Somerled unyoked the place from the tight rein of the Norse domination, and where (they say) his bones still moulder in an unmarked lair. Between the liberating of Kintyre and the secret burial, he founded an abbey at Saddell around 1160. No sense of the power it must once have wielded emanates from the ruins. Instead, tourism has collided oafishly with what it is pleased to call heritage, and strung up a dozen mediaeval carved slabs in a row underneath a transparent-and-rust canopy. You walk along the line like the Queen inspecting the Guards, staring at a faceless soldier with a bairn at his shoulder and another upside down at his feet (now what's that all about?), swords, crosses, galleys, priests, monks. They were carved to lie flat, but now they stand in their mediaeval stiffness, and they might as well be strung up on a mass gibbet. The theory is to protect the carvings. The practice is to make a farce of their purpose. Whoever carved a gravestone expecting it to last forever? The one undeniable natural characteristic of stone is that it weathers. Put them back where they were and let them go on weathering, and put the canopy where it belongs. I'm sure there must be a council tip at Campbeltown.

But I was walking the west shore, and troubling myself with insinuations of racial trespass. So, to ease the day and the footsteps northwards towards Suilven out of sight over a thousand skylines, I put Somerled from my mind and reconvened instead the journeyings of John and Catherine, wondered who they were, what they looked like (is one of them fair haired and blue eyed like myself, doused with some of that Norse blood which permeated so many Celts over so many centuries, including Somerled himself?) and what they made of this mysterious shore as they sailed towards it. And as I walked, a higher consideration imprinted itself on the Journey. The Mountains of Jura stood off the port bow and made of themselves a metaphor for the whole Journey north – mountains as milestones, and thinking of the mountains in my path from Dunadd to Suilven, my mind grew easy again and I warmed to the work, the journeying and the writing.

13

A Passable Stab at Eden

The tent looked at Gigha. And because I was lying full length with my head at the entrance, so did I. I was also writing and sipping whisky. Sipping whisky *and* writing are normally against my rules. They don't mix. They rarely distil good writing. But these were desk rules. Writing in a tent on the Kintyre shore looking at Gigha calls for different tolerances. If you can't drink Islay malt here . . . and if you can't write here . . . so save time and do them both at once. As long as you are making more words than drinking whisky, you're ahead.

The tent had one more civilising accessory, forby the whisky bottle. It was a personal stereo with two tiny speakers. Very quietly, so that the sound barely issued a yard beyond the tent, it played Bill Evans, solo jazz piano, *Who Can I Turn To*. Bill Evans's solo playing is good company for the resting hours of a solitary Journey. It strikes me as a literal translation into music of solitary travel. Its beginning and end are clear enough, but its rhythm is unconstant, it pauses to ruminate, it makes snap decisions about detours, explores occasional *culs-de-sac*, and – crucially – it is tempered (at times haunted) by loneliness. No surprise, then, that it should alight on a song like *Who Can I Turn To*, because the whole point of the Journey, whether landscaped or musical, is that there *is* no one to turn to. The absence of other shoulders to lean on is at one and the same time the restriction and the liberation. You are restricted by your own physical and mental powers and the scope of your imagination. And you are liberated by exactly the same things. When your only resources are your own, you discover a store of resources you did not know you owned.

The paradox. You look at what you have unearthed from this

108

unsuspected store, you admire its strength and its shining worth, you marvel that it is the product, solely, of your own endeavour, and it is at that point precisely that you long most fervently for someone to share it, someone to nod unquestioning understanding, someone who will take your hand and leap with you into the turbulent whirlpool because it will take the strength of two to becalm its waters. It is then that the absence of such a companion is almost too powerful a lack, the whole enterprise totters briefly, but the music sidesteps it, delves into bluesier, more melancholy grooves (and how strange the change from major to minor as Cole Porter wrote in a quite different song), and the loneliness of the hunched figure at the keyboard becomes its own resource, improvises its way through the darker shades until it evolves back into the old main theme of the Journey and resurfaces somewhere between Kintyre and Gigha and lies there on the Sound, glittering in the evening sun. Thanks Bill.

Gigha was never part of the plan, which was reason enough for it to become one. The long tented evenings looking at it, or taking the morning's first pre-breakfast coffee down to the water's edge to see how it had changed in the night . . . all that conspired to make Gigha inevitable. I took the bike.

The Gigha ferry does the fastest, tightest turns of any ferry I have ever boarded, which is a lot of ferries. The one-boat pier was vacated 15 minutes every hour by whatever was working there, to let her empty and refill. She scuttled to the island, which seemed a touch undignified in an emissary of the one they call ('they' being the tourist board) God's Island. The sound of the name – Geeh-yah – falls strangely on the ears, a Gaelic-sounding beginning with a Norse ending. You would think that with only two syllables to play with, the old island namers could have at least settled on one language. An old book about the Hebrides written by what the Gaelic language calls a 'Sasunnach' (he had better remain anonymous, lest he ever wants to return) advised that the word Gigha 'rhymes with pier'. Not in any of the tongues of Scotland it doesn't.

But whether God's island or just a benevolent landlord's, Gigha on such a June day as I scuttled over to it made a passable stab at Eden. The five single-track miles of its solitary north-south road were jewelled, flowered, birded, butterflown, all with such intensity and so profuse that I completed no one mile without dismounting to examine, immerse, climb, touch, smell and wonder. I began cycling north into what passed for the wind, a thin slicer of the sunlight, not much else. The road recalled Lismore's main artery, thickened by mercifully untrimmed roadside verges. Lismore was an old summer, at orchid time. If you have never been to Lismore at orchid time, go before you die. Lismore has orchids like lesser islands have grass, or bogs, or rocks. And Gigha had flowers enough to make me think of Lismore. A cluster of thrift rose from a thick matting of daisies, the pink mass so erect and tightly bunched that it looked like a pink geyser, a very small pink geyser. I stopped and dismounted for the pink geyser.

I stopped and dismounted again for Gigha's single standing stone. I love islands with *one* standing stone. It says to me that standing stones need the energy of landmass to sustain them. On a small island, there is energy enough for one, so make it a good and a striking stone. So in the way that my island-travelling mind tends to island-hop among old island travels, I remembered Shapinsay, which is the fulcrum of all Orkney, and as wonder-strewn a place as it is unsung. And on its lowly moorland crown, like a lone wolf baying at the moon, is a single standing stone. It is tall, perfectly erect, regularly shaped and the most exquisitely pointless thing I have ever seen. One stone. What on earth was it for? Who laboured to heave it up there, for it's a long haul from the nearest source of hewable rock? And now, by the roadside, looking as if it had been dropped off for the later attentions of a passing sculptor who might whittle it down into a serviceable milestone (but a milestone to where, Jimmy, to *where?*), Gigha's stone stood.

I laid my bike down in the grass (and five different flower species thickened the space between chainwheel and crossbar) and went to look at it, touch it, draw it, photograph it, wonder over it.

This one was no bayer at moons. It was a wayside marker. It was also leaning, a leaning standing stone, tiring, perhaps, of its own eternity? Or symbolically, in its weary aspect, it invites travellers to feel tired and dismount, and having dismounted to ponder the stone's purpose. From below the road, knee-deep in flowers and grasses, the stone presents another face, for it has split diagonally from the sculpted scoop which links its two 'heads' to its subterranean roots. With the sun on the top and flank of the stone and the 'inside' of the scoop in deep shadow, it transformed itself into two hooded figures, monkish creatures turned to pillars of salt because they looked over their shoulders when they shouldn't have.

It was only when I went to pick the bike up again that the final mystery of standing stones was revealed to me, as if some prehistoric deity had tapped me on the shoulder and lifted a veil from my eyes. Why hadn't I seen it before? They are for leaning your bike against in a treeless landscape.

The high ground lay in the north. A solitary hill, a short chain of hill forts. There was no obvious path up the hill, my kind of hill on my kind of island, so I bludgeoned my own width through all manner of growing things onto the bare summit and saw Arran to Jura, Ireland to Mull. The wind was fresher, the island airier, and from the Hebridean seas to the north and west the wind bore the sea-scents, the island intoxications, the seaboard seductions of the West, its light and its landscape; the Scotland of Rannoch Moor, Rob Roy and the Glen Ogle bridge builders was the incomprehensible province of others.

The sky hiccuped, a thin falsetto grunt, faint and high and moving. A raven on the march, ill-omen bird. The writing of Gavin Maxwell taught me to say aloud: 'Raven, seek thy brother!' to assuage the demons in the sky, although in truth, it felt as undemonish a sky as I had ever known. And anyway, it was God's Island, right? But I said 'Raven, seek thy brother!' aloud anyway, and made a mental note to look out for the next single raven on the Journey so that the ill-omen birds might cancel each other out.

The bike trundled on up the island, and if ever a landscape, a road, a day and the weather could be handpicked to coalesce into the cyclist's dream, this was mine. And it would only get better. I nosed through a half-heartedly closed gate, found a green track down to the shore where a tombolo (a sandbar with an island on its seaward end) thrust a white arm westwards. The sea laps both 'shores' of a tombolo, without (mostly) blundering into itself in the middle. These yards-apart shores were starkly different in one respect: the north shore was an unblemished virgin white, soothed by the gentlest of seas, but the south shore was foul with litter and seaweed, a harvest of plastic and rotting junk . . . other people's trash sea-borne to despoil the shore where the ill-omen bird's shadow had just fallen.

South down the island, then, wind-assisted, among small, tight farms with curving, contoured fields, past the hotel (later, later), past the famed Achmore gardens (not my taste in gardens, for all their deserved fame, but why the hell pay to see flowers on Gigha when your path is strewn with them?), a giddy pace down to the tiny harbour, a rock shore as bold and hard-edged as the north shore was soft and shy.

Further south, one of the Hebrides' many Oronsays rose to its single summit. This is the Oronsay where – they say . . . that 'they' again – St Columba first hove to, looking for a place to set up in business, but found he could still see Ireland. So he turned again and sailed north and found Iona, which is blind to Ireland. So Iona and south Mull got to service the late 20th-century pilgrim trade as redefined by the tourist industry, and

Oronsay – and Gigha to which it is all but attached – got to keep their tranquillity, and I have my own ideas about who got the better of that deal.

The island-hopper in my head was at work again, chalk-and-cheesing my way through the relative attributes of Iona and Gigha. I have been profoundly moved on Iona, a wholly spiritual experience inflicted by forces I do not begin to understand, but on its hilltop in a gale rather than cloistered in its abbey. The thing, the presence, the whatever-it-is, cannot be denied, not by me anyway. If it was a 'thing' of winds and austerity and pared-to-the-boneness that Columba sought, then he found it in full measure, and to be sure, Ireland (whatever the reason he wanted it not to be there) was under the horizon. But if he had taken the trouble to dismount at Oronsay and linger up the length of Gigha, he must surely have thought twice about that curious caveat.

The hotel again, no longer resistible, not the least of Gigha's charms for which a passing cyclist must dismount again. I took my pint of Guinness out into the garden. Ye gods! Palm trees!

I pulled out a chair, put down my glass on a table, tossed a notebook and pen down beside it, sat down, pulled the chair into the table, sat back, reached out for the glass. My arm, the glass, the notebook and the pencil were in the shadow of palm leaves. My hand passed the glass, reached the pen, flicked open the notebook, and wrote:

'Gigha. I'm having a pint of Guinness under a palm tree.'

Then I put down the pen, closed the notebook, closed my eyes, opened them again when I couldn't find the glass with them shut, picked up the glass, closed my eyes again, and drank. St Columba, what were you thinking about?

The tent looked at Gigha. And because I was lying full length with my head at the entrance, so did I. Gigha was never part of the plan.

And I had a pint of Guinness under a palm tree.

God's Island. If only Columba had known that at the time.

14

Heir Lies the Corpss

The Atlantic Ocean pokes such a long and skinny finger into the land at West Loch Tarbert that it falls only a mile short of making an island of Kintyre. Tarbert itself shrugs at the west, turns its face towards the east where Loch Fyne is not so much a finger as a whole armful of ocean, complete with dislocated elbow at Lochgilphead. Strangers get confused. The sea disappears from your port bow. You negotiate Tarbert and it reappears to starboard. That can't be right. You've taken a wrong turning somehow. So you u-turn back into Tarbert, the sea disappears from your port bow and reappears to starboard. You consult a map at last (when all else fails, read the instructions) and the confusion of sea lochs unravels itself. You turn again, confidence renewed, for you have found a way of keeping the seaboard where you want it, which is in the west. Just south of Tarbert, a slip of a road, all but unannounced, hedgehogs its way quietly round the rim of the land, a new land – no, not a new land, a very old land, but instantly different, tangibly more West Highland, less out-on-a-limb, less extrovert than Kintyre. Knapdale has no truck with the east. Its every settlement (and these are sparse and small) clings to the south and the west, facing the sun and the ocean. Inland it swells to an 1,800-feet ridge where the wrong kind of foresters have been over-zealous in their planting. But the coast is drunk on the scent of birches, oaks, rowans, hazel, and the all-pervasiveness of the sea, where Gigha appears end-on in the south, and Islay and Jura have grown wide and come close.

The old Fiat was in truculent mood, excuse enough to abandon it to the midgey shade of the lochside, and point the bike towards the sun. The roadside fingerpost said 'Kilberry', a name I have cause to know well, and where I had an appointment a day or two from now, an appointment with a woman who would unlock some of the secrets of this land for me, for is she not the guardian of an unbroken attachment to this portion of Argyll for 400 years?

But today I was travelling simply to travel, the slow movement round the coast its own purpose. Herons stood along the shore, admiring their own upturned selves in the shallows, almost as regular as milestones, and just as still. Oh, the things herons must know about their shores because of their long stillnesses. Perhaps when this Journey and its book are done, I should write an anti-travelogue, a book about being still, to see what mountains come to Mohammed. So as I brushed past and mentally ticked off the herons (seven . . . eight . . . nine . . . 13 . . . 14 . . .) I began an argument with myself. Was this kind of journeying nothing more than a symptom of the fact that my life had never found a place where it longed to be still? And would it ever? For that matter, did it ever want to? The clamour of the argument was upsetting the day, so I switched it off, and listened to the sound of the bike's wheels instead, the rich fragments of warbler concerto as my ears came within their scope then faded away beyond them, then into another wood where another warbler explored new variations of the same theme. In that way, a healthier frame of mind was restored by the time I stumbled on the burial ground of Kilnaish.

It lay – no, mostly it stood – on a gentle slope above the road, enclosed by a shoulder-high stone wall handsomely clad in furs of moss, patchworks of lichen. Two strands of fence wire threaded through rusting poles along the crown of the wall spoiled the effect, but I suppose they keep the sheep out. The grass was newly cut, but the daisies had rushed out again in the wake of the mower. The stones stood in uneven rows, a kind of random order with inexplicable gaps, the lichens were on them in swarms the way magpie moths occasionally storm a hawthorn hedge. The midday stillness of the place was irresistible.

The stones were mostly 18th century, and small, plain and slim (although I would learn later that I had missed an incised cross on an upright stone, possibly ninth century). A few were just rough stones, uncut and unshaped and unlettered, and simply planted on end, confirmation that a life had been begun and ended, without saying whose life or when it had been lived. Most enigmatic of all was one of the smallest stones, no more than two feet high, on which had been cut in careful capitals the words 'HEIR LIES THE CORPSS OF'. But the sculptor hadn't judged the size and the spacing of the letters too well, and the word 'CORPSS' began to run out of room at the letter 'R' because the angled top of the stone intruded there. So the 'P' and the 'S' put a downward curve on the word, with a second 'S' alongside the first as though to fill out the line. The word 'OF' begins a second line, but such is the profusion of lichen over the stone that not another letter is decipherable. Or perhaps none was ever carved. Perhaps the sculptor prepared a batch of stones with the same words across the top (others nearby introduce their corpses with the same form of words), and due to pressure of work – an epidemic perhaps, which struck down a township calling for several stones at once – he forgot one. Maybe it's the sculptor's own stone (if it is, it displays exemplary modesty) to which he hoped a later hand would add his name. Perhaps it marks an empty lair, and no corpss lies heir at all. Only a traveller coming curiously, 250 years later, feels cheated.

The rampant beauty of moss and lichen is slowly erasing the detail of commemorated lives from the stone, nature reclaiming the fruits of its own seeds, an exquisite and exquisitely appropriate deterioration, earth to earth. Stone-workers like the sculptor who laboured here would know that the way of all stone carving is the same as the way of all flesh, albeit longer lived. He would know that on a shore like this the shallow cut of his lettering would last 200, perhaps 300 years, and vanish. He would know it from the work of his predecessors. And if that truth troubled him at all, why not cut much deeper? The fading beauty of the stone, and the uninhibited beauty of moss and lichen is all the testimony, all the monument, that any of us could wish for. And how much more fitting is that slow regression back to nature than the frozen-stiff stones of Saddell under their bus shelter canopy? Lay them down, lay them open to the sun and the wind, the rain and the frost, the sea air and the lichens and the moss, and let them go, slowly and at nature's pace.

Ah, but there have been double standards at work in the burial ground of Kilnaish. One uphill corner has been cordoned off by a high-walled mausoleum, a quoined and finialed and spike-gated monument to how the other half died. But the gate sags open, its iron is rusted, and nature – no respecter of pompous gate pillars – had planted a rowan tree on top of each finial. The fact that one thrives and one straggles adds a cheerfully unimpressed lopsidedness to an entrance designed and built to impress. Nineteenth-century latecomers huddle their taller stones along the mausoleum's outside wall, as though there was saving grace in death by association. To reach the gate of the mausoleum you walk past a row of five of the smallest stones. One is slightly taller than the others by virtue of a curved top. The three middle stones might have been cut from a mould, and the fifth stone is smaller than even these, not much bigger than a school slate and the same shape. That small stone file looks like nothing so much as the kind of guard of honour of servants and other staff gathered at the mansion house door to welcome His Grace from some imperial adventure or other.

The joyful thing is that it doesn't matter. The guests in the mausoleum are no less dead than the unlettered *hoi polloi*, no more commemorated, no more equal in their histories.

I lunched in the other uphill corner, an empty green plot with the warm stone of the wall at my back. A cuckoo havered. Wagtails squabbled, and one made a point of perching often on the stone globe of the mausoleum's corner finial, and adding white stains of its own to the lichens.

The day stalled. The sun came and went and came again, switching shadows off and on, firing and smooring the shades of the mosses. Time was . . . well, it was passing and it wasn't. Where were all the others of Kilnaish? Was this all that was left of them and it? For that matter, where was Kilnaish? Not on my map. If this was all that remained, it's a better memorial than a row of roofless cottages. So keep the grass trim and the sheep out and let the stone go, slowly, at nature's pace; and let the living, the curious landscape-trekkers like me, pause and be warm and still two days before midsummer's day, drifting north out of Kintyre into Knapdale, heading for Suilven. It was not the pause I had planned to make in Knapdale, but the unplanned pauses have always been the springs from which I drink most gratefully.

It was not the morbid quest of the hunter-of-the-dead I brought here over the stone wall, not an excuse for tears for God's sake or any other, but rather I paused to run an appreciative eye over this small treasury of the stone-worker's art, and to read the social commentaries which inhabit its unspoken asides. To these I added my own.

> *Two standards of stone*
> *stand shoulder-to-shadow*
>   *the unlettered unsung*
>   *the lettered sung*
>   *the stone-wafered*
>   *the stone-chambered.*
>
> *The high-walled enclave*
> *of the lettered*
> *darkens at sunset the remembrance*
> *of the unlettered and lowly.*
> *The knee-high stones throw*
> *too few inches of shadow*

at noon even to cool adjacent kin.
But the chambered ones still chill
in their own spelled-out sepulchre.

A wagtail is laird of that place,
perches proprietorially high
and by her own example teaches
her adjacent kin which side of the wall
to shit on.

The burial ground had a neighbour, a *cnoc*, a low rounded hill. Stones gathered about its highest curve, as though something had been built there once, not a house, an ancient dun perhaps. But its crowning glory was not the stones, nor even whatever the stones may once have been. From the midst of that loose spillage a tree grew, and what a tree. It was not tall, not by the standards of great oaks and mighty beeches and tapering pines. But it stood alone on the *cnoc's* highest bareness and from the burial ground below it stood against the sky, and by the standards of hawthorn trees, which is what it was, it was peerless. It was so laden with white blossom that there was hardly a green glint of foliage. It had a great swelling of blossom at its waist, as though it might be pregnant, and another vigorous spread at its crown. Between waist and crown was an intermediate tier of blossom, seven or eight smaller clumps which girdled the widest spread of its limbs. It must have been a great age by hawthorn standards, for it was taller and wider-flung than any I have ever encountered, and I count myself an avid student of hawthorns, in a small and amateur way. So it was white blazes against the blue of the sky and its trunk was black and grew out of rocks, and it so imposed itself on the burial ground because of the way you looked up to it from among the small stones that you began to think it had been planted there for a purpose.

You could see in your mind's eye, the bowed, sorrowing heads muttering their dour amens, then looking up and through their mourners' tears they would see the hawthorn, high and white and blazing (if it was a June burial or a snow-drifted one), and so like the angel Gabriel that you half-expected trumpets. Or if it was autumn and the tree was not blossomed but gold-leafed and burdened with berries, then it put the burning bush in your mind and you waited fearfully, half-expecting your own hoary definition of God to bellow His Commandments. But of course, no Commandment came, although perhaps you left the burial ground muttering to yourself 'Thou shalt not kill, thou shalt not covet . . .

no . . . Thou shalt have no other gods before Me . . .' that should be first, then you went home and turned up the Book of Genesis to reacquaint yourself with the form of words, and even if God hadn't voiced the thing Himself, the tree had made His point for Him, eh?

And if it was a spring burial, and the tree was skeletally black and thorned and tight-budded and feeling the sap rise in its old bones, you prayed your thanks that you and yours were safely through one more winter and alive to the new season, and as eager for it as the *sgitheach* on its *cnoc*.

Then one more June day with the hawthorn looking very much as it did today, a new young minister came to conduct one more burial service, a child so young and innocent and blameless of the world's ills that your very Faith was rocked, and the grief of all Knapdale was inconsolable and not helped by the sight of the new young minister when you wanted the reassurance of the old one. But he told you not to weep, not to bow your heads, but to lift up your eyes. What devilry was this? Not to bow your head to show grief? But he said:

'Look at the hawthorn tree, not at your feet.

'Look at the way it rises out of the rock – the very stuff of our world – and spreads towards the four corners of heaven, which is God's world and ours to inherit. We have laid a child into the same dark place as the seed from which the hawthorn sprung. The tree and the child are as blameless, their inheritance as certain as each other because they have showed only a fair face to the world.

'Think of that tree as the means by which the souls of all buried here rise to their heaven.'

He climbed to the little *cnoc*, broke off a tiny sprig from the tree, and laid it on the child's grave, and for the first time (the tradition has been unbroken ever since) you said your amens looking not at your feet but at the hawthorn tree. The new young minister did not return to Kilnaish.

I wandered off into the afternoon, leaving the bike against the old stone wall, wearing only shorts and sandals, shirt slung over a shoulder, carrying nothing at all, the Journey reduced for the moment to a biblical simplicity, the burial ground's quietude rubbing off, I suppose. The wandering unearthed an oakwood, found its rarity value as irresistible as the stone stillness of the burial ground.

The place was its own green world, self-contained and secure, sure of itself, the way oaks always seem to be in their own company. The wood dipped into low valleys, climbed low hills, made glades for itself. You don't get many glades in the Highlands. This one astonished me with its greenness, every shade of green. I suddenly remembered that wonderful trick of Janice Galloway's in *Foreign Parts* where she evokes the vast sense of the interior of Chartres Cathedral by smothering the page with the word 'glass' in vertical columns. If I'd been given to that kind of wholly admirable inventiveness I would now smother the page in 'green'.

Oaks *demand* space. They also decline to be straight. They spread. And what they spread is green. An oakwood forms when the sun throws the shadow of one tree onto the leaves of another, but the shadowed tree must also throw its shadow onto the leaves of another, and so it goes. So it dapples. Dapple is a word invented for oakwoods in June. I walked deeper into the dappling green.

I found a secret dark brown burn. How come, I asked it, when water lies out under a blue sky, it looks blue itself, but when it eels its way furtively through something as green as this, it declines to be green, and turns dark brown instead? The burn answered my question with the sublime irrelevance of a pair of dragonflies. Perhaps, reasoned the burn, if I unleash a couple of these, he'll worry about them instead and leave me and my dark brownness alone. Anyway, what does brown mean?

The dragonflies were blue, which is like saying oakwoods are green or Chartres is glass. It's not the full story. The bodies were the blue of disgruntled Fiat estate cars, but their wings were dark blue, something between royal and luminous navy. I had never seen such a shade. But when they flew, when they caught the sun, what transilience! Bodies and wings snatched at every kingfisher shade, but at different times, so that as they flew the dragonflies reinvented themselves with every other wingbeat. In one light – with the sun right behind them – their wings showed completely clear and colourless. But then they landed, and the wings folded dark blue, the bodies beneath them glowed a vivid electric green.

How close could I get to them? If I had my camera, could I photograph them? But the camera was back with the bike. Walking with biblical simplicity precluded cameras. There were no biblical cameras. But the idea niggled and I began to stalk my quarry. I knew only this of dragonflies, that they split into one of two categories – hawkers and darters. Hawkers patrol a stretch of territory feeding on whatever crosses their path. Darters dart up from a perch as their prey passes by, and anything up to the size of butterflies is fair game. So these were hawkers. Three times I followed them up and down the same 100-yards-long stretch of burn. Three times they turned and flew back the way they had come, sometimes together, sometimes solo. They were particularly loyal to a bend in the burn where it emerged into the sunlight after some particularly dark brown eeling among the oaks' deeper shadows. After every foray downstream they returned to the same corner of the same bank by a plank bridge and lingered there close together. Conclusion: they know where they are going, and even when they are 100 yards apart, they know how to find each other again.

I started to line up questions for myself.

What's going on? Food? Eggs? Territory? Does a dragonfly have a territory? Is it a dragonfly or a damselfly? And what's the difference anyway? Why do they fly individually when they so obviously interact when they are close (but no actual contact)?

Why do they fold their wings when they land, but then open and 'clap' them slowly and continually for as long as they are perched?

A larger yellow-and-brown striped dragonfly suddenly infiltrated their corner. Their response was one of high excitement, short bouncing flights, skirmishes, but again no contact. More questions.

Intimidation?

An enemy?

Flirtation?

Piss off?

What's going on?

No idea.

I remembered one of those sublime moments which punctuate the writing of Gavin Maxwell as frequently as lesser mortals use commas. The flight of damselflies had interrupted his thoughts about the perils of his shark-fishing business on Soay, and in his book *Harpoon at a Venture* he wrote:

> *One pair, joined in that brief embrace of the insect world which seems so pathetically improbable, alighted near to me; there was a whirring rattle of wings, and they were swept away by a huge yellow-banded dragonfly. He circled me, carrying the struggling pair, and alighted upon a lily leaf close by. He did not finish his meal, but flew away, leaving them dead but still joined, a spot of colour suddenly robbed of meaning.*

My intruder was rebuffed, seen off, my spots of colour remained vividly meaningful. If I slipped back through the wood for the camera, I could be back in 15 minutes. There was every reason to believe the dragon/damselflies would still be there, or if they were not, I could sit and wait by the plank bridge for them to turn up. I went for the camera. Back at the bridge, they were waiting for me, probably saw my smug smile.

120

I sat on the bank with my feet in the burn, inched the camera towards them. I took two unsatisfactory shots from too far away and lowered into macro range, at which point they flew up into my face in protest. When last seen, they were flying away across the glade, away from the burn where they had spent the last two hours.

I sat on the plank bridge with my feet in the water, feeling the cool tug of the dark brown water, and for half an hour more I thought of nothing at all.

Later, elucidation from the library in the back of the car: there are two sub-orders of British dragonflies (thinks: do they know they're British?) – *Zygoptera* (similar wings) or damselflies and *Anisoptera* (unequal wings), the true dragonflies. Both sub-orders have two sets of wings. In the damselflies the wings are uniform and emerge from the same part of the body. In the dragonflies, one pair of wings is set further back than the other, and the hind wings are broader than the front pair. So I had seen a pair of damselflies and one true dragonfly.

Snap judgements about individual species made on the basis of colour are not always reliable. Patterns and shades often differ between males and females (but not always, and anyway, how can you tell when sunlight and shadow wreak such confusion?), and as if that wasn't confusion enough, the colours deepen as the creatures grow old. Eyes with 30,000 facets, swivelling heads giving all-round visibility, and an ability (thanks to four independently manoeuvrable wings) to hover and fly backwards . . . I think I may have to set up camp by the plank bridge some other June.

15

This Business of the Land Owning You

The sign at the roadside proclaimed my arrival at Kilberry, a useful sign for there is little sign of any village. These have not been straightforward miles, even for a car which has recovered its humour. The road-maker – no Roman he – insisted on exploring every contour, and having explored it once, it must be revisited often. And the west is forever dragging your eye away from the road when the road needs it most. A dozen miles can make light of an hour.

The landscape was classic Argyll, which is to say that it compelled a fertile mind's eye in every direction at once, including the past. Especially the past. It might occur to you in such a landscape that what the place needed amid the standing stones and bewildering carvings and great cairns was an archaeologist with the soul of a poet, and as rooted in its soil as the Kilnaish oaks. Such a person might do justice to the place in a great book. She is Marion Campbell, an eloquent 70-something, and her book is *Argyll – The Enduring Heartland*, and she was the pause I had planned in Knapdale. If anything could illuminate my Journey through the Highlands alighting with dragonfly wonder on this fascination and that, it might be a glimpse of how it feels to be bound into the same fragment of landscape for more than 400 years. For that is Marion Campbell's inheritance. She wrote in *Argyll*:

> *There is yet another kind of cairn. You will find it in a fold of hill ground where a shepherd lost his way in snow or at a steep corner where a cart overturned. These are not graves – the dead sleep in kirkyards – but we lay a stone on them to appease that which here parted suddenly from its clay.*

As we near any of them, even the oldest, plundered or excavated though they may be, you may see us hunt about for a pebble to bring in our hand; cur mi clach air a charn – I will lay a stone on his cairn, whoever he was, he was here when I was not, and I am the future of his past.

I bought Marion Campbell's book shortly after its publication in 1977 at a time when my own life had begun to nurture ambitions of a writing life beyond journalism, though I was by no means certain of the kinds of books I wanted to write. I found my role model in *Argyll* for the way it wove a sense of place with threads of poetry, humour, history, landscape, nature. But there was one crucial and less definable thread, one which confronted the past with a kind of awed respect and made it live and relevant, lifted it off the page with the highest endeavour of the writer's art so that it was as tangible as honeysuckle on a sea wind. That was the kind of book I wanted to write.

A ragged, irregular correspondence between us began with my simple fan letter. We finally met in 1995 when I interviewed her for *The Herald* and a new edition of *Argyll* had provided the excuse. And now I was back on the Kilberry road to interview her again at some length for a book of my own. A leafy track (shadows over the potholes, tricky) slipped past the entrance to Kilberry Castle, the converted tower house which was the centre of her existence for so much of her life. She lives now in a small garden cottage, taking it easier than her life had been accustomed to, slowed a bit by a heart attack and a limp, frustrated that her 'begouted' hand stops her from typing. But her mind is nimble and so is her wit and she is the most stimulating company. We had lunch at the Kilberry Inn, a portion of Nirvana after so much tent cooking. Mine host remembered me from the last time, and while he poured Marion's accustomed sherry he looked at me and said:

'Highland Park, wasn't it?'

It was, it was . . .

We talked through the afternoon and I took a tape of our conversation back to the tent on its shore. The evening unfolded into the most mesmeric sunset hour I ever knew, tall flames which flickered up the sky, up out of the charcoal-black shapes of Islay and Jura. So I slipped headphones on, put the tape player in my pocket, and walked out alone on the shore, staring out the sunset as I walked, and as I walked this was what I heard again in my ears:

The furthest back that I'm sure of is just before 1600. We haven't got a proper date, but somewhere about 1570–80–90. The younger son of a Campbell of Danna [a tiny island two sea lochs up the coast], was moved down here to take charge of Kilberry. The first one was Colin – Colin Mor, and Colin Og, his son. Colin Mor died about 1619. By that time his daughter had married a MacAlasdair, and Colin Og married some other local family – his wife was a MacDougall – so they were really in the business of infiltrating the local clans. From then on they were in Kilberry until 1790-something when the laird died childless, having executed a deed of entail under which the estate went to his cousin's son at Knockbuy which is Minard on Loch Fyne. It was that family which came back to Kilberry, not that generation but the next. The house of Kilberry stood vacant for a generation. It had been damaged by fire in the old boy's time. My great-grandfather came back and rebuilt the house, starting in 1840, moving in in 1843. At that time he was extremely reluctant to come back here. There's a desk in the castle with a little envelope in it and written on the outside is:

> *'A leaf plucked from my mother's favourite willow tree the day I left dear, dear Minard.'*

As if he was being shipped off to Australia! We've got his diaries which are mostly about the weather because he was purely interested to find how different the weather is here from Loch Fyneside. He hadn't appreciated there would be a climatic difference between the coast and the loch!

The place was new to him. He and his brother had come over for the shooting and found bits of the castle they could camp in. It really was pretty derelict. So he set to work to rebuild. Lord Cockburn, who was a friend of his wife's family, came to visit them at Ardpatrick while the house was being rebuilt. And there's a piece in his Journeys . . . he mentions being taken to see the rebuilding and he was horrified that they were coming here to such a bleak and desolate place when they had land on West Loch Tarbert, as indeed they did right down to my father's time. Lord Cockburn couldn't understand why they didn't build a commodious modern mansion instead of coming to this benighted place! The trouble was that this place was entailed, and in order to sell it they would have had to raise an action in the Court of Session and get the consent of all the relations, which they obviously weren't going to get.

The thing was . . . the land had been divided up like cutting a cake.

The whole of south Knapdale was the centre of the land, and when whichever earl it was was given the job by James IV of cutting up the Lordship's mainland possessions, he went to work, keeping the centre as a royal hunting ground up on top of the hill. So all the estates ran in like wedges. You got one wedge or three or four according to how lucky you were that week. You might get two rotten wedges or one good one. What with intermarriages, years going by and one thing and another, we got these four bits. Great-grandfather sold the two northerly ones in order to pay for rebuilding the house.

He hung on to Achaglachgach where he built a villa – I don't think Lord Cockburn would have approved! – a slightly gothic baronial villa with a sandstone tower. It's still standing – quite nice too. It was designed to be occupied by a Great Friend of Great-grandfather's who came up regularly from England to shoot with him. Great-grandfather died before it was finished whereupon Great Friend said he wouldn't be coming and we were left with a half-built villa to dispose of. Nothing happened for 20 years, when it was finished, and consequently the house has given nothing but trouble ever since.

It was sited by my great-grandmother walking about and choosing the view. She was a MacBean, one of the Jacobite MacBeans. She had kinsmen who were bankers in Rome and had been bankers to the Prince in Rome – a curious Campbell connection!

But then, if you go back a little in the Minard family, in the 18th century Campbell of Knockbuy, who was quite notable in his way as a farm improver, was locked up in Dumbarton Castle in 1715 – at his father's behest! – to prevent him doing anything foolish. And in 1745, with all that forgotten, he got a militia commission from the Duke and was given command of the troops on the Moor of Rannoch. And that is how the Appin Stuarts got their banner back to Appin. It's also how the Appin Stuarts got through the moor to raid Blair Atholl; because the commander didn't get his boots on in time to stop them.

There's a beautiful account in Sir James Ferguson's Argyll in the 45 of Knockbuy and Robertson of Struan chasing each other through Struan's wood. Struan kept dropping incriminating papers out of his pocket as he ran, and Knockbuy, peching after him, kept stopping to pick up these valuable pieces of intelligence to transmit to the authorities. The two of them had probably written them together! The amount of disinformation provided to the Government was considerable at that time. Knockbuy was court-martialled for neglect of duty. But he explained to the court that he was a poor old gentleman of 55, and couldn't possibly be out on the terrible Moor of Rannoch in the month of April. The court agreed – not guilty! But don't do it again! And he died at the age of 97 on a jaunt to Edinburgh.

He had a boot in each camp, very firmly. His colleague on the Moor of Rannoch was Campbell of Glenure who also had a boot in each camp. Well, for goodness sake, if we hadn't learned by that time to keep a boot in each camp where were we? After all we got done over in 1685, done over again in 1709, 1715, 1726 . . . by '45 you'd expect us to have a little sense!

But as to this place, they acclimatised, presumably settled in, but why they should become so fervent about it I really don't know, but they did and they do. I know my father put the place beyond everything else. And I went through considerable struggles to hold on to the farms.

It was left to me when I was eight, when my father died. He died just at the beginning of the great crash and slump and we couldn't afford to stay here. Mother and I trekked about for three to four years, living in hotels, living with relations, anywhere but here. The place was put on the market and of course didn't sell. Until some time in 1931, a cousin of Father's became very ill with pernicious anaemia, and decided that as she didn't have long to live she wanted to spend her time at Kilberry. So she sold up her house in London, scooped up a considerable amount of money from her father's family who were East India traders, and bought Kilberry. We came back here with her, with Mother to keep house for her, which was difficult for my mother.

She had to be carried into the house. She couldn't walk. For the first few months she was carried up and down between her bedroom and the main floor. And on fine days she was carried outside, wheeled out in a bath chair towed by a pony! And she lived for seven years, at the end of which she could walk about two miles. On one walk to the Post Office she caught her foot and fell and broke her hip and that disheartened her immensely. She didn't last long after that, but she had her seven years at Kilberry.

Difficulties were considerable immediately after that because she had left it to me. We had no idea she was going to do that. [The 'difficulties' stemmed from the fact that noses in the wider family were a bit out of joint.]

Then the war broke out and that put an end to the nonsense. I went *off to the forces. Towards the end of the war – in '44 – I had been ill, a couple of times in hospital, felt very rotten and unable to cope. Once I came home to convalesce, I realised my mother was seriously ill and had worn herself out with trying to help the war effort, trying to give our people her rations and other silly things. So I came out of the forces and was immediately confronted with the question of being called up again, which didn't appeal to me in the least. So the only thing was to have an urgent occupation here, and the only occupation available was to run the estate, for which I had not been trained. But I had been a pay clerk!*

I brought in service methods of bookkeeping and found it was relatively simple – I only had about 18 employees! So I weighed in. I don't think I did too badly. I had 13 years of running the farms. My mother died within a year or so, so I was very glad I came home when I did.

There were very hard times indeed, but my world was governed by wanting to keep the estate together. So much so that when I eventually decided I had to sell the farms, or at least some of them, I put the whole thing, the house and all, on the market. And it was in the middle of doing that, trying to keep the garden looking nice, the house looking nice, the farms all on top of themselves, that I started having Dark Twin. [The Dark Twin was her extraordinary 1973 novel which invented a Bronze Age matriarchal society. It was the result of a series of fragmentary waking dreams which she began to write down without knowing what sense they might ever make. Over several years they amounted to a pile of loose-leaf pages which she reordered and made sense of, though she is no nearer explaining the source of the dreams. I first read it just before I met her for the first time, a gift from the author. She described it as 'off the wall' and she wrote of it in a letter: 'People either love it or hate it and that includes me from time to time . . . It upsets Anglo-Saxons who don't know what it's all about, which I find reassuring.'] It was the extreme stress and strain and distress of throwing it in. Because I really felt that I was giving everything up. I'd sacrificed the thing I wanted to do in order to come home and run the place and now I was chucking it. It was very traumatic indeed. The dreams were written out of the trauma, an escape of some sort, from stress.

I switched off the tape and slipped off the headphones and walked in silence for a while. The sky was orange and so was the sea. I had walked up from the shingle shore onto a short stretch of machair, found it was host to a small nesting colony of little terns. Some of them rose in the air, that jaunty, bouncing flight which characterises all terns. A few grew anguished and screeched a protest. I pulled back, saw them settle again, sat and watched through the glasses. Other terns were working the Sound, a few travelled between fishing ground and nesting ground, the sand eels glittering orange too, and breathing their last 50 feet above the waves in the terns' beaks, not knowing what had hit them. Then I felt it again: 'I had that strange too-fullness of the heart which the sensory sum of my surroundings would often bring.'

I don't know how long I sat, but I saw the sun sink behind Jura and the afterglow grow smoky, and I was still sitting when I began to shiver. It was not cold, but the air felt recharged and invigorated. The tern colony had gone quiet but gulls still drifted down the Sound and a red-throated diver cried, eerie, unchancy crier that it is. I stood and turned my back on the islands and began to walk back. I switched on the tape again and heard my own voice ask:

'When did you become aware, as a child, of your history?'

> It was something that was taken for granted, I think. There was a lot of talk about it. Father was very interested in history, pre-history, and so was Mother, and they discussed what they knew a lot.
>
> And there was a great deal of pressure to look after the people on the estate: you must do this and that for people. Mother had been brought up in Shropshire by a generation back: she'd been handed over to her grandmother to be brought up while her parents were in India. So she was tapping back into an 18th-century way of thinking about the estate. But there was a lot of conflict between her and Father about that because Mother thought you should tell people what to do. Father knew you couldn't tell people what to do; you had to ask them, and I have heard them squabbling about this:
>
> 'But why don't you go and just say they've got to?'
>
> 'Because it won't work!'
>
> On the other hand, Father would have gone without a coat to his back if he'd needed something for the estate. Indeed, Mother would too. She struggled to keep everything after his death. She was very distressed, for example, because the children would miss the Christmas party. She used to send money to somebody for the Christmas party or we'd run it when we were here. Although she hadn't got money herself. She was wondering how to clothe me, clothe herself, but she had this obligation to it.

Me: What was it about . . .?

The Highland Edge from Sheriffmuir – Ben Ledi (left), *Stuc a' Chroin, Ben Vorlich*

Ben Vorlich, centrepiece of the Southern Highlands skyline

Red deer hinds on the hill above Loch Lubnaig

Snow clouds mimic Ben Ledi's shape on its summit

Cultivation strips, Glen Ogle

The 'back' of Stuc a' Chroin from Glen Ogle

Exquisite little pack bridge, Glen Ogle . . .

. . . and the hidden art of the bridge builder from below

Wintering whooper swans gather on frozen Loch Dochart

Dunadd 'crouching the way a hare crouches in a field'

Dunadd, midsummer night

The Dunadd footprint . . .

. . . boar . . .

. . . and bowl

High summer – a hidden corrie of Glen Orchy

The River Orchy slips over winter rocks

Marion (*correctly anticipating the rest of the question, as she did constantly throughout the interview*): *I don't really know. It's difficult to analyse. It is this business of the land owning you, not you owning the land. That definitely is basic to it. I think even the most . . . I was going to say toff-ish . . . stuck-up . . . incoming . . . that sort . . . do feel some sort of obligation to the land itself.*

It's not something you just strap on with a title deed, though, is it?

No, no indeed. It's very difficult for people who haven't been indoctrinated from the cradle! I've known dear, kind people who have bought estates and thrown themselves into the business of being a good landlord, putting up the most shattering clangers. They know what needs to be done! No point in repairing the old village hall – we'll build a beautiful new one! And funnily enough, no one goes to it!

As well as being fundamental to your life, is it also a burden?

Oh, it is. In my case, my dear Aunt Ivy left me the estate, but she also left a very complicated will in which she'd made small bequests to a great number of friends. One hundred pounds for so-and-so, £200 for the next one, all of which would have been very useful to them, and the residue was for me. But there never was a residue. They didn't even get their full £200, poor old biddies.

As for relinquishing the farms and so on, well, it was very difficult indeed. I might easily have gone out and topped myself but fortunately for me, just when it was building up to final dissolution of the estate, Mary Sandeman and her mother moved in to live with me. [Mary Sandeman was a lifelong friend who remained at Kilberry for the rest of her life. She died a couple of years ago.] I think I sold one farm. The effect of selling that farm, which I had been running, was really like having a boil lanced – the relief! That was one page of the ledger that I could turn. It was the effect of that one that made me say: 'Come on, you're going to sell the others.' There was no going back. I went ahead and did it.

I did have to force myself a little to become dispassionate and not get emotional about it. I minded very much about the Highland cattle, because I had been working on re-establishing a Highland fold and I had got some good beasts. I sold them to the incoming owner who immediately announced she couldn't be bothered with all this herd-book nonsense and stopped making entries and sold the cattle as quickly as she could . . . which was tiresome because I had put a lot of effort into getting the right stock together. Fair enough, she had bought it, she could do what she liked with it. But I minded that.

I very much minded the disruption to the employees. I couldn't . . . one couldn't make any condition about them being employed by the incomers. I gave them as good references as I was able to give. They did all find jobs, but I didn't like seeing that happen.

I minded the home farm dispersal sale a lot more than I thought I would. I thought I would be glad to see the home farm go, because it was the last burden. But in fact I found it very distressing. Because we rouped the stock at the farm, which meant I was standing on a kitchen table with the auctioneers as the beasts came out and walked round us, which was trying.

On the other hand, it was quite a funny sale. We were not at all sure we were selling the right calf with the right cow! We labelled everybody – stuck numbers on them – and the big cross-cattle went to work at once getting this nasty sticker off; and we were running round putting second and third stickers on them pretty well right up to the moment they went into the ring.

'Now,' says the auctioneer, 'we come to the bull.'

The Kaiser had been watching proceedings from over his half door nearby. So Jimmy just went and unbarred the door and out walked the Kaiser. Scene two: the policeman is up on the shed roof! One look at this Aberdeen Angus rolling out, not on a halter or anything, just Jimmy's hand on his shoulder, and the policeman shot straight up onto the roof, smartly followed by one of the auctioneer's clerks. And the Kaiser walked round the ring of his admirers, looked at them, bowed right and left, and he was eventually sold for a couple of hundred pounds more than I paid for him and went off to gladden the hearts of ladies I forget where! We needed the laugh.

Now . . . it's all changed very much. All the farms are owned by different people . . . I mean they're all individually owned. I can and do rejoice that mostly it's not my roof that needs renewing. I do get people coming to me all the time asking 'Do you know where the water supply is?' Mostly I do. There are things I see happening I don't like, like the field drains going back. But when I was farming we always had fairly labour-intensive places. Usually everyone had an old uncle we could shuffle out and clear a drain if there was nothing else he could do. Old bodachs who could scythe were very good at it, whereas the younger generation couldn't. And you did consciously try to find jobs for these people. And you didn't try to pack them off into an old people's home where they couldn't keep their dogs . . . which I think is one of the worst things that happens to a shepherd.

Or if he went into a council house he couldn't keep a dog either, which disabled him from helping at the lambing. But if he could live on – in whatever degree of squalor – and keep his dog, he could still help at the lambing and someone would ask Old Dougal to lend a hand – and the community would keep itself integrated in that way.

When Great-grandfather came back here he had four full-time employees on the home farm and the manager. Great-grandfather himself worked in the fields and worked a lot with people who were quarrying stone. He liked stone work so he used to go down to the quarry and work with the old man down there, so he was sort of half a hand. But come harvest, they had 30 or 40 day workers. Everybody turned out and they were paid pennies – but paid. They ranged from grannies to grandchildren, some men, but mostly women. Interestingly, the top women got paid the same wage as the top men. But it was a question of skill. They were cutting the corn with sickles and some of the women were obviously better at it than the men. These were the task force that came from far and wide for harvest, potato picking and sheep washing. Now the farm is run by one man. The high ground has been sold for forestry.

Do you regret what's happening to Highland estates now?

Yes I do. I suppose Eigg is the supreme example of horror at the moment. I feel sorry for the people who are living there, who can't just up stake and go somewhere else. Or they can but they don't want to. They're entitled to think that's their home and that's where they live and have some decent conditions to work in. I think it's very difficult for incoming landlords to pick up the way things are done, because the way things are done looks terribly inefficient. And some of them are inefficient. On the other hand, over the bit, that's the only way that works. So there's a strong tendency to stick with it, as there was a tendency to stick with . . . well, run-rig, you name it. If it ain't broke, don't change it. There does seem to be a terrible tendency to bounce in and make all things new without waiting to see what's going on. And of course there is a tendency to write off the countryman as a stupid peasant, which is rather dangerous. I've no

131

doubt my ancestor who came down from Danna wanted to do things differently, and was told he couldn't!

I think we have lost an awful lot in the loss of community. Every now and again, community suddenly works terribly well, and you think, 'Oh, goodness, I wish it could always be like this!' It's the small things – the local sheepdog trials, the local WRI, things that people are running for themselves. I would like to see this place supporting itself more, the community supporting itself. I don't want to see it at the mercy of incomers. I want the local voice heard. There are people who can make the local voice heard. I'd like to see them carrying their weight and expressing the feelings of the community. I'd like to see more of the acclimatised population if I can put it like that, having a say in running things. I'm a little scared of earnest people with ambitions for 'improvement' coming in because I think they usually improve the wrong things. I don't want to see us becoming a backwater, but nor do I want to see us becoming a dump for geriatrics.

You've got to have new blood coming into an area, as it has done from the beginning of time. I think probably tolerance is a lot of it.

I was glad I didn't sell the house. I would have had to move away and that would have been traumatic. I had another 40 years there, without the farms, and found plenty to do. Then I moved down here (other Campbells, cousins, now live in the castle) and still drink from the same spring. It makes more difference than you might think. And I've got the same view, same woods, same birds, so it's a very happy solution for as long as I can cope on my own.

Can you articulate why the spring is important?

It's difficult to put into words. The taste of a spring is something you do notice more than you realise. It's a conditioning thing from childhood. You find it in a lot of the songs of exile. And it's the basic flavour of life; if you're used to limestone springs, say, or as here to soft water springs, it must affect all the food you eat. It's a token, a convenient symbol of continuity, but it's more than that. You notice the flavour when you come back.

But I still don't understand how my family got so intensely bound into this place when they were imported to it. I can so feel for the people who were cleared, but to get so bound up in a place where you were dumped – it's so strange. My father always made a great point that no one was ever cleared from Kilberry. I believe that is true.

The tape fell silent, and even before I removed the headphones, the sound of my own footsteps rushed into my ears and I realised where I was and what I was doing. Without the islands and the sunset and the terns for diversion, and with Marion Campbell's quiet, measured voice unravelling the threads of a 400-year-old legacy in my head, as it were, I had walked back to the tent without a thought about how I had got there. From that small stock of books which I had stashed away in the car for the wheeled part of the Journey, I fished out her *Argyll*. I knew what I was looking for.

As for the dirty, dwarfish, ignorant hillman – I sometimes feel that we who live among the hills have indeed fallen under enchantment. We are fo geasa, *under spells, that imprison us within walls of glass. We are trapped in our beautiful landscape, which must be kept exactly 'as it was' (but when?), an exquisite fossil; and fossils are, by definition, dead. Beat as we will against its shell, those who gaze lovingly on it cannot see us. We have become 'People of the Green Hills', living underground among the old dead in the cairns, our music occasionally echoing to the outside world, our cairns sometimes opening to let others dance with us and forget the passing of time; we cannot assert our existence in any terms convincing to that outer world. It would frighten them to think we are not as they imagine – they stand close to use and talk as if we could not hear.*

There is nobody there, they say, nobody we can ask about what to do with this place, we must try to invent uses for it – sheep farming, forestry, tourism, superquarries. If there is anyone left there, they must be stupid beyond redemption or they would have got out long ago. What life could anyone expect in such a place? You couldn't stay there all winter, with nothing to do and nobody to talk to.

Look at their miserable houses, they say – low-roofed, thick-walled, small-windowed; but remember they knew no better, they'd never seen proper brick houses. Let's stop using the gloomy slates and those coarse stones, put in nice picture windows and paint the outside a cheerful pink. When the winter winds come to strip the tiles and encrust the glass with salt, we'll be snug in our city apartments.

Let us, by all means, ensure that any surviving children are got out of this deadly isolation, into bigger schools and larger communities, where they can be fitted for modern life instead of stagnating here and occupying houses that could well make pleasant holiday cottages.

133

*We hammer on the glass wall in vain. There is nobody there, they
say, and isn't it beautiful?*

And then there is this which (a) I wish I had written, and (b) I have
written out to keep in my pocket, by way of stimulation, as Stevenson
would say:

*I should be sorry to leave the impression of dwelling on bygones to
the exclusion of present and future; I would prefer to see the past
used as trees use their fallen leaves, a compost to feed future roots.
History has moulded the present and will colour the future of
nations as of individuals, whether they study it or not. Only the man
who has lost his memory confronts each day in bewilderment,
unable to draw upon inherited talent or acquired skill; and even the
amnesiac may find his hands moving of themselves in arts he does
not know he knew. A nation that ignores its past is in the same sorry
case; sorrier still is the case of the country whose history is fed to it
through alien minds and the fogs of prejudice.*

So that was the pause I had planned to make in Knapdale.

The long Highland twilight of midsummer was on my shore, and my
head was so full of all that I had been listening to, that the idea of sleeping
held no charm at all. I put on a jacket, pocketed the hip-flask, and with
my step slow and hands-in-pooches, I walked back the way I had come
through the West Highland midnight for the tern colony. On the way
there, this occurred to me:

Simon Schama wrote a book called *Landscape and Memory* which
included this observation:

*. . . it seems right to acknowledge that it is our shaping perception
that makes the difference between raw matter and landscape. The
word itself tells us much. It entered the English language, along with
herring and bleached linen, as a Dutch import at the end of the 16th
century. And* landschap, *like its Germanic root,* Landschaft,
*signified a unit of human occupation, indeed a jurisdiction, as much
as anything which might be a pleasing object of depiction. So it was
surely not accidental that in the Netherlandish flood-fields, itself the
site of formidable human engineering, a community developed the
idea of a* landschap *which in the colloquial English of the day
became* landskip . . .

So, about the same time that Colin Campbell came down to Kilberry from Danna to initiate a unit of human occupation, a new word to describe what he was about to embark upon had come alongside on an east coast quayside. And dare I suggest to Mr Schama that it was more likely to have been east coast Scots which imported the word rather than colloquial 'English' given the enthusiasm with which my own native shore traded with the Netherlands, the way our dialects battered back and forth across the North Sea.

Landscape – people in place on the land, and honouring that sense of place, and being shaped by the land even as they shaped the land. It was never truer of anyone than it is of Marion Campbell and her portion of Argyll.

16

Dunadd

Midsummer night, the lingering end of the longest day, and for as long as the venture had been in my mind, the fulcrum of the Journey. In the original blueprint, I had planned a midnight vigil on the summit of Ben Nevis. But the nature of the Journey had changed. Such a grand gesture suddenly seemed as grotesque as it was inappropriate. I was neither in the frame of mind for the slog of the pony track nor the company of crowds of revellers. The prospect had shadowed the previous few days like the shadow of an eagle on a running hare. The Journey had evolved. It had its own rhythm now, its own surreptitious demeanour, its own quiescence. Where there was company, it was company of my own choosing and relevant to the purpose of the Journey.

'Well, you won't be alone there,' Marion Campbell had cautioned when I told her something of the spirit of the Journey and the Ben Nevis notion. It was all the dissuasion I needed. It was on the second late-night trudge out to the tern colony that I confirmed to myself the obvious alternative, so obvious and right that it seemed at once as if the decision had been taken out of my hands. Here it seemed was purpose: Dunadd.

I was disappointed to find another car at the end of the Dunadd track, then found the sentiment ungracious, and consoled myself with the idea of the number of cars which would be scattered around the foot of Ben Nevis. But I was still low on the hill when I met the car's owners coming down. They had stayed for the *sunset* and had no intention of staying for *sunrise*. I stopped to watch them go, and didn't move on until the sound of the car had died.

Now, where were the grey-robed folk?

A soft shape coalesced out of the darkening, low and purposeful, flickered across the path and swerved violently away from my suddenly revealed presence, a short-eared owl, the first since Sheriffmuir. The shape hardened, unnervingly close, the orange eyes burning out of its deepest shadow, its wings low, then it was gone and its going reinforced the utter silence of its flight. I walked on, and as I walked with my head full of old Flaming Eyes, I heard the voices again, hooded and robed and sandalled, the sense that I was one of their number, able to communicate in their quiet-voiced tongue, yet neither dressed like them nor aware of their purpose. It is as though they usher me past some feature of the hill which is either dangerous and demanding of an escort as they see it, or so sacred to them that by the sense of their presence they divert prying eyes. They were with me at the foot of the gully, and we began to climb it convivially enough. Halfway up, the moon appeared, a vertical crescent about one-third full, stitching my moon-shadow onto my footsteps. At once, the shadow was the only companionship I had. I neither heard the grey tribe go nor sensed them turning. It was as though they had contrived first the owl and the sight of the moon to divert my attention for Dunadd's guardianship to fall in, perform its escort duties, and fall out again. Their presence was wholly benevolent.

I reached the summit of Dunadd at a quarter to midnight, pleased to have the company of the moon to lighten the vigil hours, and was greeted by a shooting star, hurtling into the north, a beacon for the Journey to follow. The sky was still light from west to north, the twin points of Ben Cruachan sharp on the northern skyline. You place your feet in the stone footprints, raise your eyes, and you see Cruachan. Is that why the footprints lie where they do? It would be too much to expect the midsummer sun to rise between the summits of Cruachan.

Midnight. I produced whisky. I toasted the land and the names of a handful of people who I thought would like to be associated with the hour. They included Marion Campbell, and my great friend George Garson whose mosaics and stained glass and paintings and drawings so often incorporate moons like the one which now stood over the Sound of Jura.

There was still enough light to write. There were still enough midges to torment the stillness of mind and body which writing requires. I heard a sheep cough on the Moss below. A cuckoo called, just once, as though it was a clock sounding 1 a.m.

The sky was all but cloudless. The moon had no intentions of shadowing me through the short night. It was setting. A yellow afterglow still clung to the north-west, and above that, and stretching as far round the compass as north-north-east was a wide band of the palest blue you wouldn't call white. The east was a profound grey, but host to one vivid star. Such clouds as there were stood on end, slim diagonals. They showed brown against the yellow and pale blue corner of the sky, otherwise white or silver.

I watched the moon sink, on end like the clouds. Once the foot of its crescent was below the skyline (a hill of Jura I think) the rest went down like a diving shark's fin. The last of it sank at 00.12, and I was sorry to see it go, but I had climbed on to the summit with my moonshadow.

Far below, and far out across the Moss, the coils of the Add still showed pale in the darkest mass of the land. Oystercatchers – the best of companions for solitary trekkers – caroused down on the riverbanks. Were there otters too, nosing vee wakes, blunt and bubbling amid the coils of the river snake?

A light wind skipped up the crags from the sea bringing coldness with it and banishing the midges at a stroke, a mixed blessing. I was now taking a glove off to write. The farmhouse lights went out. A fox barked, unmistakable three-syllable yelp, and provoked an answer. Fox and moon lodged in my mind, and aided by that pointed switching off of the farmhouse lights and the constant sound of a hidden spring, rekindled an old half-memory and made a half-poem of it; I wrote as much of it down as I could before it became too dark to see the words on the page. In the morning I tidied it and plugged its gaps.

> Memory drinks deep where wells
> are sweet draughts and granite cool,
> past tense made perfect, time reinvented
> whole as before it was spent.
>
> Moment surfaces meniscally slender:
> that glance before first kiss milkily
> infiltrated that chilled clarity; that sound –
> baying hound fox-foiled and far
>
> (the vixen safe below the barn
> and under that moon, plated
> and memory-crafted onto the tar-black
> granite-cold meniscus of the night well).
>
> Night owl's slight scowl at the fox
> limping home, grateful moonshadow caught

cobbled on the way to the barn. Damn
the distant dogs, the owl and I concur.

And you: your nod's understood
in your absence, and damn your distance too,
I tell the owl as we add your testimony
to the weight of evidence against

the culpable huntsmen. The night
unclouds again the drinking memory
and sweetens, follows again the spoor
of vixen and the Highland moon.

All is all but healed again
and granite-cool, save that your nod
catches again and again in the eye
of memory and I crave

that time again (I repent)
whole, as before it was spent.

Headlights on the track down from the road, two of them, in single file, two motor bikes; company, at 1.30 a.m. I saw the bikes circle near the Fiat, saw it illuminate briefly in their lights, saw the bikes stop, the lights go out, the engines cut, heard the voices. Trouble? The voices started to climb the hill. Did they sense the grey folk? I had clambered into a bivvy bag half an hour before to keep the wind at bay and lie and watch the stars. I clambered out again. If there *was* trouble, I wasn't going to meet it lying down and hamstrung by a sheath of orange plastic.

The nearest voice emerged from the top of the gully. I called a greeting.

'Ah, company!' said the cheerful reply. I relaxed. No trouble then. We shook hands, introduced ourselves with first names. I produced the whisky. Hail fellows, well met.

It was a complicated story. They were from Edinburgh. They had biked over to the West without knowing where they were going. One of them was booked into a hotel, the other was planning to bike through the night back to Edinburgh. The booked-in one drank heartily from the bottle. The biker-back-to-Edinburgh took a sip.

I told them what I was doing there, and why I was doing it. Oh, a writer. Do you make a living out of that?

Why is that always the first question?

Yes, I make a living, of a kind. No I don't do anything else. (What else would they have me do?)

The biker-back-to-Edinburgh decided to take his leave. The booked-in one asked if I minded if he stayed for a while. He was a GP, German, but working in Edinburgh. I clambered back into the bivvy. He had a good sleeping-bag down on the bike, and thought he should get it. It would get colder, I agreed. I saw the back-to-Edinburgh bike retrace its tracks up to the road, heard its engine dwindle into the night leaving only the voices of owls and oystercatchers in its wake. The GP was back with his bag and made himself comfortable. The bottle passed between us a couple of times.

I dozed. I started awake, staring at the stars, and wondered where I was. A snore nearby. I stood to get warm and woke the snorer with the rustling of the bivvy bag. He decided to go down. It was too cold and he simply couldn't afford to get ill. Did I mind being left on my own? I did not. We shook hands, he thanked me warmly for company and whisky and said:

'Have a good life, Jim.'

Presently the bike opened its throat and lit the track, and vanished. I looked up at the stars again, and to my quite irrational joy, realised that I had dozed off under the constellation of Cygnus, the Swan. I couldn't have invented that in my wildest dream. The Swan, sentinel over Dunadd on midsummer's morning.

Two gulls crossed my hilltop at 3 a.m., the first of the morning's wings. Others followed, moving from their roost towards the sea and the tide's uncovering of the fertile shore. At 3.15 a cuckoo began the dawn chorus. The day was roused. A robin stirred and joined in, the first singer.

I crossed the top of Dunadd, moving sunwise round its plateau crown, until I stood over the wildest side with the uncultivated acres of the Great Moss below me. I heard larks. I heard larks as I had never heard them before. From my perch in the clear air, I had a vivid sense of the song rising from the land, drawing level with me then rising on above, columns and columns of it, larks in the clear air. I stood stock still, in a kind of stupefied wonder.

A thrush flopped almost at my feet, bounced over the summit turf, stabbed at it and produced breakfast. Two clouds, crossed like a saltire in the north sky, glowed orange, the first confirmation of the sun under the horizon. It was 3.30, and it was light enough to write again. I suddenly realised the stars had gone, all of them except Venus. Cygnus had flown.

I went to the slab with the footprints, the bowl, the boar and the indecipherable slogans, and asked its meaning. The half-light was conducive to the offering up of solutions, the summer solstice the most propitious of hours for the unravelling. Not a whisper, not a clue, not a shred of understanding, a comprehensive nothing.

Since about 1 a.m. I had been watching off and on a peculiar cloud formation in the north. I had seen it grow from next to nothing into the shape of dove wings, saw the wings converge into a tall compact mass like an inverted elm leaf, saw it begin to disintegrate. Now I saw its last tiny shreds dematerialise and vanish. One more comprehensive nothing.

Cruachan was a hard shape against a pale sky again, but it played no part in the sunrise, no symbolic orb blazing between its twin peaks. Instead, it rose well to the east of north and without spectacle. There were a few pink preliminaries. A red horizontal bar, a searing electric-fire red, flared across the east then faded and the sun, pale yellow and dazzling, heaved up and Knapdale threw summer shadows again. I was back at the car before 5 a.m. and there was ice on the windscreen.

I drove without a plan, navigating by instinct, sleepily negotiating the burgeoning morning. I think I entrusted myself utterly into the safekeeping of the old Fiat in that morning hour, a trust it repaid with its sweetest demeanour. It chose the direction and the destination. By six o'clock I was washing strenuously in the River Orchy, sleepless and hungry. But every nerve jangled like taut guitar strings as I immersed myself in a quiet pool, every sensation homed in on that exquisite cold. I bathed with the enthusiasm of mute swans, so that the pool rocked and small waves slapped the bank. I had stepped from the most intimate embrace of night into the free-for-all of the river and the sun lurching over the mountains. I had bridged gulfs of the darkest blue air I have ever seen, and fingered the old stone footsteps, tracks beyond comprehension in the oldest snow of the world.

I brewed coffee and ate breakfast on the riverbank. It was a moment to relish life. I shared it with a dipper which came close to my stillness and rocked on a stone, flirting with his own self in the shallows. Then he stood still, cocked his tail and sang. Then he flew, low and fast upstream, chirping as he flew. It was as if he paused to sing for my benefit, a concerto for one.

I sat while the morning warmed, easing away the frost – midsummer frost! – steaming, then drying out the grass and heather. For much of that time, I had my hand cupped round a mug of coffee, but I drank little. The cup warmed and the coffee steamed, and I sipped at it, but it was soon cold, and I made some more and did much the same thing. I was alone under Beinn Dorain again, keeping the company of Glen Orchy again, making a pause in the Journey again, and I was locked into a stockade of my own thoughts, which were threefold:

One: A sense of participating in the past. I had chosen Dunadd instead of Ben Nevis, 177-feet-high Dunadd instead of 4,406-feet-high Ben Nevis, and I had seen further from Dunadd than I could ever have seen from the Ben. Because I was looking not into distance but time. Because I was seeking not height but depth. Because I was working towards a closer bonding with the land, not an aloofness above it. Because if I had reached for Ben Nevis in the midst of the Journey, Suilven must surely suffer by comparison at the end. So I reached as deep as I knew how, then deeper than I knew how, into the corpus of Dunadd. It has occurred to me more than once – as it must have occurred to thousands of others who have stood there – that the Dunadd slab looks like a burial slab. As far as I know, it is not. It is part of the hillside. But my wildest guess (and it seems mine is as good as anyone's) at the meaning of the lettering on the stone is that it says (in the manner of that land's burial grounds)

heir lies the corpus

that it means the collected body of wisdom and knowledge of the (then) unborn nation, Scotland. If I could stretch your credibility and mine a little further, in the particular circumstances of that midsummer night it says that the past teaches us the wisdom of thinking small. And that put Marion Campbell back in my mind, for in *Argyll* she wrote:

> *'Three things,' said an Irish philosopher, 'three slender things that sustain the world: the slender green hair of young corn, the slender thread of milk from a cow's udder, and the thin stream of spun wool from a woman's spindle.' In the legends it is always a small thing that overcomes, a homely thing that defeats giants or enchanters. It could be that the day of small things is near, coming upon the world in a groundswell rising against super powers, anthill cities, faceless manipulators. Starting from claims of the right to do one's own thing, and for the search for clean air beyond the smoke, a tide begins to set towards the shore of small countries everywhere . . .*

And I say 'amen' to every syllable of that.

Two: It is a fundamental, enriching thing to do, to lie out under the stars and watch them at work far from the tainting, dimming glow of city lights. It should be done, not just at the summer solstice, when the process is tolerably comfortable, but at every season, to remind ourselves of night, of night forces and night creatures, and of our own only half-forfeited right to keep their company. Nothing makes you more aware of yourself, of the way you move through the land, of your strengths and vulnerabilities, than time spent alone with your own resources in the embrace of nature's night.

Three: The Journey was considering reinventing itself again. I was tiring of summer, after three weeks of the driest June for 30 years, and July and August pressed weightily down on the horizon, storm clouds laden with all the artefacts of tourism-bedevilling, of head-high bracken, of no other shades but green and blue, of rain and midges in more or less equal proportions. It was not enough to move through the land and recall old seasons. I wanted the Journey to *taste* all seasons. I wanted the scent and shade and breath of autumn and its winds, its billowy restlessness, the land's exquisite dying. I wanted the battening down of winter and its hard edges, its cold intensity, its tracks in the snow.

The Journey stalled. It stalled that morning as the heat grew and I retreated for an hour into the tent to lie on something warmer than Dunadd's rock.

I worked fitfully into the afternoon, stripped to a pair of shorts, getting up often to walk down to the water's edge. Once I stepped in and swam out through a deepening pool until I could feel the tug of the midstream current. Even the river felt lethargic, and I swam ashore again, more disgruntled than invigorated. I returned to where the debris of the work was scattered around the tent – a couple of books, sundry notebooks, a loose-leaf binder, a bag of pens and pencils, the hand tape-recorder. I sat down again for the fourth or fifth time since lunch, just as three cars drove into the short stretch of grown-over track between my tent and the road. They were a convoy. They disgorged 14 people and began to erect three huge tents. One of the adults ambled over affably and said:

'Lovely day. Not disturbing you, I hope?'

It was the tourist season. They were tourists.

'You're okay,' I said. 'I was just about to strike camp.'

'Oh, that's lucky,' he said, and he turned to the woman who had stepped down from the same car:

'Over here, Fi. The gent's just going. The barbie can go over here.'

The road end at Glenorchy. I swear the Fiat pointed itself south back across the Highland Edge without any assistance from me. Mind you, it is Italian. A couple of days later, a national newspaper carried the following report under the heading 'A prayer for the world as police foil the travellers':

> *A lone figure prayed for the world from an ancient fortress yesterday after police had ringed the Dark Ages stronghold of Dunadd, near Lochgilphead, Argyll, in a round-the-clock operation lasting one week.*
>
> *They had feared hundreds of New Age travellers were heading for the site for a pagan festival at yesterday morning's new moon. But only Mr Andrew Connel turned up to sit in a circle of stones and recite a prayer to the 'Great Spirit' he had scribbled on a page from a school jotter.*
>
> *Mr Connel, a 47-year-old honours graduate who now lives in a commune at the so-called 'Pollok Free State' at the side of the M77 extension in Glasgow, chanted his appeal for salvation from the fort, which dates back to 500 AD.*
>
> *The chants came in a howling wind and pouring rain at one minute to five – the exact moment when the new moon was at its fullest. He apologised to police and locals for bringing them the threat of travellers, who have caused trouble in other parts of Scotland, after news of his plan was broadcast on the Internet.*
>
> *He said: 'I published a pamphlet asking innocent people with a like mind to join me in prayer at the full moon. But someone advertised it on the Internet and another movement only interested in partying got to hear about it.'*
>
> *Police, who had heard that hundreds of hippies from communes in other parts of Scotland were heading for Dunadd, the ancient crowning place of Scottish kings and the capital of Dalriada, asked Argyll and Bute Council for an order prohibiting 'trespassory assemblies' and asked for a five-mile exclusion zone round the site.*
>
> *Officers had been drafted in from throughout Strathclyde to man checkpoints. They may ask councillors to extend the order today after hailing the operation as a great success.*
>
> *A senior spokesman said: 'I am very pleased with the operation and we are continuing to monitor the situation. If we need another order, we can get one very quickly.'*
>
> *He added the success of the operation could be judged on the fact there was no trouble and the travellers stayed away. Last year, there was trouble when hippies moved onto a site a few miles away and refused to move for almost one month.*

Where, oh where, did we go wrong? Do the grey folk of Dunadd know they amount to someone else's definition of a trespassory assembly? Andrew: don't stop praying to the Great Spirit. Just leave the Internet out of it.

17

The Wild West

Wild is a word I use warily in a Highland context. So often what is perceived as 'wild' is merely empty, neglected, often purposefully so. To return to Schama's definition of the word 'landscape', he had added:

> *. . . In the Netherlands, the human design and use of the landscape – implied by the fishermen, cattle drovers, and ordinary walkers and riders who dot the paintings of Esaias van de Velde, for example – was the story startlingly self-sufficient unto itself.*

I doubt if that was ever true of Highland Scotland where 'human design' laboured to its most lasting effect to achieve the clearance of 'fishermen, cattle drovers, ordinary walkers and riders' from the face of the land, likewise the great forests. Before all that, before the wreckage which post-dates the Unions of Crown and Parliament, people did redesign the land, but in a small way, because the land was sacred and because in the West Highlands of Scotland it was such a powerful force. It still is, of course, which is why tourists and climbers and holiday-home buyers still magnetise there. It is why painters and photographers pore over it, why travellers and travel writers who inhabit lesser landscapes are moved by it to the point where it makes mincemeat of prose, and slaverers of poets. It has all been going on a long time.

And here I was, having recoiled from the prospect of high summer, resuming my own Journey where I had left it, re-examining my motives, reassessing my understanding, and my lack of understanding, of the land I travelled. Why, for example, did I just wave to the Rannoch Rowan as

146

the recalcitrant Fiat grumbled past? What was that all about? No one ever instructed me to do that, but I have been passing the Rannoch Rowan for 40 years and I don't remember a time when I was unaccustomed to waving to it.

Superstition? I don't think so. I walk under ladders.

Tradition? Not that I'm aware of, although I have instructed others that it should not be passed dismissively nor treated lightly.

So what? Why acknowledge a roadside tree growing out of a rock when that landscape is full of the massive gestures of mountain and moorland and cruised by eagles? Why smile on a runt of a rowan?

It is something to do with being wild. It is something to do with daring, of standing up to forces before which strangers have wilted and natives fled. I want its blessing on my travels, its approval of my motives, and of course it affords neither. It's a rowan tree. How often have I heard that! How often have I explained that the rowan is *the* tree in the Highlands, the guardian of thresholds, the vanquisher of evil spirits and ill omens, and countered scepticism by pointing out that it matters because people believe it matters. I am one such. The Rannoch Rowan matters. If I ever live in the Highlands, I will live with the shadow of a rowan on my wall.

And wildness will be the root of the comfort I derive from that shadow. The rowan embodies and symbolises our old faith in nature. It is nothing to do with superstition. It is in the acknowledgement of the oldest bond of all, or at least the oldest that man can acknowledge, our place in nature, our existence as just one of the creatures of the landscape. Our existence has become our isolation. We are, mostly, aloof from nature, double-glazed against its consequences, houses lit and alarmed for security, our phones mobile enough to summon help when we fall off mountains. Yet we like a rowan in our gardens to ward off we know not what, but better to have one anyway, and God help anyone foolish enough to uproot or fell one.

I draw great comfort there. It means wildness in our species is not wholly extinguished. We need our glimpses of Eden, and in the West Highlands, where that great bareness has been inflicted on the land, we need it more than most. So I wave to the Rannoch Rowan and the wave acknowledges its wild survival and asks that something of that quality rubs off on the traveller, something of its spirit accompanies me on the Journey. So I crossed the Moor, the treeless, wolfless Moor of Rannoch, and because it had passed this way before in the course of the Journey, the Fiat reined itself in under Buachaille Etive Mor, one more carriage creakily grateful for the coaching inn at Kingshouse, the horses panting for breath.

Sarah Murray was an extraordinary Englishwoman who travelled alone through the Highlands in 1796, well, sort of alone, as her book *The Beauties of Scotland* reveals. There is, for example, an introductory chapter headed 'Advice for the Traveller'. I've often thought I should read it aloud to the Fiat, but it might take offence, more offence than usual, that is. The chapter begins:

> *Provide yourself with a strong roomy carriage, and have the springs well corded; have also a stop-pole and strong chain to the chaise. Take with you linch-pins, and four shackles, which hold up the braces of the body of the carriage; a turn-screw, fit for fastening the nuts belonging to the shackles; a hammer, and some straps.*
>
> *For inside the carriage, get a light flat box, the corners must be taken off, next the doors, for the more conveniently getting in and out. This box should hang on the front of the chaise, instead of the pocket, and be as long as the whole front, and as deep as the size of the carriage will admit: the side next the travellers should fall down by hinges, at the height of their knees, to form a table on their laps; the part of the box below the hinges should be divided into holes for wine bottles, to stand upright in . . .*

Tch, tch, wine bottles upright! Now, if you are a bit strapped for cash, as my own expedition unquestionably was . . .

> *If a traveller would like to save a great deal of money, and render a servant more useful than on horseback, put a seat for him behind the carriage . . . You will say, perhaps – if the servant be stuck to our backs, how inconvenient! not to be able to send on for horses. If you travel for pleasure, you need not be in such haste; and besides, how few men are able to ride 100 or more miles a day, for two or three days together? also, when you get into countries where you are obliged to take your horses wherever you go, there can be no sending on for fresh horses. But the most solid reason with many for adopting this mode of conveyance for a manservant is the very considerable sum of money it saves. To me, the convenience is not to be described, as by my man's being at all times at hand, he was ready to discover if anything was amiss, and to assist in setting it to rights . . . With my maid by my side, and my man on the seat behind the carriage, I set off . . .*

Mrs Murray was not overly complimentary about Kingshouse ('. . . my

148

petticoats tucked to my knees for fear of the dirt which was half an inch thick on the floor . . .') but with the aid of her maid and her 'independence in point of linen, blanket, quilt and pillows . . .' – that is, she brought her own – she passed a tolerable night.

The Fiat and I were stopping only long enough to water the horses. We were servantless, maidless and without even a wine rack. We would just have to make the best of it. I cannot speak for the car (I can, but I don't see why I should), but the rest of the resurrected expedition was in its autumnal element. Not only that, but autumn had surpassed itself by calling down the shades of winter early, so that the fiery grasses were smoored with snowcaps, the watersheets and rivers silenced by ice. The relentless greens and blues of June were extinct, and as we pulled out of the Kingshouse car park and broke into a canter under the Buachaille, Glencoe was looking like itself again.

I have lingered too often in Glencoe, and so has my pen (a whole book, *Glencoe – Monarch of Glens*, with photographer Colin Baxter, and a chapter in *Among Mountains*, several newspaper and magazine outbursts) and the Journey had decided not to linger there. But the weather on the big summits looked so outrageously furious that I couldn't resist a fast stomp up Beinn a' Chrulaiste, the unsung Glencoe, a bit of a plod, but a matchless perch from which to eyeball the Buachaille, to gawp at the great 'vee' of the Pass of Glencoe, and to spin and gasp at the mass of Rannoch Moor, seething quietly to itself.

The summit was broad and bouldery and powdered with snow, too early for the ptarmigan posing on a skyline rock, for they were still dressed for summer, doubtless fooled by the Indian summer which had lulled the first half of October and prepared no one for what followed at once. Indian winter. It is not that the summer plumage of a ptarmigan is gaudy, just that its ability to keep pace with the seasons by gradual moults is almost flawless. The rich brown and black of summer mottles through autumnal grey-browns to winter white. Its rock-stillness can fool passing boots and eagle eyes into thinking it is a still rock. It fools more boots than eagle eyes, but this pair on their rock didn't even fool the boots. They were brown and they should have been white.

What a vile day on Bidean nam Bian across the glen! Storms convulsed that singular mountain mass of shoulders and arms (and the bunched fists of the Three Sisters which reliably darken *Scotsman* calendars). The top 1,000 feet was obliterated, clouds poured down and winds thundered up to meet them and burst them apart as they fell. Snow and raw black rock showed fleetingly through the holes. You couldn't pay me to climb there on such a day. I have seen the day, and my folly went mercifully unpunished. But I still love to climb to a perch such as this where I can watch (like one of Bruce's camp followers) the elements at war, the oldest unresolved war of them all. This is where the landscape survives, quite undesigned, more or less the way it was born, looking older of course, but then don't we all. The passage of people here is as irrelevant as the passage of ants across a rock. We climb, we gasp, we come down, some of us don't live to come down. Not one of us could sustain a week of winter nights like the ptarmigan can.

I have always felt magnetised towards the Glencoe mountains. They repel as many as they enthrall, but in my mind their allure only grows. But I also love its low ground, and walk eagerly there and often. Nowhere else that I know of – apart from a brief acquaintance with Switzerland – lets you in *under* the mountains so close that you sense the enormous rooted power burrowing deep and ever deeper under your feet, so that even at almost sea level you feel elevated.

I don't like the way Glencoe is managed now, but that too is a theme I have aired too often. I will say only this. That just as Paul Errington argued 'Of all the native biological constituents of a northern wilderness scene, I should say that wolves present the greatest test of human wisdom and good intentions' . . . so Glencoe presents the greatest test of human wisdom and good intentions in the matter of management of 'wild' Scotland. When the old low-lying fertility of the glen is worked and wooded in a small way again, and its thoughtless sheep are replaced with a handful or two of cattle, and human life is restored in some appropriate measure to the low ground, and cramming tourists into the Glencoe Visitor Centre and taking their money is not the first priority of management here, then human wisdom and good intentions can take a bow. But I am not holding my breath.

The view from North Ballachulish back to Beinn Bheithir and the west end of Glencoe is the most impressively Alpine in the West Highlands. So how come the second ugliest bridge in the western civilised world was permitted to be built in its shadow? The Ballachulish bridge is a monster, made the more monstrous by its setting. For long enough it was unchallenged in its monstrousness, but that was before the most warped consortium of minds ever let loose in the Highlands since Cumberland unfurled the Skye bridge. Ballachulish's offence is slight by comparison, and actually embodies one point of principle, its solitary saving grace. It's free.

The Corran Ferry. Now that's how to bridge the narrows of a sea loch or a sound. A patient queue, time to look around, have a pie or a pee, scent the salt air (have it thump wetly onto your lap if you open the window too wide on the wrong sort of day for salt air scenting). Watch the ferry's crab-wise gait head-butt the waves and remind yourself of the Ardnamurchan poet Alasdair Maclean's assessment:

> . . . *a kind of mobile decompression chamber where various kinds of pollution were drained from the blood and I was fitted to breathe pure air again.*

It seems strange to be on the ferry and not be bound for one or other of the two destinations with which it is forever linked in my mind – the Lochaline ferry to Mull or the Loch Shiel home of my friend of many years, the wildlife writer Mike Tomkies. But Mike is uprooted (although you can take a boat trip up the loch to visit 'A Last Wild Place') and Mull is not on the itinerary, not this trip. 'In winter's gloom,' Mike wrote, 'one comes close to the animal state oneself.' He knew more about that than anyone I have ever met or ever heard of. The work he undertook here and on Eilean Shona on the coast, in Canada before all that and in Spain after, showed me what is possible, how close the bond between man and nature *can* be, even now. He still comes back, quietly and alone, for a week days or a few weeks at a time, living in the old campervan he calls *Mi Caballo* – My Horse. The place – and its golden eagles – has a hold on him. I think of an old boxer who can't resist one more bout, one more crack at the title, as much to remind himself of what it feels like as to win. Working with golden eagles was what he did best, undisputed heavyweight champion of the eagle world, and nothing else in life gets close to it. Now, at 69, a brush with cancer has 'catapulted me into old age' as he put it, he is contemplating Spain again, Spain where he buried his father, Spain where he trekked after bear, lynx, wolf, and golden eagle of course . . . But there is a bit of him in these hills which he can only ever reclaim by returning, which I can share by association, by reading his tracks in the snow of the world.

The ferry clatters ashore. The Fiat handled the next few miles itself while I rummaged in my mind among the souvenirs of our treks together, of long whisky-fuelled nights, the fraternal clasp of a hand on the shoulder . . . *mi amigo.*

The Fiat hurtled west, towards Ardnamurchan Point. It could begin again then, the Journey. The wind and the rain thumped into the car. The black hole of the Ardnamurchan night opened its throat and swallowed us whole. We were Jonahs to its whale.

18

A Lunatic Ocean

Hurricanes concentrate the mind. I hugged bare rock and held on. The Atlantic looked angry with Scotland, angry and grown mad. It bore its grudge ashore with lunatic frenzy. 'A Lunatic Ocean' I wrote in a notebook later, thinking I had made a cute anagram out of such adversity but I was a 't' short and a 'u' too many. But lunatic is what the ocean was. Three rocks away, and noticeably better bedded down than I was, a tightening of knots cowered on a ledge – that's knots as in wader birds, not knots as in fankled ropes.

I told the knots aloud (not that they could hear so close to the bared larynx of the banshee) that I was disappointed in them. You are named knot, after all, I told them, after Kanut, or Canute as he has been unforgivably anglicised (but he is not alone in that unhappy circumstance, I added mischievously), because of your daring in the face of tides. What is the matter with you, I demanded, cowering there like so many sheep? Get up and turn back the tide. And at that the Lunatic Ocean heaved one wave 50 feet higher and further away than any of its immediate predecessors so that it splintered a lurching shade of green across a ledge which I had assumed five minutes ago was the safest proximity to the storm I had come down to watch. One way or another, that behemoth among waves galvanised the knots and me. I crouched with acute caution, backwards among the rocks, then up the rocks until I had put one more tier of absolute safety beneath my feet. The knots shook themselves, reassembled themselves, then flew, low as the wavetops plus a foot, and vanished in search of an easier legend to live up to.

I have been twice to Ardnamurchan Point, both times in a hurricane.

The first one was an official hurricane with a name – Nellie, I think, or maybe it was Melba – but this second one, though anonymous, felt like no less a hurricane. I had considered the day's possibilities over breakfast (that's breakfast in 'bed and . . .', with walls and a roof: if I had planted a tent last night it would have been sailing past Mike's old place on Loch Shiel by breakfast), decided the Point of Ardnamurchan would be worth looking at (and why did the expression 'one more nutter for the lighthouse' lodge in my mind as soon as I stepped outside), and swore I heard the Fiat groan through the double glazing. We compromised. I only drove it as far as the sign which proclaims END OF PUBLIC ROAD with the word END in fist-sized capitals. It is one of the more pointless road signs in the world, a bit like hanging a notice on the gates of the Garden of Eden saying ADULTS ONLY.

I put on thermal jacket, waterproof-windproof jacket, waterproof-windproof trousers, wellies, gloves, and told the Fiat: 'You wait here.'

It watched me Gromit-eyed as I headed for the Lunatic ocean. Why bother, it was saying? Wait here and it'll come to us.

I had fled from summer protesting the omnipresence of green and blue. Here was the entire repertoire of grey from almost black to almost white by way of almost green. I have never before been aware of menace in colour. It was not the tiers of waves, stacked up and cruising like sharks though they were, which frightened me – and I was frightened. It wasn't the faintly ludicrous image (poets should not be let loose on this stuff – too high octane) of a second Giant's Causeway, recast in water and climbing down towards the land rather than towards the ocean. It was the colour, the relentlessly working and reworking versatility of that remorseless GREY, armies of it, battalion after battalion, storm after storm of stormtroopers, all of them aligned in short waves and long, and unleashed with crushing power on the rocks of tiny Briaghlann, the rocks and the gaunt grey lighthouse of Ardnamurchan Point. It wasn't END that should have adorned the warning sign at the road, it should have said GREY in capitals the size of behemoths.

I took as much of the thing as I could, swallowed as much salt air as my lungs could handle, as much bellowing wind as my ears could contain before the force of two simultaneous earfuls met in the middle of my head and blew my brain back to Kilchoan. For as much of it all as I could, I watched the lighthouse. It is in the nature of lighthouses to shrug at hurricanes. Ardnamurchan shrugged heroically that day. I have never seen such magnificently pointless shrugging. Ardnamurchan Pointless. Pointless of Ardnamurchan. It sounds like a pseudonym sent in to *Points of View*.

153

Lighthouses are among my favourite things. I suppose I like uncompromising natures. On my desk as I write is a postcard of Turner's painting of the Bell Rock lighthouse off the Tay estuary (a long way off, in truth, rooted on a half-sunk skerry, shrugging at seas in every direction). The painting is among the annual Turner watercolours exhibition at the National Gallery of Scotland in Edinburgh. The paintings are so light-sensitive that they are only brought out in January. Every year, you see the same faces in the gallery, people who make a small January pilgrimage from Fife or Stirling or West Lothian, renewing auld acquaintance with their favourites. Groups from amateur painting classes go together to marvel, to wonder at how he could make watercolour of all subdued artforms glossy and glorious. It is inevitably – it being Turner – painted during a storm, one particularly lunatic wave is swarming up the entire torso of the lighthouse, clutching with its claws at the verandah round the very light itself. The lighthouse – of course – is quite untroubled, but the wretches crewing the three distant sailing ships would be cowering in the face of all that fearfully piled black-grey-which-is-almost-green-but-at-heart-it's-terminal grey. I used to watch that same light, a 30-miles distant blink of light from the window of my childhood home in Dundee, and invest dreams in it. Lighthouses and I have got on well together ever since. I don't compromise very well either.

Ardnamurchan is westmost Scotland. The Bell Rock is east of eastmost Scotland. But they shrug at adversity in much the same way. I shrugged at the Lunatic Ocean and went in search of shelter, not as much lighthouse as I sometimes think I am.

Hurricanes purge. By late afternoon it was done, the ocean grown sane. The sky was shredding, letting in yellow light, scraps of blue, shades the ocean snatched at eagerly, patchy salvation, light relief. I squelched up onto the high ground above Sanna and found the Cuillin, white to the waist. It was as if the sky had thrust a lid down on the land while the hurricane smote, the tighter the lid, the more the hurricane boiled, the more utter the purging of the land. Now that it had boiled itself away, it had blown the lid clean off, ripped it from the land. The land stood and looked at itself in the sudden light, shook itself like a sodden dog, and steamed.

Inland Ardnamurchan was brown, striped with white. The brown was every scrap of battened down land gasping in the aftermath of the onslaught. The white was every gully from crack to cataract, on every crag the length and breadth of the peninsula. Even on lowly Meall Sanna where I stood, the map shows three burns emerging from the crags on its seaward side. I counted 14.

Water is everywhere on Ardnamurchan. What isn't craggy, rocky volcanic bits and pieces is high, lochan-strewn moorland. These two landforms have one thing in common. They leak. Given that the watershed of the peninsula is long and narrow and slopes, mostly steeply, to the sea, they leak quickly. Now they leaked furiously, from every pore, and every leak was white.

Alasdair Maclean's book, *Night Falls on Ardnamurchan*, was based on his crofter father's diaries, and records how every entry over many years began with the weather. If he had still been alive, this day's entry would have made dark reading. When weather forecasters talk about 'the possibility of structural damage', and their remarks are addressed at the body of the nation, it invariably means dire consequences for those who live on the extremities of the land – wrecked crops, flattened outbuildings, or at least roofless ones, trouble at the bank.

Mostly the people of Ardnamurchan have turned their back on all that. A few travel long distances once or twice a year on the Corran Ferry, to touch native rocks and scent the past, draining away the pollutions of lives lived elsewhere fitting themselves to breathe pure air again. But it wasn't Maclean's sentiment which impinged on my thoughts as I wandered the hills and the shores and the road-ends of Ardnamurchan over three glittering days which followed in the wake of the storm. It was Marion Campbell's pointed irony: 'There's nobody there. Isn't it beautiful?'

Ben Hiant is the summit of that land, a dark and abrupt hill with a summit which looks as if a second hill had been added on top as an afterthought. On a day of any visibility at all, it throws far sightlines among islands and mainland mountains, for all that it falls short of 1,800 feet. Many a hemmed-in Munro summit is blind by comparison with Ben Hiant. Mull masses in the south, Coll and Tiree lie low in the west, Muck is close in the north, and beyond it stand ascending ranks of islands – Eigg, Rum, Skye. Resipol and Rois-Bheinn stand proud of the mountains massed in the east.

The summit at noon, a hard wind, the autumn's coldest, niggling the Sound into white wavetops, the sea dark blue, bruising showers flaying the uncertain shapes of the Western Isles, moving north-east and fast. If you climb from the north where a half-hearted track crosses the moor and cuts across a five-mile loop in the road, and contour the hill to the north-east, the summit breaks you in gradually and saves the island view for the last few spectacular yards. Eyes widen with the seascape, trying to accommodate so much light at once. Always, with the West, it is the light. I think it was that, as much as anything, that Maclean was getting at. He was one of those who travelled back regularly to touch the native stones. I think his 'various kinds of pollution' were drained as much from the eyes as from the blood. The West is forever demanding that you *look* more often, and more intensely, and it is the light which makes the demands. In the east, the light moves at a slower pace and the sea is unrelieved by islands. Colours are more durable. Maclean was long domiciled in the east. It was his eyes which would need purging, as much as the blood.

A tiny headland of Mull was what I was looking for, because I know so well the view from the other end. That headland points straight at Ben Hiant, and turns it into a Schiehallion-ish pyramid, an unlikely configuration if you only know the mountain from Ardnamurchan.

It is not hard to find the headland, because it is fingerposted by a lighthouse. Rubha nan Gall is the Headland of the Stranger, and one of my favourite places anywhere. It is a great comfort to an east coast mainlander by birth to cross the breadth of the country and find (on more or less the same latitude as my native Dundee) an island headland named for you. To stand on Ben Hiant's summit for the first time and see the lighthouse across four miles of open water, miniaturised to the size of a fencepost (while my mind's eye remembers the day I patted its huge white girth and admired its reflection rooting it into the shallows of its own shore), was to draw one more perspective in the three-dimensional map of my own country which I carry with me everywhere, in my head. It is a map with the simplest philosophy behind it: if you know the mountain from the lighthouse, it matters that sooner or later you must have a grasp of the lighthouse from the mountain. For much the same reason, I want to sail out to the Bell Rock lighthouse, and look deep into the estuary of the Tay to the wooded Dundee hillside where the high window of my parents' old flat used to gaze seawards at an improbably distant flicker of light.

The idea frees understanding of landscape, and lets light in on my own life, sheds light on my own tracks in the snow of the world. It matters to me to know where I've been.

Inevitably east, dawdling along Loch Sunart, the road utterly empty, the day flat and grey and cold and threatening snow. Autumn, where were you? I saw a woman getting out of a car at Salen, an event quite unprecedented in the day's history. I waved, an almost reflexive gesture, an acknowledgement, nothing more. But it produced such a breadth of smile in response, a smile set in a frame of long dark and wind-blown hair that my own gesture seemed suddenly mean. I wanted to reverse, re-enact the bend in the road and make more of the moment. But she had already disappeared and I had turned north, the old Fiat dragging me away from my train of thought. But the smile of the encounter stayed in my head, a talisman for the day. Snow if you want to, I told it.

I waved again as the road crept into Acharacle, but it was the waters of Loch Shiel I waved to, a greeting for *mi amigo*, wherever he was at the moment. I had not planned to stop here, but as usual, the unplanned pause was particularly welcome. It was prompted by a road sign. 'Dalella', it said, and the name so charged me with the electricity of memory that the Fiat was rumbling quietly down its narrow and unassuming *cul-de-sac* with no effort on my part. There are times when that car takes matters out of my hands. It stopped at the pier, the road end, and let me out. Dalella, 1981, November . . . Dalella. What was I thinking about? I had met Mike Tomkies for the first time earlier in the year when he was passing through Edinburgh, shortly after the publication of his *Golden Eagle Years*. I was a journalist, and we had arranged an interview. I had been much impressed by his books, but I didn't know what to make of *him*. But then an Edinburgh hotel lobby was hardly his natural habitat. Now, after some correspondence, he had invited me out to the house he called Wildernesse, eight trackless miles up the loch. It was raining. The lochside was tussocky, bouldery, strewn with fallen trees, and punctuated with bloated burns. On it went, and on, for hours. At one point, I saw the green rooftop of Mike's house far up the lochside, a reassuring glimpse. I next saw it about two hours later.

I called a greeting at the door. He appeared, looking a bit dishevelled.

'Good God, I didn't think you'd come in this. I was in bed, listening to *The Archers*. Late night last night.'

Somewhere about three in the afternoon, he told me he had a rule that he never drank until after dark. He squinted out of the cottage window. 'But it's pretty dark now, isn't it?'

That weekend was the beginning of one of the great friendships of my life. When we parted company, he walked a little of the lochside with me, before turning to walk back to the cottage. I stopped after a few yards and watched him, a moving fragment of his own landscape, as appropriate to it as eagles. It is easy to make snap judgements about such a man, based on his surface demeanour. His depths and strengths are well hidden. He handled an extraordinary species of solitude there, and bouts of black loneliness were as much part of it as the exhilaration of the golden eagle days. Years later, when I asked him a question about handling loneliness, he said:

'You can't handle loneliness! You have to have something which transcends loneliness, to make you forget about loneliness. You've got to have a work ethic, get up in the morning with a purpose. And if you can't do that, you're only half alive.'

Mike Tomkies is as alive as any other man I ever met.

Dalella, 1981. That's what I was letting myself in for.

I used to haunt this coast. Long before I knew Mike, I used to hang around the headland west of Glenuig, Samalaman Island with its terns, Smirisary Hill where I dreamed dreams about nosing a small boat into its tiny cove, Smirisary Hill where I used to sit with the loch at my back and the sea in my face and watch otters, divers, terns, islands, and wonder how I could cast adrift from the anchors of newspaper offices and write a living out of landscapes like this. I was oblivious to the fact that on Eilean Shona, a mile to the south of where I liked to sit, a man I had never heard of called Mike Tomkies had begun to do just that. Then, on one of my Glenuig treks, I wandered up the coast, saw a footpath cross a bridge at a place called Polnish, saw how it unfolded across the map to the sea and an enigmatic pairing of words – 'Peanmeanach ruins'.

So I crossed the bridge (a stone bridge, the width of footpath), and wandered the three miles to the sea. The high sections of the path were stone-flagged. The path had been important, once. The path curved and dipped, and 'Peanmeanach ruins' was below me. It was a single row of cottages, detached but close together, and facing the sea. They stood on the further edge of a long flat and low-lying sward, drained by two burns. The cottages were roofless. The situation was engulfed by an aching melancholy. There's nobody there, and isn't it beautiful.

The Highland Clearances had made their first impact on my consciousness. They had touched the embryonic writer's consciousness, too. So many years later, with that forlorn row of rooflessness in my mind, and coloured by many island explorations which unearthed more and more rooflessness at the end of more and more footpaths, I had brought an idea back here and wrote it. What I wrote is told in the next chapter.

19

The Campbell

People drifted over the years to the bottom of the island like the fruit in an imperfect cake. The recipe for island life was lost, likewise the art of the baking. It was no one's fault. Or perhaps it was everyone's fault. Certainly it had become the pattern of the island's tide and no hand sought to stem it or turn it. It was a place perpetually in waiting.

The old crofts at the North End had grown decrepit.

Wind and sheep and starlings and nettles were all the energy which inhabited North Crofts now. Winds were their roofs now too. Starlings rode the winds down to nest in the alcoves where the old box beds had rotted. Nettles rooted in that corner where a basket of peats had fed the blaze at the hearth of the island.

Everywhere, sheep shat and stank and these were all that moved across the North Crofts where once 12 chimneys reeked over half the island, or if the wind was in the east, and because the houses were so close to the shore, the reek reached the working boats a mile out.

So the islanders had drifted down their desultory destinies – east and south to the Mainland, west to Nova Scotia, opted out or cleared out to . . . what? A new life? Opportunity, jobs, lights, bustle, success, wealth? A new death? Exile, homesickness, tidelessness, saltless air, no heron or otter below the house, no boat hauled up? No Gaelic words in the mouth?

Mostly, of course, they would have preferred to stay. But mostly they had gone one dishonoured day in 1870 when preferring to stay had ceased to be an option. When MacPherson had cheated them all, tricked them all out of their houses saying there was such a glut of fish at the South End they must all hurry down with every available boat and barrow and bucket. It was a windfall of herring such as they had never known. But when the North Croft folk got there, there were no fish, and when they returned it was to find MacPherson gone and their houses ablaze. Only the laird's factor was there, on his horse, and if he had once stepped down from it, he would have been done to death on the spot, but it was MacPherson they had reserved their bile for, and nurtured it more than 100 years for hadn't he been one of them and colluded with the factor's lackey for whatever he had bargained?

It was not an exceptional occurrence on that seaboard. MacPherson was already on a westbound ship while the islanders were still standing incredulously among the charring embers.

'He must have seen the smoke as he sailed,' an old one said. 'He must have seen the very smoke of his own roof.'

The few islanders who lived beyond North Crofts and the few who in time found a way back when a marginally kinder regime held sway, had drifted together into the single village street facing south. Now, a few crossed north over the island only to gather sheep or driftwood or peat. But the cables across the Minch had snuffed most of the village peat fires and lit the street, 'mainland kindling for island hearths', as the seer had prophesied.

The natives accepted the fate of North Crofts now as the way it goes on such islands. Their passivity infuriated incomers who paused there and mostly there was little evidence to suggest they cared much either for that low skyline dereliction or for those few visitors who spent a blue summer week among the fallen lintels dragging the hapless township through video camera viewfinders.

Among such visitors might come a more thoughtful one whose dreams would have the skills of restoration (an architect or a stonemason, say) to shore them up. Such a visitor might grapple with the realities of rebuilding, laying in services, working the land (a thrawn parcel of bog, rock and machair), the nuts and bolts and mortar which hold the framework of that simpler, slower life in place. Perhaps a jaded writer or an eager composer would see something, sense something conducive to his life's work, and come raking among the fallen stones seeking stories, stanzas, symphonies. Sooner or later one would ask at the Post Office or the guest house or the pub about this house or that and the islanders would cast down their own defeatedness about their answers like a shroud.

The blue week would pass and the visitors' daftness with it, the islanders reasoned, but only because summer after summer proved them right. The ferry spilled the dreamers up the pier, spilled their questions, then it took them back with no answers, only doubts, and winter after winter, North Crofts wilted a little more. Soon no house would shelter even a starling and the houses would have winds for walls as well as roofs. Sheep stepped in over broken doors, doorless lintels, a useless hinge.

The Campbell came one blue week off the ferry, up the pier, booked into the guest house for a week, walked out to North Crofts on his second day. He began his week the same way as many a tourist, watching the birds and otters, assessing the ruins, gazing out to sea in the manner so diagnostic of people with nothing more to do on the shore but gaze out to sea. The islanders assessed him diffidently, saw the same daft dream in his eyes, paid him little heed beyond the usual instinctive courtesies. Soon enough he would come into the bar, order whatever he was having for himself ('and have one for yourself, Mr Urquhart'), and shift a halting conversation from the weather to the kind of tourist season it might be, to the crofts out by, and who might one have to talk to about such-and-such a house?

The regulars would exchange knowing glances and a well-practised routine would fall into place, not malicious, not co-operative, not interested. Which croft? Oh, number 12. No, no, Davie, that's eight. No, 12 now . . . wasn't that old MacPherson's place that went to Glasgow, or was it Nova Scotia? Twelve's been down a long time now, man, a long, long time, haye!, a long time. Who to speak to? Well, that would have been the laird's office, the factor's place. That was then, of course. Now? Who would know about number 12 now? Does he still have an office, the laird? Donald, would he still have an office, the laird? Why ask me, man? Murdo, you knew the son, surely? No, no, not the son, the grandson, and he was no more concerned about the North Crofts than his grandfather, the old fart, excuse me Mr Campbell. Now? I don't know if it has a laird, never mind a laird's office. I haven't seen a factor out by since the King's day, man.

And so it would go on until the Campbell man, or whoever, had the daftness knocked out of them by exasperation, and went quietly home to Slough, or Stirling, or Southend. Wherever.

On Campbell's last night at the guest house, all had gone according to the pattern, and he had hardly mentioned number 12 North Crofts since the first time. He talked a lot about birds, about books, and knew much about both, and had a way of embroiling the islanders in his bar-room philosophising which they liked. There were a fair few who fancied themselves as philosophers on the island. There always were, and at least it made a change. He had been an architect in Canada mostly, but now he wrote about birds and otters and other scraps of nature. Oh, he was a fine man, Mr Campbell, a fine man, haye! For a tourist.

And because he had caused more than one husband on the island to comment to his wife over supper what an interesting chap he had seen in the pub that night – nothing more than that, but that was enough – Mrs MacPhail had dropped in by the guest house on the morning of his departure to question Mrs MacQueen, who was really from Partick, but sounded so like them now after 24 years that you had to keep reminding yourself she wasn't really an islander. 'What was he like, Davina, this Campbell man?'

Mrs MacQueen, however, was uncharacteristically flustered.

'Well, I'm not sure, not now. That is, I was sure enough until he signed the visitors' book this morning before he left, but he spent so long at it that I almost trembled to read it. See for yourself, I don't know what to make of it.'

Mrs MacPhail didn't either. She read: just 'Campbell' in the name column, 'Alberta, Canada' under address and 'Exile' under nationality. Under 'remarks' where folk write 'friendly and comfortable, many thanks' or 'we had such a lovely time' or 'you made us feel so much at home – we'll be back, promise!', there was this:

'The hollowest epitaph to a man's life is the dereliction of the house which spawned him, the saddest of headstones to mark his being is a fallen lintel. The tomb which out-demeans a pauper's grave is the one sealed by the slump of timbers and the deranged slates of the roof which sustained a life. When the nettles stifle his hearth and overwhelm the bed where he sowed the seed of his sons and daughters, that summarises him. This was a life, it says, so lived that its legacy is too futile to count, too flimsy to brook continuity, a cup drained of hope.'

Mrs MacQueen, who never liked to be proved wrong about a guest, said:

'The thing is that he didn't seem like a rude man. He was polite and friendly and quiet and neat and punctual for meals. You can't ask much more than that in a guest, can you?'

Indeed, Davina, you could not, Mrs MacPhail was saying and concluding that whatever his purpose in this admittedly discreet outrage (he had troubled to take a fresh right-hand page so that it could be removed easily without troubling other visitors who signed the book) he had not intended it to follow him home. There was no address, no first name, or perhaps it was Campbell something and there was no second name.

The island was quickly agog. It didn't take much. A community council meeting was advanced by a week. Usually they were deferred at the least excuse like a good film or a big match on television. Theories and speculations criss-crossed the council table loudly. MacMillan, maybe the oldest man on the island – though who knew? – startled them all and their clishmaclavering when he said quietly:

'The thing is, the man is right.'

That unleashed a silence, a rare thing at such a gathering. Outrage, or something perilously close to it, inhabited that silence, except that Mrs MacQueen, who had been privately impressed by the dignified eloquence of Campbell's insult or whatever it was, not to mention the demeanour of the man himself . . . Mrs MacQueen shouldered the ominous lull aside to ask calmly of the old man:

'What do you mean, Euan?'

'All I'm saying is: never mind the way he has chosen to convey the message – and it has harmed no one as far as I can see – but I've looked at the words and I cannot fault them. The North Crofts is the disgrace of the island. It was the disgrace of our past. Now it is the disgrace of the present.'

'You're out of order now, Euan.' The bark was Urquhart's bar-room best. 'Language like that is not going to assist the council to reach a consensus situation . . .'

'Oh damn your consensus situation and your wee committee mind, Murdo!' MacMillan had made a second silence. No one barked back at Urquhart. MacMillan drew a deep breath, raised a hand in acknowledgement of his rudeness. Urquhart's nod acknowledged in turn. Certain transactions among such close and age-old friends could always be conducted wordlessly.

Euan MacMillan continued:

'We all know why the old houses were made ruinous. But why do they still rot 125 years later? Who has fought for them? Not me. Not any of you. Number ten was my father's house, and his father's. The dream I have dreamed most often in my life is that I should die in that house.'

'But Euan,' said Mrs MacQueen, 'you've been back on the island – in the village – 40 years, man.'

'Yes, and as the Campbell has put it, that summarises me.'

The door opened softly, a small head peered round it down by the handle, the five-year-old son of the secretary.

'He's back,' said the boy, and he withdrew his head which was all that had advanced into the room. As it withdrew it left a wedge of summer spilled across the floor. Dust danced in its light like an enchanted cloud of midges.

MacMillan said:

'The Campbell!'

The council's eight members rose as one and went out to the door and stood in a gaggle in the sun. There were three identifiable silhouettes out by number 12 North Crofts – a Land Rover, a tent, and the figure of the Campbell going energetically between the two.

'What's he up to?'

'Damned if I know.'

'More birdwatching?'

'He said he wanted to photograph the otters.'

From Mrs MacQueen: 'I wonder if he'll need a room?'

From MacMillan: 'No, Davina, I don't think so. I think he's moving in.'

The old man walked home then, while the others swung their heads after him, then back to the bizarre silhouettes, then back after MacMillan.

'Meeting adjourned, I think,' said the secretary. It was to Urquhart's they adjourned it, the whisky loosening the tongues to ever greater and further fetched improbabilities. Campbell did not join them that night with his philosophising.

After three feverishly gossiping days and a hastily convened sub-committee meeting, three community councillors including MacMillan walked out to see Campbell and inquire as casually as they could what his business might be.

'Mr Campbell . . .'

'Oh, hello.' (Cheerful enough.)

'You're busy there, eh?'

'Aye, busy enough.'

'We saw you were back, and when you weren't in the bar, and didn't seem to be needing a room, and we were wondering . . .'

'We . . .?'

'That is, the community council, we're here by way of a . . . a . . . delegation.'

'The fact is,' said MacMillan, wearying at once of the perfunctories, 'we saw your entry in Mrs MacQueen's book.'

'Ah, yes,' said the Campbell.

'Now this, Mr Campbell. The community council is curious about your intentions.'

'Right,' said Mr Campbell, laying down the stone he had been hefting in both hands. He wiped them free of dirt and grit and addressed the old man directly.

'What I am doing, Mr MacMillan, is moving in.'

'Have you permission?' demanded Urquhart.

164

'No, I have not.'

'Well now, you'll need it, won't you?'

'Whose?'

'Well, there's the factor and . . .'

'Ah, the factor. Hasn't been here since the King's day. The laird's grandson is a disinterested fart, if he is still alive, and the factor's office may or may not exist. I think that was the advice you gave me, more or less.'

'Planning permission,' Urquhart said testily while MacMillan shook a weary head.

'How long since the planning authority was here? Before or after the factor? No, I think I'll take my chances with them when they find out, if they ever do, and meanwhile, I'll just put the walls back as they were, or at least as close as I can. I do not have the building skills of those who put them up the first time. All the timber I need is either in the ruins or on the shore, and there are enough slates left to put up more than one good roof.'

'And then?' asked MacMillan.

'Live in it.'

'But why?'

'Why what?'

'Live in it. Why here?'

'Ah. That might take a while for me to explain adequately. Meanwhile I will live as fittingly here as I can. And there is the question of a debt.'

'A debt?'

But his back was to them at last, bent to the burden of the stones. MacMillan led the others quietly away.

It took a year. He worked with painstaking care, disassembling a new stretch of wall if he was dissatisfied. He was just as painstaking in his respect for the island way of life, or as MacMillan observed, he seemed born to it. The first Sunday, and every Sunday, he walked to church, offered polite greeting, then returned to his tent, where, as more than one watching pair of eyes confirmed, he did not a stroke of work and stirred only once to stroll out to the low water mark in the evening. That mollified the few island hearts still set against him.

The second week, the community council met again.

'Can he do it?'

'Do what exactly?'

'Can he just turn up like that, rebuild the place and move in?'

'I feel disposed to let him try,' said MacMillan.

'What if the authorities find out? Are we culpable in any way?'

'Who's going to tell them. Are you, Murdo?'

'Me? Hell no. I rather like the man. But you know how word gets around in the islands without a word being spoken.'

The council adjourned unresolved. A few days later MacMillan was seen to walk alone to North Crofts, seen to be talking at length with the Campbell. Once two voices loud and laughing eddied across the machair where an oystercatcher danced away startled on the wind. Tea, then drams, were poured. Bonds were forged. Bonds, thought MacMillan, too comfortable for an islander like himself to have been forged so soon with an incomer from a distant shore. Then these words were heard by at least one pair of straining ears:

'Well, goodnight Mr Campbell and thank you for your hospitality.'

'Goodnight Mr MacMillan. It's been my pleasure. And it's just Campbell. My name is Campbell MacPherson.'

MacMillan nodded.

'I had begun to think that might be the case. I think I understand the nature of the debt you feel, Campbell, although I'm not sure that it is your debt to shoulder. Everyone on this island has a debt to shoulder when it comes to the North Crofts. Don't overburden yourself, man.'

'Thanks, Mr MacMillan. I'll try and remember that.'

'Euan,' said the old man, and shook the Campbell's hand.

MacPherson! That dark shadow fallen again on North Crofts! And hell-bent on rebuilding number 12. The word was on the island's lips before MacMillan had crossed it and closed his door on the whispering night.

Another meeting, the third in a month, the secretary on her feet, bristling:

'I understand he's a . . . a . . . MacPherson.' The word had to be dragged from its lair behind hissing teeth. It was no meagre ordeal she was inflicting on herself, she who restricted her contributions at such meetings to a clipped account of the minutes of the last meeting. She trembled and her face twitched but her courage was up now and Moses himself couldn't have silenced her.

'I just thought – well, a MacPherson (easier this time, like the second time you swear) at North Crofts of all places, and I'm sure I speak for my late father, God rest his soul, and to answer Mr MacMillan's question of the meeting of the 12th inst., the reason the cottages at North Crofts have remained derelict all these years is, I believe by way of a sacred monument to this island's darkest day – and it was a MacPherson's darkness. It was the Lord's wish that the houses have remained as they are, and that is why Mr MacPherson's actions are unseemly and unholy

166

now, and I have heard from my sister in Nova Scotia that there was a MacPherson from hereabouts in the churchyard there and there was a grandson who went out to Alberta that was an architect and that is all I have to say.'

MacMillan exploded out of the council's speechlessness:

'Jesus suffering Christ, woman! No wonder Sassenachs think all Gaels are savages. And do you hold every Englishman responsible for Cumberland and every German for Hitler and every American for Mickey Bloody Mouse?

'Did you ever stop to think *why* MacPherson acted as he did?

'Did you ever consider that perhaps he had very little choice in the matter?

'Do you ever address your corrupted mind to what that particular MacPherson out there at North Crofts is trying to do and the sense of honour which is driving him?'

'*Honour!*' shrieked the secretary who had never been told she had a corrupted mind before, she was such a model of logic and control.

'Yes, honour.' MacMillan was calmed again, placing his words levelly. 'Let me tell you about him. Let me tell you that he grew up with his grandfather's guilt engraved on his heart, so often did he hear its remorse. Let me tell you of the childhood nightmares he endured and in particular the one in which his grandfather, the same MacPherson who inhabited 12 North Crofts, came home to find the factor and three henchmen had bound his wife and three children in a corner of the house and it was made very clear what would happen to them if he did not persuade all the folk of North Crofts out of their houses at a certain time of the following day. That he was to tell them the fish story and persuade every last one of them out of the house for the laird wanted no blood on his hands, but if he declined or resisted, or attempted to incite rebellion, the blood that would be spilled was the blood cowering in the corner of his own house, and a wound was cut in a child's arm before his very eyes?'

MacMillan gasped for his own breath and composure but he saw in his pause that he had won them over.

'A sacred monument! What's sacred about fire and sheep shit? It's a monument to nothing but our own darkness, not the wretched MacPherson's, a monument to our own disinclination to face up to the past and put it in its proper place – and you should minute this so that you remember it – which is *behind* us. Goodnight fellow councillors, I'm off to talk to my friend, Mr MacPherson. And I will tell him he has no debt to this island. And I will tell him that he labours not in debt or in darkness but with his name absolved from all guilt and in enlightenment.'

167

He stood and his kicked chair lay where it fell. The slammed door burst back into the room off its faulty catch. The half-open space let in sunlight and reason and the skirl of curlews.

MacMillan, once he had apologised again, this time to the secretary and the council as a whole (which he did graciously and eloquently and with flowers in the case of the secretary), determined then to be the bridge between the villagers and the Campbell-that-was-a-MacPherson's driven rehabilitation of North Crofts. He spent much of his time there and became an integral force in the rebuilding process and MacPherson's wellbeing. He advised about the lie of stones, the rhythm of the labour, the set of timbers, about floor stones, about rounding the corners of the walls so that the wind went quietly by, about the wisdom of small and deepset windows. The architect in MacPherson understood that principle well enough but commented 'a pity with such a view', to which MacMillan responded, 'If it's the view you want, go to the door, and if the weather is too bad to stand at the door you won't have a view anyway.'

So the old blunt and hunched profile of number 12 North Crofts grew low and robust on the flat northern skyline of the island. MacMillan went deftly between the cottage and the village, advising of progress and quietly extolling the qualities of 'The Campbell', always 'The Campbell', and banishing forever the old ghosts which had haunted the darkest recesses of island minds for more than 100 years. Long before it was finished, the house was known as 'The Campbell place' and the bridge MacMillan had built was sturdy and bore the goodwill of all islanders. And then it was finished.

Forty-two people, which was the whole island, crowded in and admired and blessed the work and offered a small presentation for the wall. It was a framed copperplate scroll of a text which began . . . 'The hollowest epitaph to a man's life is the dereliction of the house where he lived . . .' and the whole thing was attributed to 'Campbell of North Crofts' with the date he signed Mrs MacQueen's visitors book.

'So what now, Campbell?' asked Urquhart as the housewarming began to peter out with the dawn.

'What now? Well, Euan is going to be my neighbour, just as soon as we can put number ten to rights.'

'Is this true, Euan?'

'It is Murdo. Campbell's debt of honour has been the impetus for the salvation of my own dream. And after that, who knows.'

So they rebuilt number ten North Crofts much as they had rebuilt number 12, but this time it took less than six months for every able-bodied man in the island volunteered his labour at some point, and every day islanders gathered round with advice and tea and whisky. At MacMillan's own request, the second housewarming furnished a second scroll with the same text. He hung it over his hearth 'to remind whoever comes after us – Campbell and me – that what summarises us is that we put roofs back and unstifle old hearths'.

The council had agreed at the outset to convene a special meeting after a year of new life at North Crofts to review the position. Motions for the meeting suggested that authority should be informed, otherwise the council was condoning a breach of law, possibly several breaches. But the mood of much of the island had swung behind MacMillan's counter motion, the like of which no one would have credited the island with right up to the day Campbell set foot on it. It was that of the 12 houses at North Crofts, there was enough workable stone among the ruins and enough workable land to rebuild eight crofts, and that they should do just that, as an island, and select occupants from the island.

The room was quiet for a moment. Then:

'Can we do that?'

'Two houses is one thing, but eight?'

'Will we get away with it?'

'What if the planners . . .?'

'What if the sheriff's officers . . .?'

'What if . . .' interrupted MacMillan, 'we just do it? It seems to me that the thing about Campbell was that he just did it because there was a good reason to do it and no good reason not to do it. If you remember, none of us advanced such a reason, although we had assumed for long enough that there was such a reason.'

Seven heads nodded at that. They would just do it.

It took two years, two more after that for the planning authority to find out, six months after that for them to decide that they would all have to be demolished, two hours after that for an eager press and television campaign to mobilise behind the islanders, two years after that for the planning authority to grant retrospective planning permission. The laird, believed to be in Jersey, did not respond to communications of any kind. Six-and-a-half years was all it took to turn the island tide. By then, Campbell MacPherson was dead.

MacMillan had gone in to see him, knowing him to be uncharacteristically depressed, with a dram and an enlivening evening's company in mind. He opened the door, called a greeting, and entered. At once the coldness of the house troubled him. The fire was out. Campbell was missing. The pages of a manuscript were on the table at the window, longhand and typed, a fragmented account of life and wildlife during Campbell's short and galvanising time on the island. It began with the now familiar words from the visitors' book, but beyond the known paragraph, there was this:

'So when I came to North Crofts, I knew I would not just have to sweat and bleed amid its wounded stones and stinging, stinking foundations, not just contend with the disapproval of the islanders, but also be seen to repay what John MacPherson had been judged guilty of here . . . that, particularly would be a slung albatross about the neck of the enterprise. He is judged the destroyer of North Crofts. Only I can rebuild . . .' and there the paragraph hovered like a questing kestrel, its mission unfinished. Half-hearted pencil marks had scored out the paragraph, as though Campbell had begun to distrust the sentiment perhaps, and a hard specific line was through the words 'the disapproval of the islanders'.

Then MacMillan found:

'It is so much more than a house I have rebuilt. I have been beachcombing through the driftwood of my life, to salvage that which might be put to a worthier purpose, and so stacked the odds against myself because I knew I would only heal in sustained commitment to a new and irrevocable beginning. I had thought to be assisted only by the hospitality of the landscape, the anthem of its winds, the generosity of its seas, the scope of its unfurled skies, the neighbourliness of its birds, the furtive kinship of its otters. It would be assistance enough and more than I have been used to.

'But I had reckoned without *human* warmth, acceptance, kindness, friendship. Grandfather left no hint of these.

'So the building was made easy for me, and I know now that the albatross is not in the building – for anyone can be taught to build – but in the living with what is built. I have tried to live with what is built, but I fear I have built that old ugliness back into the place. I have built the stench of sheep back into it, I have built a home for ghosts, a small mausoleum for others who died on distant shores. I am no part of it. For all Euan MacMillan's shepherding kindness, I am not born to it, and I doubt whether I can live with it.'

MacMillan sat by the window of the chill room, passed a hand across his white hair, shivered, and felt for the first time his 80 years as a burden.

'Oh, Euan, oh man!' he said aloud. Any ear which had heard the words would have heard the melancholy of his island race laid bare.

MacMillan read among the loose pages again. Typed pages were followed by what seemed to be a complete little essay, still handwritten. The old man read:

170

The tide flowed and flowed and drove the press of the wader birds into the tightest of shoreline corners, between the closing jaws of the tide and the caves. They crammed ever tighter, an inches high forest of red legs which muddied and rinsed, muddied and rinsed with every new-flung wave and its retreat down the beach.

My eyes drifted up to a high, speeding falcon, tinily detached, I followed it until the distracting black pitch of my new roof grounded the flightpath of my gaze. I wondered about that roof. Could any mere assembly of old stone and slate and timbers acquire powers beyond the sum of its parts? Not just a domestic atmosphere which evolves with continuous habitation, but an unnerving 'personality' (I need a better word here . . . houses don't have personalities, only persons do yet it troubles me as much as a personality) of its own which evolves counter to human habitation? I have survived thus far – two years – by countering the discomfort with one naïve truth, that there are stones, slates, timbers, and that these sheltered me well enough for the first six months until, subconsciously, I stopped marvelling at what had been done here and the flimsy reassurance of home caved in, denuding pretence, and I began to accommodate doubt.

So I have set about establishing a benign presence, so that stones, slates, timbers, and whatever else it is which bedfellows here might acknowledge my good intentions and relax their hold. It seemed at first that there was a truce of tolerances at least, but it was neither the new beginning I had craved nor the harmony my discordant life had demanded.

I turned again and again to the birds. They had helped to lure me into the enterprise that first week when I stayed at the guest house. I had imagined them then as neighbours, kaleidoscoped 100 yards beyond my threshold with only the machair between us. How they have sustained me!

Consider the madness of the winter redshanks. Redshanks are 1,000-times-a-day cowards as they sprint up the sand ahead of each new wave, 1,001-times-a-day heroes as they sprint back down through the broken aftermath of wave after wave. But as the tide heightens there are more camp followers than heroes and cowards, 200 birds in a space fit for 20, so that the sprinting is the work of the handful nearest the water while the also-rans stand or stab seaweed or vie for the right to compete in the next chase and its brief bounties.

At a sudden unsounded alarm, half of them fly, no less tightly packed in the flying than in the beachcombing, a pied panic. Ten seconds south along the shoreline, banked east with clockwork discipline, herring silver now at a sudden whim of the sun, banked north again through the casts of fishing terns, banked west again, thrust braking red undercarriages out at the same hazard-strewn runway they have just left.

Now – what chaos! Those left behind, the unpanicked hunchbacks and morose wrack-stabbers, have sped down the beach to fill the empty tideline spaces left by the fliers. The flock readjusts by its own laws, subsides into a redefined – continually redefining – pecking order of sprinters and stabbers and hunchers. The tide gnaws another yard from their feeding ground. The press of birds crams closer.

My mind is drifting today. I am cast off with the fliers. For the brief duration of the flight, I know the fearful liberation of the flock. I have been fed, provided for by the reliability of tides. At this last gasp of the tide's highest encroachment, all birds must snatch a last sustaining mouthful. Feed then fly so that the others behind on the shore may feed. Fly, even knowing that flight puts the flock in the marauding path of peregrines and skuas, the confident exhilaration of controlled flock-flight, tinged with the fear of the downwind falcon none of us can outfly. At home, I have commanded my flock of stones to fly, fearful of downwind falcons.

Now in my drifting mind the tide has rolled far, far back. The sea is half a mile back. A single redshank stands rooted and alone in a square mile of sand. His head is deep in his spine, one foot clamped to his belly, his balance meticulously shifted to centre on a single webbed sand-anchor. I am he. Sand-stranded, my anchor hooked perilously in sand and liable to drag dangerously, restful only between the rush of tides I found so unbearable, aloof from the press of the tribe I shunned. Or am I that waltzing tern, a bird of passage, wounded perhaps and reluctantly resigned to the hospitalisation of this shore, under that troubled roof?

My mind has drifted back to the high tide again where a solitary knot stands on the last rock the sea has not yet devoured, perhaps I am he? Knots won their name from Canute for their daring in the face of the tide, a notion lent some substance by this lone bird keeping its head while all around danced to the tune of the tide. The sea did go back, of course, but not before the bird-who-would-be-king suffered a drenching crown of foam and fled in search of an easier inheritance to live up to.

The tide has lunged hugely forward at the last, then lain brimful and slack and all birds have flown. A tern tiptoes past, pauses to hover and dive and catch and swallow, tiptoes on. Far out, gannets fish supreme. I am alone again and I am shorebound, and fearful of downwind falcons.

MacMillan shook his head, rose and went out into the island to summon help to search for The Campbell.

They found him in a cave along the shore at low tide when the sea pulled back with his beloved birds loud and bright beyond the cavemouth. He had drowned, by accident or design, inside the cave. They put him in the old burial ground where none had been laid in 100 years. The stone said: 'Here lies the corpse of The Campbell.' No dates, no other words. MacMillan said to the gathered islanders: 'He was the man who rekindled the hearth of the North Crofts and the heart of this island. He vowed on the island's behalf that the houses of North Crofts would never decay again. That summarises Campbell MacPherson.'

Euan MacMillan walked far out over the low tide sands, where a calm yellow-and-grey sunset held sway, fingering in his coat pocket a single frayed piece of paper. It was The Campbell's entry in Mrs MacQueen's book which she had removed and brought to the community council meeting years before. The old man considered it in the yellowing light.

'Name – just Campbell.

'Address – just a province in a land halfway across the world.

'Nationality – none. Not to know where you belong, Campbell. It's the greatest burden of all. And yet for all you have done for us there was no belonging here for you either.

'I think maybe you were a bird yourself, man, a species we thought was extinct from here long ago, but called back by nature, race memory, whatever, to put down a new nest, reclaim an old territory, so that others coming after you might flourish, make a new flock.'

On a cliff at the edge of the wide bay which marks the natural boundary of the North Crofts land, a peregrine falcon kicked out from a ledge and went eagerly among the flocks, downwind.

20

The Last Sentence of a Dream

Gavin Maxwell had his first harpoon made in Mallaig. He went shark hunting with it, an abortive adventure, abortive but idealistic, for his ambition was nothing less than the regeneration of a moribund island – Soay, snugly moored under the Skye Cuillin. Good things came out of it eventually. The waters between the south of Skye and the mainland became the centre of his universe, and with his account of the shark fishery he discovered what he was good at, which was writing books. He put the landscape of the Sound of Sleat and Loch Alsh before the eyes of millions, mesmerised them in *A Ring of Bright Water.*

I am among the mesmerised. I began – like most of the rest of us – with the book he called 'Ring', but he so flamboyantly embraced and enriched the literature of the Highland landscape that he became a kind of apotheosis for my own writing ambitions to aim at. The fact that I haven't got close is no hardship to bear. No one else has done either. Later I took my enthusiasm for his work a stage beyond, and began working on a biography, only to discover that Douglas Botting was several years ahead of me, and because of his personal friendship with Maxwell, had access to personal archives whose locks would have taken me years to unpick, if indeed I penetrated their family defences at all. My consolation is that Botting's book is all that I could ever have wished of my own, and fitting tribute to the life that was lived·here.

It was a life strewn with abortive ventures, major and minor disasters, but touched here and there with magic, blessed here and there by the sublime, and couched and chronicled in the immense scope of his own writer's gifts. From time to time, I wander back here, in the nature of pilgrimage, homage, and because it is here more than most places that I too feel that 'strange too-fullness of the heart'.

The ferry from Mallaig to Skye gives you just enough time to pin down two of the fixed points in his landscape – Isle Ornsay on the Sleat shore of south Skye, and once the ferry is out in mid-Sound, Sandaig itself, his Camusfearna, over the starboard stern.

More lighthouses, one on either shore, and there is a third hidden from here behind Glen Arroch's hills, where it all ended for Gavin Maxwell, and where his memory is besmirched in the most disagreeable manner imaginable, the unforgivable imprint on his island home and the wider landscape of the Skye Bridge. Eilean Bhan, the White Island, off Kyleakin, might have become the best kind of memorial to Gavin Maxwell. Instead, it has been hinged to the mainland by the bridge and grows derelict at the hands of vandals and neglect.

The Journey alighted on Skye, and while the ferry traffic convoyed north up the Sleat shore, I pulled into the pier café and let it go. The pier café is Skye's answer to Crianlarich's station tearoom. Islanders and hitch-hikers mingle agreeably and ferry passengers while away the space between boats. For many people who only come once, it is their first and last impression of Skye people. On that score alone, it reassures me greatly. I am very fond of Skye people. I am very fond of Skye. Two or three times a year, and for over 25 years, I have found excuses to be here. Now I have one more, an extravagant diversion in the Journey to make a point, and (of course) to be here just for the sake of being here, as so often before.

A ragged parallelogram of roads encloses a cross-section of the Sleat peninsula, 12 square miles of high lochs among low bare hills, crags and peat bogs, with – around the edges – scraps of old woods, and even a few people. With a still, gentle day at my disposal, cold and sunless and pent-up as though the land had inhaled a great breath and awaited some kind of signal before releasing it, I hauled out the bike for the succession of strenuous pechs and giddy descents which the topography demands, bottom gear and top gear and very little use for anything in between. I crept west, up from the Sal Mor Ostaig corner, uphill all the way to Loch Dhugaill, my mind on nothing but that climactic moment when the road begins to level out, and Skye unwraps the Cuillin, frescoed and sculpted in watercolours and in gabbro. No matter what the mood of the mountains, that first revelation always exceeds expectations. Now the great ridge heaved over the hilltop, battleship grey and sea-going, the most exciting skyline I know. All my days on Skye, from my very first to my very last, I know I will never get used to it, know that wherever I travel on the island (and however persuasive are its many other charms),

I will travel anticipating the next appearance of the Cuillin, wondering what colour it will be this time – white, yellow, pink, purple, brown, grey, blue, or quite black?

I left the bike by the loch and walked out a mile across the crown of Sleat to the gentle summit of Sgurr na h-Iolaire, Peak of the Eagle. You find that name on crags and ridges all across the Highlands, although few are quite as featureless as this. But the land falls away easily from its summit in every direction, gentle gestures to set before the Cuillin. An eagle might stand here, feel the tug of an onshore wind, step onto it with wings wide, then, working the shafts of mobile air, climb 1,000 feet in a minute, pull in its outer wings to a curving 'W' shape, and cut a 100 miles per hour shallow glide across Strathaird and vanish against the rocks of Gars-bheinn. I know such a thing might happen. I was 20 yards away, two years ago, when eagle and I surprised each other, and that is just what happened.

The road dives into the sea at Tarskavaig, where the landscape ingredients of well-worked crofts, trim houses, the Atlantic beyond, and the Cuillin beyond the Atlantic have fused into a much photographed and much reproduced representation of the crofting way of life. In my own head, it says: 'There *are* people here, and isn't it beautiful?'

The road goes on diving, porpoising up and down above the shore like an otter on the march until it reaches the bridge at Ord, where otters *do* march. A few months before, I was taking part in a radio programme on the subject of otters on Skye with my Skye-based friend, Andy Currie. As the producer and presenter were coming from Bristol, I took the precaution of wandering down to Ord early, to satisfy myself that there still were otters around. I parked, put on jacket and wellies, prepared for a long search or shore and river, and looked up to see an otter cruising into the small bay, headed for the river and the bridge. I was on the bridge and leaning over when he got there, saw him adjust his sea-going stroke to cope with the shallows, saw him emerge and climb the riverbank, and deposit a glistening spraint on the grass. I whistled down to him. He looked up, scratched his chin with a forepaw, looked up again, then wandered off upstream, swimming the pools, paddling the shallows, until I lost him among the otter-coloured rocks and shadows. I thought:

'Well, at least I can show them a fresh turd,' went back to the car, took off jacket and wellies, and headed back over the hill for coffee. That evening, it took us about four hours before we found one, far round the shore of Loch Eishort in the very last of the daylight.

I walked the bike back to the top of the hill, pausing often to admire the scraps of old ash wood, scanning the sky for glimpses of eagles (found

176

none), breathing hard up the last steep slog to the top, turning for one last look at the Cuillin as they darkened into the late afternoon. I blew them a kiss.

Dusk at Isle of Ornsay, a stoat jigged and reeled across the road and hit the crest of a dyke, turned on its heels and took the dyke at a flat-out sprint, a thing to marvel at. The inn above the tiny harbour is one of my favourites anywhere, as is the walk along the shore to the headland. At low tide you can walk out onto the island with its two cottages and inevitable lighthouse. Gavin Maxwell thought he'd rediscovered Camusfearna here and lived here briefly, but after the fire at Sandaig, it was Eilean Bhan up the coast which turned his head. I would have settled for Isle Ornsay. I would always settle for Isle Ornsay. I love it best in winter, which is also how I know it best, when sodden squalls hurtle up and down the Sound, and it lies low and hunkered down in the crook of Sleat's arm, and the lighthouses of this island and Sandaig across the Sound chatter to each other silently through the night. Curlews and shelduck, mergansers and herons, oystercatchers and all manner of other fly-by-nights plowter in the low-tide mud. There are seals in the bay, and harriers on the hill. There are otters, of course.

Across the Sound, Beinn Sgritheall whitened, a handsome mountain profile, and the brooding backcloth to Gavin Maxwell's stage. I am apt to watch it from Isle Ornsay through slow mornings and lingering dusks. It is such a store of memories for me, but one in particular stands clear of them all. I have written of it in detail elsewhere, in a small book published a couple of years ago called *The Heart of Skye*, and there is no need to repeat the detail here. But it centred on a kind of apparition at Sandaig during yet another pilgrimage to Maxwell's Camusfearna in which a man, a boy and – I *think* – an otter appeared on the shore, then disappeared without trace.

I had pitched my tent further down the shore, and long after dark I walked the beach listening to the sounds of the October night, uneasily reconvening the day's ghosts. I hardly slept, and at something like 5 a.m. I gave up the unequal struggle, packed breakfast, and set out in the pre-dawn dark to climb the mountain. I had no clear idea of the easiest route, so I went straight up for as long as that option was practicable.

Strenuous physical activity took over from strenuous mental activity, and I climbed harder and faster than on any other mountain, before or since. I paused after an hour or so, looked down and round and saw Loch Hourn in a trance, a landscape of dreams. It lay so perfectly tranquil in its black ring of mountains that it looked as if it had been newly painted.

Again the notion of a stage set occurred to me. The Knoydart mountains, with Ladhar Bheinn for their centrepiece, were inked in, too black to be convincing, not real mountains, but effective as a stage set. The loch was pale blue, shading to turquoise as it neared the mountains, milkily opaque, and the changes of colour and texture worked into its water through dawn and sunrise were the exclusive preserve of gods, not writers. But every now and then the climber would pause and turn and gasp, then turn and climb again.

I found my way round the mountain to the upper reaches of the Allt Mor Santaig, that mountain burn which feeds the waterfall which Maxwell called 'the soul of Camusfearna', then ripples in a glittering arc to the sea, an arc which became, in certain lights, a ring of bright water. That form of words first entered the language in a poem by Maxwell's sometime soul mate, Kathleen Raine.

He has married me with a ring, a ring of bright water

The mountain grew bare, and towards the summit the burn flirted as much with the underworld as the overworld. The cloud cap which the mountain had worn all night, began to evaporate to reveal the snow cap underneath. At last, in the very summit rocks themselves, I found the place where the burn issued above ground for the first time, as much ice as water. If the Allt Mor Santaig fed the soul of Camusfearna, then here was the womb of the soul, and Highland mountain-tops come no more portentous than that. I patted the summit cairn at 8 a.m. and had breakfast.

The cloud cap, I now realised, had not evaporated so much as slipped. The sun poured through higher clouds and lit the eerie merging of snow and cloud yellow and green. For a few moments it threw my shadow onto the cloud and made a Brocken Spectre of it, that ghostly phenomenon of mountain light which throws a rainbow-coloured halo round a watching shadow. I had only ever seen it twice. I will never see it in a more profound mood of wonder.

The thing faded. Hot coffee from a flask restored a more practical demeanour. From here I could see Sandaig Islands, Isle Ornsay and Eilean Bhan, a trinity of lighthouses built in the classical manner first devised by Robert Louis Stevenson's father . . . for the Bell Rock. He could hardly have imagined that more than 100 years later, Gavin Maxwell would come down a treacherous hillside footpath to the Sandaig shore, push open the door of the long-disused lighthouse keeper's cottage, and launch a literature of that landscape through which his lighthouses glowed like beacons. And what would they both make of that glowering untidal wave of concrete which springs from the Kyleakin shore, bows high into the air above the lighthouse, and crash-lands onto the eastern shores of the island? Stevenson would probably have laughed off such an outrageous idea. Maxwell, I would imagine, would have sworn that if it happened, it would happen over his dead body. It has so happened, Gavin.

Kyle of Lochalsh doesn't know what to do with itself these days. It lived and breathed for the Skye ferry for so long. A barge called *Yorkshire Lass* was rummaging around the ferry pier where the waterfront was being reinvented to do something else. There was talk of a new freight service to the Western Isles, but most of the talk was about 'the bloody bridge', its outrageous tolls, the sustained campaigning and non-payment protests, and just the general outrageousness of its very existence, its very ugliness. I have always loathed the very idea of a bridge to Skye, the very idea of making a peninsula out of an island, not just an island, but the island the Skye folk call The Island, in a manner which suggests it should have capital letters. The abstract quality of island-ness inherent in an unbridged and encircling mass of water cuts no ice at public inquiries, falls on deaf ears in Government quangos. But it is part of the lifeblood of islands. The history of islands is delivered to their thresholds by boats – the Vikings to every island off our shores; Columba to Iona; Charles Edward Stuart to Skye; Mendelssohn to Staffa. And it was not by bus that the cleared folk left Suishnish nor the transit camps in Tobermory. You cannot tell me that an indefinable part of Skye is not already dead because it has been irredeemably bound to the mainland in concrete.

I walked out along the approach road to the bridge from Kyle with the intention of photographing Gavin Maxwell's house and the lighthouse. A north wind was hammering down the Sound, making the long lens difficult to hold steady. So I wedged it in two stones on top of the wall which borders the approach road. It was while I was leaning there that an older man stopped his brisk walk to ask:

'Are you not going down to the lighthouse? It's easy. I'll show you.'

And with that his slipstream towed me along the road to a point he had marked out as the easiest place to jump over the wall. He duly jumped. I would guess he was 70. I jumped after him, and at once I landed on a different world. It was jungly with long heather and brambles. We stood in the lee of the wall for a moment and discussed Gavin Maxwell, Eilean Bhan, the buildings and the otters, and the bridge. He was, he said, a Kyle man. He thought the bridge damned ugly, and the tolls a hideous imposition. If it was a pound, then local people would probably accept it, though he would never accept the look of it. Neither, I suggested, would Gavin Maxwell. I had said the right thing.

He would never had let the island go, said my new friend, never. He loved this place. It reminded him of his childhood.

It did. Maxwell said so himself, in *Raven Seek Thy Brother*:

> *Deeply as I had been impressed by Isle Ornsay, I felt drawn to Kyleakin as I had to few places in my life – and this despite its nearness to the summer scene. I have since tried to analyse this feeling of profound attraction; at first I thought it might be due to nothing more complex than the fact that Camusfearna, with all its echoes of past unhappiness and loss, was out of sight. But I think now that it was a far call back to childhood, for the long, rough heather, the briars and the outcrops of bare rock might have been those surrounding the House of Elrig where I was born, the house that obsessed my childhood and adolescence and came to represent the world. The land surrounding Elrig was a wilderness in which the close-cropped green turf of Isle Ornsay would have found no place, but at Kyleakin I felt as if I were coming home.*

It was here that Gavin Maxwell planned the last adventure of his life – a wildlife sanctuary where people could observe a cross-section of Highland wildlife at close quarters, and on the adjoining island where eider duck already nested, an eider farm. But Maxwell died before his ambitions were wholly realised and the venture died with him. And now his island is dying too, and that troubled my escort greatly, as it troubles me.

'I come out here every day,' he said, 'to make sure things are all right. Twenty lads got into the lighthouse one day last year. They were all high on drugs. They were swinging on the weather vane. They didn't know where they were. They could have dropped off into the sea. I phoned the police. They were very quick.'

He showed me where the eider farm had been, describing its strips of bunting and toy plastic windmills which (as the Icelanders have known for centuries) induce the eiders to nest in big colonies from which commercial quantities of down can be harvested.

We found the overgrown stone on which had been carved a single name and a date, grown all but illegible with the passage of time and the spread of lichen. It said:

TEKO 1969

the last resting place of the last of the Sandaig otters.

'There should be an otter sanctuary here on the island,' he said, 'where people can come and watch them. The house could be a restaurant – I don't know – but look at the view! The walled garden could be restored, The wee building where the generator is could have something which told you about Gavin Maxwell.'

We wandered up to the generator shed. The door was off it, and thieves and vandals had begun to strip it. He tutted and shook his head.

'The otters are beginning to come back, you know. Oh there's plenty people think they're vermin, and we should get rid of them, but I tell them, "The otters were here before you". An otter sanctuary, and something to honour Gavin Maxwell's memory. And you could restore the lighthouse and reopen it. Can you imagine the view from up there?'

I could, but only because the crown of the bridge replicates it, and from quite a few feet higher.

He showed me the plaque on the lighthouse which proclaims the work of Stevenson the elder, the garden that swarms with daffodils in the spring, the entrance to the pipe which the bridge builders let into their construction so that the otters could still move 'between' the islands (the bridge approaches obliterate the idea of either of them as islands now), the old pier where the old generator and all the house's furniture must have been hauled ashore – hauled for it was not a pier at all but a slipway of the shore's own stones.

The house itself was boarded up and had new padlocks on the doors, but that was all the maintenance anyone had done there. Slates were missing from the roof.

An incipient decay pervaded what Eilean Bhan had become.

A verse of Robert Louis Stevenson's lyric to the *Skye Boat Song* crept into my mind, but I 'heard' it as if it had been spoken by Maxwell's own voice:

Billow and breeze,
Islands and seas,
Mountains of rain and sun;
All that was good,
All that was fair,
All that was me is gone.

And the chorus . . . the 'Speed bonnie boat' bit:

Sing me a song of a lad that is gone,
Say, could that lad be I?
Merry of soul he sailed on a day
Over the sea to Skye.

I went back the next day, hopped over the wall and went prospecting round the shore. 'The otters are coming back, you know,' the old man had said. They had been absent during much of the construction period, but now they had found their own way back, and I found the first traces of them at the water's edge, spraints and 'tunnels' where they had writhed through the heather. And I began to think.

The lure of Gavin Maxwell is a durable one. Many people still make the arduous trek down to Sandaig by way of pilgrimage. It is inevitable that many more will take advantage of the changed circumstances on Eilean Bhan to experience the sense of his life here and touch its artefacts. The fact that the otters are coming back will hardly detract from their enthusiasm. Without a care-and-maintenance presence at the very least, incipient decay will become rampant decay. But a care-and-maintenance presence is hardly a fit memorial to the life and works of Gavin Maxwell.

I think the old man had it the wrong way round . . . the house should be devoted to Maxwell's life, and the old generator shed some ancillary purpose, whether shop or office or snack bar or potting shed. But it is Gavin Maxwell who would draw people here, not a restaurant. The islands as otter sanctuary with viewing hides, the lighthouse as seabird observatory, and a living presence on the island so that it is managed properly and its buildings kept safe and secure. But its first and overriding purpose would be to do justice to the life of Gavin Maxwell.

Maxwell and the World Wildlife Fund established the Edal Fund after fire destroyed Sandaig and killed Edal the otter in 1968. The fund's purpose was to prevent the extinction of Britain's otters. I think it is time for the millions of Maxwell's admirers around the world to follow that example. The Teko Fund would rehabilitate Eilean Bhan, restore the buildings and the gardens as Maxwell had evolved them, and serve Maxwell's highest purpose, which was the wellbeing of otters. And through the unlikely agency of 'the bloody bridge', Gavin Maxwell would have the kind of memorial he deserves.

An epilogue to Maxwell's *Raven Seek Thy Brother* concludes a single-page account of the Sandaig fire thus:

Tonight at the last sentence of a dream I stand in thought before the Camusfearna door. Someone someday perhaps may build again upon that site, but there is much that cannot ever be rebuilt.

The sentiment is also true of Eilean Bhan, but there is no reason why we should have reached the last sentence of that dream. A small stone, two inches by an inch by an inch, sits on my writing desk, not two feet in front of my eyes. I reach over it every time I put a new piece of paper in the typewriter. I picked it up at Sandaig during that extraordinary October, and I have written on it, the form of words taken from another rock on the Sandaig shore:

EDAL

Whatever joy
she gave to you
give back
to nature

Starting, I think, at Eilean Bhan.

AUTHOR'S NOTE. A few weeks after I wrote this chapter, and just as the book was going to press, it was announced that Eilean Bhan was to be handed over to a trust. The impetus for reprieve came from the Born Free Foundation, a wildlife conservation organisation founded by Virginia McKenna and her late husband Bill Travers who both starred in the film of *Ring of Bright Water*. The foundation's eleventh hour intervention persuaded the Scottish Office to withdraw the island from an auction of surplus property after sustained local protest. The foundation proposed a wildlife sanctuary and a visitor centre at Kyleakin. The Scottish Office undertook to make the island buildings wind and watertight. It seems there is life left yet in Gavin Maxwell's dream.

21

Normally Impassable

Fiats are illiterate. Nothing else explains the alacrity with which my hitherto tired and tiresome estate skipped past the biggest warning signs in the Highlands. They were ten feet high, they intoned gloomily on the subject of the road ahead – one-in-five gradients, hairpins, a summit at 2,053 feet, and the curious coupling of words 'normally impassable in winter conditions'. It was winter. Impassable and normal. Would today be normal? It was 25 years since I had last crossed to Applecross and I remembered little. Certainly the warning signs had grown more conspicuous. The Fiat thrust eagerly on up the first gentle mile, rising of course, but cannily. Then there was another warning sign, 'normally impassable in winter conditions'.

Then there was the first twist, a marked steepening, and the road contrived a glimpse of what it had in mind. The oldest marriage in the land, the 2,000 millionth anniversary of that match made in hell (or at least in fires in the bowels of the earth) between Lewissian gneiss and Torridonian sandstone, characterises the mountains between here and Suilven, my Journey's end, and as I see it, the ultimate consummation of that age-old marriage. On the Bealach na Ba, the mountains stood around in blackened cubes. The road's problem, and now the Fiat's, was not to get through the cubes, but *over* them. Distance is irrelevant here. Height is all. You *must* climb.

The terrain had a curiously liberating effect on the old Fiat, which had not been at its best since Ardnamurchan. No, it had not been at its best since about 1993, but in the context of the Journey, it had consistently underachieved. Now it grew young. It girded its loins, which is rare in Italians, and, faced with something like a pass over the Dolomites, started devouring hairpins with relish. The climbing grew relentless, mesmerising. Then a jaw opened in the mountains and inhaled. More behemoths. Some perverse gravity was winching me up and into the jaw. Then the gradients got really steep, and the hairpins so tight that I suddenly remembered what a real hairpin looked like, and realised why hairpin bends are called hairpins. It was an illuminating moment.

The Fiat grunted, dug in, rebuked me with an Italianate oath on one deceptive stretch which was much steeper than it looked. *Third* gear? Forget it. Second then, the revs kicked back in, the car willing. Another hairpin, first in the middle of the bend, not smart. Remember your old police driving course: be in the right gear *before* the bend, practise car sympathy at all times. 'Car sympathy' would have involved an hour-long detour round the coast. The tightest hairpin of all: just as I reached it my eye was caught by the sight of that gaunt, black jaw, but *below* me now, a black yawn. At the exact moment you want to stop to gawp at it, a sign materialises and tells you in the most unambiguous terms not to stop or park. First, 180 degrees of hairpin, then the one-in-five bit you were warned about and had forgotten about, the warning was so long ago, back in that other life down there were roads were wide and level and had straight bits. The cruellest thought of all lodged irretrievably at the front of my mind right there, right then: this is no place for a clutch cable to go.

It relented. Straightened, levelled out, let in light, pronounced its own summit and lay there in the sun panting for breath. I parked, switched off the engine, got out and looked around. I owned the only car in the world.

Away to the north the world widened and sunlight blazed on a flat snow cap. There was an indicator beside the car park. It said among other things, 'Ardnamurchan 50 miles'. Fifty! Is that all! It had taken half a season. So I waved to my former self from the summit of the Bealach na Ba to the lee of the lighthouse rocks in a hurricane.

The sun was throwing things down through the clouds above the black cubes, a full set of buttresses with black sails where the wind was going berserk. I resisted the temptation to sit on the car park's two park benches. Sea views were lost in sea fog.

Down was easier, wider open, no jaws, then fields, then trees, then what's-all-the-fuss-about Applecross on its shorelines shelf, then the long and kinky miles down the coast to Toscaig pier, on a small sea loch between bare and birchy crags. As end-of-the-road as Ardnamurchan.

A bit of a scudding, squally wind, a snivelling thing, not nice to be out in, whistled round the car and the pier, and kicked up small slapping waves. Two ravens roughed up the wind, the pier, the lochsides. A knotted thing on a rock untied itself and a cormorant stood there, then went fishing under the pier.

I had lunch where I sat, thinking the weather would lift. Besides, I was hungry and it was late for lunch. As I ate, and notebook-scribbled with the other hand, my eye drifted from time to time through the open window and up to the nearest skyline. Three or four times I looked along that hill edge, and on the fourth or fifth time, intuition suddenly informed the looking. Intuition said I should get the glasses and have a look at that blip in the middle. Intuition thought it might just have moved. Intuition was right. The glasses showed a pointed rock with a golden eagle on either side.

I have done a lot of eagle-on-rock watching in my time, and it can be the most frustrating pastime on earth. Four hours is the longest I have put up with watching an eagle not move. But I was comfortable enough where I sat, I was halfway through lunch, I had work I could be getting on with, and music I could play, and ravens and a cormorant for diversions. I would just sit, and run the glasses along the skyline from time to time.

It took an hour and a half, by which time I was fed and watered, fed up with the work. The ravens and the cormorant had gone. I was cold and bored. Intuition nudged me again and I picked up the glasses, and moments later, the male eagle stood on the rock, then landed softly on the female's back, and they mated. Then they flew, a couple of wingbeats then a few climbing circuits of languorous soaring, then far across the loch to the opposite hillside to a rock where she perched and he disappeared.

I looked back at the hillside where they had mated, found a line up through the trees, and climbed it. I found nothing which looked like a nest, which I was pleased about – too conspicuous by far if it had been so close to the pier – but I stumbled on an old path crossing the hill. A sign on a deer fence gate said 'welcome' and that the woods were being managed by the Forestry Commission. The fenced-off ground was growing the right kind of trees and keeping out sheep and deer. Good. Another gate let me out, and I crossed the line of an old pass over the watershed to Totaig. There was the old familiar green turf which spoke of abandoned pastures, and the inevitable cluster of shoreline ruins. A couple had been turned into holiday homes, a couple of others into stores, or bothies. There was an orange swing in front of a restored house, a catamaran in the back garden; the pasture was studded with heaps of stones which the old inhabitants would have gathered to make the land fertile. The slipway was like Eilean Bhan's, just a flattening of shoreline stones with the bigger rocks heaved or dragged off to one side or the other.

I don't know which is worse . . . the caved-in walls and littered evidence of the old edge-of-the-land struggle, or the fact that it has been turned into playthings. There's nobody there, and isn't it beautiful.

We hit thick cloud at the top of the pass, which induced a nervous vertigo into the Fiat's sensibilities. We gingered on, the only car in the world again, taut with anticipation about the direction of the next hairpin. The car guessed them all correctly. We went down into the daylight and that other world where the roads are wide and level and have straight bits. I wondered if people who cross that road regularly ever become blasé about it. I would think not.

I had made up my mind about Torridon some time ago. For as long as the idea of the Journey had been in my mind, I saw it as gradual unfolding progress towards Suilven. The approach would be geared to give Suilven its due, and to bridge the gulfs of blue air between. Torridon, it seemed to me, was barrier not bridge. Torridon, and indeed all the land between Liathach and An Teallach, is an airspace crammed with mountains. People, where they cling at all, cling to the very periphery of all that. Climbers enter, the rest go round. I had thought that to go in, to trek through all that in winter especially, was to risk being trampled underfoot by a herd of buffaloes the size of mountains. In Torridon, the mountains come at you in herds. None of them is content with one summit, none of them is commonplace. They jostle for space which does not exist, a too-fullness of the landscape, and they are miserable with winter daylight, throwing shadows on shadows. The Journey had opened my mind to mountains with spaces, mountains which stand apart amid the gulfs of blue air. Now, nearing Suilven, was not the time to be surrounded by Goliaths without so much as a sling.

Besides, Torridon is its own book. An Teallach is its own book! Torridon is deeply embedded in my yesterdays, and with good fortune it will grace my tomorrows. But the Journey was a different creature, a different way through the landscape. So I turned east and drove round, not even risking a dusk confrontation with An Teallach. I have met it before in unprepossessing circumstances, and had it blow away my sensibilities to other mountains for weeks.

So I drove round, and crept into Ullapool in the dusk instead, found it as I always find it, calm, self-contained, sure of itself, working for its living, affable and welcoming. Ullapool in winter is the ultimate antidote to Highland tourism, Aviemore or Tyndrum, say, in midsummer. Eddie Cochrane was wrong. There is a cure for the summertime blues, and the summertime greens for that matter. It's Ullapool in winter. It pulls a chair into the fire for you and is as pleased to see you as it is surprised. In the morning, the sun was switching itself off and on, mountains donned and doffed cloud caps and snow caps, the light was hard and soft and patchy and mobile, and Stac Pollaidh bathed in it.

Stac Pollaidh is two things. It is the most eccentric mountain in the Highlands, and it is a monument to the most crass school of mountain management imaginable, the one which says that it is a service to tourism to put a car park at the bottom of the mountain and signpost the way up. Its eccentricity is lovable. Its management is loathsome.

Stac Pollaidh and I go a long way back. But since our first association almost 30 years ago, we have been like passing strangers, no fault of the mountain of course.

From afar, Stac Pollaidh looks like something perched. It is so *up there*, as if its top was nothing to do with the rest, but rather something that had paused there, something some passing god had put down, then forgotten where he'd left it, and presumably got annoyed at himself because he hadn't finished it yet. And from afar it is black.

From below, from its wretched little car park, it is grey and pink and regressing into sand. Climb it, and you understand as never before the principles and forces which shape and shake down mountains into the raw stumps we know them as. Stac Pollaidh is still at it. Its lobster claw pinnacle lost its claw years ago, but old photographs show it clearly. Other pinnacles and hangers-on have tottered and fallen off, rotted and died. Bits of the path that snakes up among the high stonework are pure sand, and now and again, according to one Stac Pollaidh veteran I met, the path changes route, which is disconcerting if you climb from memory.

I stamped up into the stonework. Cathedral roofs – the more implausible, overdecorated ones – look like this, I'm sure. But Stac Pollaidh is dying under the weight of feet that the car park builders have pointed here. When it levels down to a sand dune, don't say you weren't told. Do something. Dig up the car park.

Reaching the summit ridge changes the world, for suddenly, you see north, north out of Inverpolly and into Assynt. Assynt is rock and water, water and rock, and miles and miles of space. And enthroned on all spaciousness, like a recumbent wild boar on a hearth-rug the size of Rannoch Moor, prostration incarnate, is Suilven. You don't want to go back down the mountain, down to the road, into the car, thread a path up the finicky coast road to Inverkirkaig, walk in six miles and shin up the flank of that masterpiece in the north. You want to fly. You want golden eagle wings (and no other wings will do, not for this flight), you want ten cruising minutes at 2,500 feet, then you want to dip a starboard wing so that you come in at the creature above its boar snout, perch gently on its forehead and ruffle its ears with your hook beak.

Threading a path up the finicky road, then, wondering about the use of low stone walls instead of safety barriers on a blind single-track bend cut into a cliff 20 feet above the high tide, then you think: 'Why not stone? You make damn sure you don't hit them.' But I can't see it catching on on the M8.

Suilven craned over the bits and pieces of the intervening landscape, reinventing itself (Stac Pollaidh did that once, circling round its western flank, when it became an aircraft carrier, bow on), the way a good sculpture does, telescoping itself closed until one sensational moment when it became a single, stupendous monolithic dome. Then the road buried itself again, the mountain leant back with the sunset on its frosty pow, and I promised myself an early breakfast after an early night.

22

More Reasons for Hills

In my head three images – Suilven from Stac Pollaidh, elongated and pressed down; Suilven from the coast road, the dome; Suilven from the east, an old winter, and after the long moorland miles the tail of the boar straight and erect and puncturing the gulfs of blue air like a Matterhorn.
   In my head four lines:

> *Gulfs of blue air, two lochs like spectacles,*
> *A frog (this height) and Harris in the sky –*
> *There are more reasons for hills*
> *Than being steep and reaching only high.*

In a sense these lines, which begin Norman MacCaig's poem *High Up On Suilven*, also began the whole enterprise. I was never easy with the school of thought which some of my early climbing companions brought along with them, that a hill is not a hill until it's climbed, the curse of the Munro-bagging fraternity. I began searching out not the summits but the reasons for hills, and as a matter of instinct, for I was never told to go among mountains that way. So as I walked out the last few miles of the Journey, bound for an unknown point 'High Up On Suilven' (and because the long walk in above the Kirkaig hides Suilven beyond a hill shoulder for miles so you need to think of something else in order to avoid a madness of anticipation), I began to enumerate reasons for hills. I made a top ten, but I couldn't agree with myself on an order: number ten is as valid as number one.

One   *They lift the landscape into the realm of skies (and help to explain flight).*
Two   *They reveal the unlifted landscape.*
Three *They make high-living lives possible – eagle, fox, ptarmigan, mountain hare, arctic willow. All right, then, Norman, frog.*
Four *They memorialise the forces which make landscapes.*
Five *Nature is a sculptor.*
Six   *They accommodate the gods of the ancients.*
Seven *They remind us that some things are beyond our understanding.*
Eight *Hill forts, sacred ground.*
Nine *They help migrating birds to navigate.*
Ten   *They look good to me. I think clearly there.*

Word of the Falls of Kirkaig reached me long before I reached the falls, for the river was high and full-throated. You have to divert down to the falls; not today, though. The sense of them is enough, their gurgling roar, and once you're above them, the river is close to the path again, contemplative and placid, considering it is an abyss which it contemplates.

I found a dead shrew on the path, frozen to death as far as I could see. It bore no wounds. I looked up from the stiff little mite in my hand and saw Suilven. Reason five: nature is a sculptor.

I looked down again at the tiny lifelessness in my hand, a life of weeks, days perhaps if it was particularly unlucky. I looked up to Suilven, a life of forever, or at least as near to forever as you or I will ever understand.

I spooled the river back to its loch, found a niche in a lochside bank and sat. I spoke Hazlitt aloud:

> *Out of doors, nature is company enough for me. I am then never less alone than when alone. I cannot see the wit of walking and talking at the same time.*

Suilven was end-to-end from the lochside, but because the loch was lower than the mountain's moorland plinth, it had become a rearing boar, rather than hearth-rug boar. It had also become a boar in a suit of armour.

The day was one of sunlight in spasms. I reached the loch in one of its steely grey phases, but other mountains were lit. Cul Mor billowed above the nearest skyline, where a black rock reclined in a Henry Moore-ish pose, its back to the mountain, pretending it wasn't there. Then Stac Pollaidh tried to steal the show, hurling a plume of cloud eastward, going through its repertoire of impressions – steam train, dragon, volcano. Sun backlit the mountain black, the cloud white.

I considered the greater mass of cloud, saw that it was dragging slowly east with clear skies beyond. If I stayed at the loch long enough, the cloud might drag far enough east for the sun to light up Suilven and persuade it to slip off its nightcap of cloud. I moved round the loch while I waited, found it windless in its narrowing western corner, sat again. A single raven coughed across the sky from behind to Suilven to far past Cul Mor. Still seeking your brother, eh?

Then there was nothing. I wrote in *Among Mountains* about the first true silence I ever encountered, far out on the Moine Mhor of the Cairngorms. Sitting under Suilven, as though to serve the purpose of pilgrimage, I slipped into a second silence. The stone shore, the surface of the loch, the countless hill burns and rivulets and springs, the heaps of rock and heather moorland offering up the mountain mass of Suilven to the sky . . . none of it breathed so much as a sigh. A two-minute silence for Norman? I looked at my watch. Two minutes dawdled past and became four, five, and still the silence held. The sun touched Suilven's flattened boar nose and began to inch east, gilding the armour plating. Norman MacCaig called it 'my masterpiece of masterpieces' to which, doubtless, nature as sculptor replied '*your* masterpiece?', to which he would doubtless have deferred, urging nature not to take offence, he was only making a poem. It's *both* your masterpieces, for in what proved to be a ten-minute unbroken silence I thought of you both equally, and thought that you had both achieved your highest endeavours here, that Suilven memorialises you both.

Some headstone, though, Norman. Not bad for a poet.

The silence died with a small wind in my ear, a ripple on the loch. Suilven was gold, but it wore the cloud cap still, and slightly askew, as if it had slipped over one ear. The boar snout sniffed the Atlantic wind. I took some photographs and set off for the mountain, not knowing what more there was to achieve, or to commemorate that the silence had not already served better. Half an hour later, I dug a boot into the flank of the boar and climbed, the cloud gathered and fell down the mountainside in avalanches of flimsy grey, and smothered the last steps and rites of pilgrimage from the eyes of the world.